MW00657811

SELF-CONTROL AND CRIME OVER THE LIFE COURSE

Carter Hay

Florida State University

Ryan Meldrum

Florida International University

Los Angeles | London | New Delhi
Singapore | Washington DC | Boston

Los Angeles | London | New Delhi
Singapore | Washington DC | Boston

FOR INFORMATION:

SAGE Publications, Inc.
2455 Teller Road
Thousand Oaks, California 91320
E-mail: order@sagepub.com

SAGE Publications Ltd.
1 Oliver's Yard
55 City Road
London EC1Y 1SP
United Kingdom

SAGE Publications India Pvt. Ltd.
B 1/I 1 Mohan Cooperative Industrial Area
Mathura Road, New Delhi 110 044
India

SAGE Publications Asia-Pacific Pte. Ltd.
3 Church Street
#10-04 Samsung Hub
Singapore 049483

Copyright © 2016 by SAGE Publications, Inc.

All rights reserved. No part of this book may be reproduced or utilized in any form or by any means, electronic or mechanical, including photocopying, recording, or by any information storage and retrieval system, without permission in writing from the publisher.

Printed in the United States of America

Cataloging-in-Publication Data is available for this title from the Library of Congress.

ISBN 978-1-4833-5899-4

This book is printed on acid-free paper.

Acquisitions Editor: Jerry Westby
Editorial Assistant: Laura Kirkhuff
Production Editor: Kelly DeRosa
Copy Editor: Rachel Keith
Typesetter: C&M Digitals (P) Ltd.
Proofreader: Dennis W. Webb
Indexer: Marilyn Anderson
Cover Designer: Scott Van Atta
Marketing Manager: Terra Schultz

MIX
Paper from
responsible sources
FSC www.fsc.org   FSC® C014174

15 16 17 18 19 10 9 8 7 6 5 4 3 2 1

SELF-CONTROL AND
CRIME OVER THE LIFE COURSE

SAGE was founded in 1965 by Sara Miller McCune to support the dissemination of usable knowledge by publishing innovative and high-quality research and teaching content. Today, we publish more than 750 journals, including those of more than 300 learned societies, more than 800 new books per year, and a growing range of library products including archives, data, case studies, reports, conference highlights, and video. SAGE remains majority-owned by our founder, and after Sara's lifetime will become owned by a charitable trust that secures our continued independence.

Los Angeles | London | Washington DC | New Delhi | Singapore | Boston

BRIEF CONTENTS

DETAILED CONTENTS

PREFACE

A compelling conclusion has emerged in the behavioral sciences: Self-control—an individual quality we all possess in varying degrees—is a remarkably powerful predictor of how our life will unfold. This one simple attribute touches nearly all aspects of life, affecting how we approach the world and how it treats us. These dynamics first emerge in early childhood, and by adolescence and adulthood our self-control is affecting such pivotal things as whether we break the law, how we do in school, and whether we succeed in an occupation and develop rewarding interpersonal relationships. Indeed, our self-control also affects our ability to avoid life's great hassles, including addiction, bankruptcy, poor physical health, and even criminal victimization. These events and developments all rely, at least in part, on our ability to thoughtfully assess daily risks and temptations and then behave in ways that restrain impulses and advance long-term interests. For those who do this well, life often proceeds quite smoothly; for those who do not, the complications may be frequent and severe.

These conclusions follow from countless behavioral science studies spanning many decades. Our approach to that research has been from the perspective of criminology, our "home" discipline. Criminologists have studied self-control extensively since 1990, the year that saw the publication of Gottfredson and Hirschi's seminal work *A General Theory of Crime.* That book argued that self-control was *the* singular factor most responsible for explaining criminal involvement. Gottfredson and Hirschi's work triggered a seemingly limitless supply of articles, books, and chapters on self-control. This was all for good reason—just as Gottfredson and Hirschi predicted, effects of low self-control on crime turned out to be quite powerful. Moreover, criminologists have been fascinated by its equally powerful effects on many of the family, peer, and school variables that *also* affect crime. As these impressive results piled up, the concept of self-control took on momentum, visibility, and a larger-than-life presence in criminological theory. This prompted one fellow self-control researcher to cleverly dub self-control the *"Tyrannosaurus rex* of criminology" (DeLisi, 2011, p. 103).

As we all know, however, things did not end well for the dinosaur version of *Tyrannosaurus rex,* and there were problems for its criminological counterpart also. That is where this book comes in. It first was envisioned many years ago when we recognized problems in the criminological approach to self-control—problems that undermined its future insights and usefulness. Admittedly, these were not *cataclysmic* problems—nothing like the giant asteroid that struck the Earth and triggered atmospheric shifts that left dinosaurs extinct. They were, however, problems nonetheless. Three in particular most captured our attention and inspired our search for solutions.

The first involved how the *extraordinary volume* of new self-control research had overwhelmed prevailing theory in this area. Theory is supposed to organize what is known about something and then guide future research, but in this instance, that was not happening. Gottfredson and Hirschi's theory was published 25 years ago and has not been updated since. Moreover, their theory was—by design—an unusually parsimonious and concise approach; for example, it cited only a single cause of individual self-control (exposure to high-quality parenting) and offered few details on how low self-control functions with other facets of life to affect behavior. By the late 1990s, research was zooming past the theory's predictions to consider issues it had neglected or not envisioned. Indeed, in many instances, researchers were testing hypotheses that Gottfredson and Hirschi had flatly rejected, especially in reference to the biological basis of self-control and the idea that self-control is dynamic over the life course. Regarding these issues and others, Gottfredson and Hirschi had in some sense told future researchers "don't go there." Many criminologists were woefully bad at following those instructions—they *did* go *there.* When they did, new empirical findings piled up faster and faster. And yet, the theoretical framework for organizing those findings remained unchanged and could not incorporate the new insights. In the world of science, this is a big problem.

There was a second problem (although there are terrific exceptions to it that we discuss): Criminologists often proceeded as if we were the only behavioral science studying self-control. This could not have been further from the truth. The explosion in self-control research over the past two decades knows no academic boundaries—it spans a diverse list of disciplines beyond criminology, including psychology, sociology, economics, behavioral genetics, cognitive neuroscience, and psychiatry. And importantly, just as criminologists often ignored the research in these disciplines, those disciplines ignored our research in criminology. Every school of thought—sometimes even those existing within the same discipline—seemed to proceed as if others barely existed. The end result is that too much self-control research is fragmented, narrow, and discipline-specific; the hard-earned insights emerging from any one perspective largely have not been incorporated into other perspectives.

The third problem inspiring this book relates to the issue of public policy. The overwhelming majority of self-control research—across all the disciplines—approached self-control as a variable that could explain individual differences in criminal, deviant, and harmful behaviors. Very rarely did researchers take the next step of asking (and empirically verifying) how we could use this information to inform policy efforts to reduce these behaviors. And yet, fruitful opportunities clearly are possible on this issue. Given the powerful way in which self-control shapes behavior, along with society's obvious interest in reducing the suffering from harmful manifestations of low self-control, we can reach but one conclusion: Self-control theory and research *can* attend to key issues of public policy, and this should be done with depth and precision.

There certainly were other problems, but these are the three that stood out to us: Empirical research was zooming ahead of prevailing theory, researchers were using narrow discipline-specific perspectives, and along the way, nobody was talking much about policy. With these limitations clear in our minds, we embarked on the writing of this book. Our goal was to use its chapters to answer questions that are fundamental to understanding the connection between self-control and behavior. These are the questions we sought to answer:

- Over the life course and across different arenas of life, what behaviors are significantly affected by self-control?
- What causes a person to have high or low self-control to begin with?
- Once a child or adolescent develops a certain level of self-control, does that level of self-control remain fixed or does it fluctuate over the life course? And if self-control fluctuates over time, what specific events and experiences drive this?
- When self-control affects crime, *why* does it do so—what exactly is the causal sequence by which low self-control is translated into actual criminal acts?
- Are the effects of self-control uniform across different individuals and environments, or, alternatively, do the harmful effects of low self-control depend on other factors?

We knew that extensive rigorous research had been conducted on each of these questions, but there was no mechanism or framework for bringing it all together. Our goal therefore was to write the book that would do so. And true to our beliefs about the scholarly limitations we described above, our approach would be built on three major priorities: (a) to incorporate the new insights and innovations that have accumulated in recent research, (b) to build an integrated perspective that truly captures the multidisciplinary nature of modern-day self-control research, and (c) to place public policy issues at the forefront. Regarding the last, a key principle guided us: Self-control research is much more than fanciful ideas that are interesting to college professors and their students; instead, it can be the basis for refined policy efforts that combat pressing problems faced by individuals, communities, and governments.

The chapters that follow are the end product of these efforts. The book is designed to provide an engaging and entertaining view on the science of self-control. Most important, we wanted it to be accessible and informative to a wide swath of readers, ranging from students taking their first course in the behavioral sciences to graduate students and scholars conducting their own self-control research. Writing for such a broad audience was a novel experience in that we have spent our careers writing dense, technical journal articles read mostly by

xiv SELF-CONTROL AND CRIME OVER THE LIFE COURSE

professional researchers. Reversing course and writing for a broad audience that includes nonspecialists, however, was a refreshing, enlightening, and elevating experience. It prompted us to keep an eye on the big picture, rise above the minutiae of conflicting arguments and findings, and ask ourselves (a) what the important things that we suspect or know are, (b) why these things are important, and (c) how they connect to people's real lives. True enough, we will cover rigorous issues of research and theory throughout, but this is done with a clear, conversational approach to writing that emphasizes the interesting aspects of the material.

Ultimately, we think readers will discover the same thing we did: When it comes to self-control and behavior, there is much out there to learn, and it is often fascinating. The range of topics we cover is remarkable: There are the small children in a lab trying their hardest *not* to eat a marshmallow (and the researchers who followed up decades later to see how they fared in life); there is the Russian explorer on an Antarctic expedition who, in a weakened state, mustered the self-control to cut open his own abdomen and perform a life-saving appendectomy on himself; there is Phineas Gage, the 1800s-era railroad worker whose brain was pierced by an expelled railroad spike (he survived but was plagued by self-control lapses that have modern-day neuroscientists still studying his brain injuries); there are stories of self-control transformations, where individuals previously marked by major self-control deficits turned around their lives and pursued a new course. And then there is the possibility that collective advances in self-control have fueled the advancement of human civilizations. That argument comes from Steven Pinker, an acclaimed Harvard psychologist. He provides a scrupulously researched narrative on a multiple-centuries-long "civilizing process" in which human societies became attentive to how a collective sense of self-control could shape their futures, allowing them to more efficiently and peacefully navigate the inherent challenges of life. One thing is for certain: In studying these topics and others, we learned an extraordinary amount ourselves. We look forward to sharing that knowledge with readers.

ACKNOWLEDGMENTS

For any book, the authors owe a debt of gratitude to a wide array of helpful individuals, and this certainly is true for us. The ideas and arguments we present here were a long time in forming, and their origins can be traced to countless interactions we have had on the topic of self-control and criminological theory with valued coauthors and mentors who work in this area. Over the years, we have read one another's work, conducted studies together, fired emails to one another across the country, and batted ideas back and forth at the annual meetings of the American Society of Criminology. We are indebted to too many such people to list them all here, but we want to especially acknowledge Charles Tittle, Mark Stafford, Jim Short, Walter Forrest, Alex Piquero, Jacob Young, J. C. Barnes, and Frank Weerman.

Many thanks also go to the SAGE staff for their patience and expert assistance throughout. Chris Gill heard the first pitch for this book several years ago; that pitch was far from compelling, but he kept it on his radar screen and helped it ultimately get noticed. Also, Jerry Westby has been terrific in expertly marshalling the book through this process, and Laura Kirkhuff, Kelly DeRosa, and Rachel Keith helped greatly in the production and editing stage. We are thankful also to the reviewers of earlier drafts of the book for their helpful comments and suggestions:

J. C. Barnes, *University of Cincinnati*

Michael P. Polakowski, *University of Arizona*

Brie Diamond, *Texas Christian University*

Jennifer Wareham, *Wayne State University*

Rebecca S. Katz, *Morehead State University*

Paul Becker, *University of Dayton*

Nadine M. Connell, *University of Texas, Dallas*

J. Mitchell Miller, *University of North Florida*

Curtis R. Blakely, *Truman State University*

A special thanks also goes to Samantha Ladwig, a doctoral student at Florida State University, for her impressive research that contributed to many sections of the book. And many thanks go to colleagues, students, and Dean Tom Blomberg at Florida State University in Tallahassee for their support for and interest in our efforts, along with thanks to Lisa Stolzenberg and Jamie Flexon at Florida International University in Miami.

And last, I (Carter) wish to especially thank my wife Jennifer and our two children. They have heard countless tellings and retellings of the stories and study descriptions that follow. They have been eager and supportive all along. Most important, when it was time to step away from the book, at least momentarily, they always provided the needed distractions, entertainment, and companionship.

⊰ ONE ⊱

INTRODUCTION

———•∙◆∙•———

L ife is filled with temptations, but many carry the risk of negative consequences. Sometimes the consequences are trivial and emerge far in the future, if at all. In other instances, the risks are more severe and immediate. A struggling college student, for example, may lack the willpower to study for final exams that are critical to staying in school. Or a paroled offender may want to smoke pot with his friends—an allure that must be balanced against the possibility of a failed drug test and a return to prison. Whether big or small, each temptation calls on us to assess our options and make a decision—do we seize immediate benefits, even at the risk of incurring costs we may later regret? Or do we resist, taking comfort in knowing that we protected our long-term well-being?

This book looks at decisions people make every day through the lens of the behavioral sciences. These decisions fundamentally deal with the concept of *self-control*, a quality that captures one's willingness and ability to assess temptations in terms of the benefits they offer *and* the costs they impose, and then behave in ways that advance one's interests. Philosophers and writers have studied self-control for some time (Elias, 1939; Smiles, 1866), but attention to it has intensified in recent decades across many academic disciplines. It goes by many names across this research—"self-control" pervades in criminology, but other perspectives describe the same behavioral process using terms like "willpower," "self-restraint," and "self-regulation," or "impulsivity" and "risk-seeking" (qualities marked by the *absence* of self-control). Regardless of the label used, however, two striking empirical facts about self-control have emerged. These facts inform all the following paragraphs, sections, and chapters.

First, there is a growing recognition that the challenge of self-control is inherent to the human experience—there is no escaping the temptations that challenge our self-control. Whenever desire meets a situation in which acting upon it is possible, temptation ensues. A battle in our mind is then under way—one that pits immediate benefits and pleasures against long-term costs and risks. In modern life, this battle plays out constantly over the course of a day. In an ingenious study of about 200 adults, Hofmann, Baumeister, Förster, and Vohs (2012) documented this pattern impressively. Subjects were asked to carry beepers throughout the day, and each time an alarm sounded, they reported the presence or absence of their desires at that time or shortly before. It turns out that subjects confronted desire roughly *half the time they were awake.* The most common temptations involved eating, drinking, sleeping, sex, and activities that distracted them from work or school. This result is what might be expected from this largely middle-class sample. For a different sample—one drawn from substance abusers or professional burglars—the specific temptations might be different, but the larger conclusion would be the same: "Desire pervades everyday life" (Hofmann et al., 2012, p. 1329). Thus, although none of us set aside time on our schedules and calendars to "put my self-control to the test" or "contemplate temptation," we will—inevitably—devote time to exactly this challenge.

And then there is a second striking conclusion from this research: Individuals vary *greatly* in how well they handle the challenge of self-control, and the consequences of poor self-control are extraordinary. As we discuss, when faced with temptations, those with high self-control (a quality that can be reliably measured at an early age) often envision—sometimes quite consciously—the well-being of their "future self" (Silver & Ulmer, 2012). They then make decisions that maximize its interests—they give in when it makes sense to and resist when it does not. They seize upon reasonable benefits in their environments and avoid immediate and long-term consequences; ultimately, individuals with high self-control competently advance their health, happiness, and security.

Compared to their high-self-control counterparts, those with low self-control do not fare well. They either do not consider this future self or deemphasize its interests (instead focusing on the needs and desires of the "present self"). They are easily seduced by immediate enticements, even those that should—upon minimal reflection—highlight annoying or devastating consequences to follow. As a result, people with low self-control often find themselves in predicaments across the major arenas of life. And, of course, this group garners extraordinary attention from behavioral scientists, policymakers, and the media.

What sort of "predicaments" are we speaking of? As the title of our book suggests, we are especially interested in crime, and research tells us there is good reason for this. Criminology has arguably devoted more attention to self-control than any other field of study, and this follows from the natural connection between self-control and the temptations of crime. Many crimes represent temptations in which there are immediate, obvious benefits but also consequences that are perhaps less certain or obvious. Benefits of crime include, for example, money gained through theft or the "justice" that comes from assaulting a cheating or disrespecting person. As enticing as these benefits are, they coexist with major costs, including arrest, loss of reputation, and injury (given that people who are assaulted sometimes retaliate). Criminological research in recent decades indicates that, relatively speaking, those with low self-control prioritize immediate, obvious benefits over uncertain but sometimes severe long-term costs. As a result, they are more likely to commit violent and property crimes, use illegal drugs, and enter the criminal justice system.

As we will discuss, however, low self-control also predicts involvement in harmful and self-defeating behaviors that are *not* criminal in nature. Low self-control is linked to, among other things, dropping out of school, being a victim of crime, developing health problems, accruing debt, and experiencing harmful accidents. And these effects are notably long term in nature. As Moffitt and her colleagues (2011) showed in a recent report published in *Proceedings of the National*

Academy of Sciences, a child's self-control during the first 10 years of life is a robust predictor of critical adult outcomes, including physical health and the accumulation of wealth (in this case reported at least two decades later when subjects were 32 years old). Simply stated, many of the undesirable things people do—to themselves and others—follow in part from deficits in self-control.

If the entire story were just this simple—temptation is every-where and those with high self-control live better lives—then this would be a much shorter book. However, these empirical realities merely set the stage for delving more deeply into the interesting com-plexities of self-control—complexities that are considered daily by an army of behavioral scientists from all over the world and from a wide array of academic disciplines. Every year, they contribute new insights to what we think of as one big self-control jigsaw puzzle. In some cases they add new pieces to the puzzle that nobody was aware of, and in other instances they shed light on where to position older, well-established pieces. As active researchers in this area—as schol-ars who spend a good part of our day thinking about self-control research—we have come to appreciate a basic fact: Much is known about the self-control puzzle, but there still is much to learn, and there is value in reliving the provocative and insightful process that brings us to our present state of knowledge.

That is what inspires this book. Its fundamental goal is to not only describe in rich detail what we know (or strongly suspect) about self-control, but also pave the way to considering exciting possibilities in the years to come. A key challenge in writing such a book is knowing where to begin. There are so many critical pieces to consider, and each one is interrelated with the broader whole; understanding any one issue requires at least a little understanding of many issues. The key, there-fore, is to describe the self-control puzzle sensibly, not jumping too quickly into its most difficult parts, but also not unnecessarily dragging through its most basic ones.

With that in mind, we use this introductory chapter to provide a concise foundation for the discussions that follow. In building this foundation, we emphasize the definition of self-control that guides us and the key perspectives and priorities that inform our approach.

A DEFINITION OF SELF-CONTROL

Academic volumes are notorious for devoting 300 or 400 pages to an idea or concept without ever directly specifying what it means. We are eliminating that possibility by defining self-control sooner rather than later. We should emphasize that we are not seeking to break new ground when it comes to our definition of self-control—we approach it much as it has been defined in prior research. Across the literature, self-control is often described with different words and phrases, but we see these differences as largely superficial. When scholars speak of self-control or its various synonyms, they generally speak of the same basic activity.

At its core, self-control is a practice in which individuals deliberately *act upon themselves* to alter their immediate urges, impulses, inclinations, or temptations (and any other word you can think of that conveys the idea of a craving or compulsion). This is done to bring responses into line with higher-order standards that correspond to a person's values, morals, social commitments, and long-term well-being. As Baumeister and his colleagues (Baumeister, Heatherton, & Tice, 1994; Baumeister, Vohs, & Tice, 2007) have emphasized, central to this is the idea of *overriding*—an impulse to behave in one way is replaced with a different behavior that adheres to a higher-order standard. Thus, when a given man feels an impulse to assault someone who has disrespected him but overrides that impulse to adhere to higher-order standards, self-control has been exercised. And those higher-order standards can come from a variety of sources, including moral values ("Assaulting people is wrong; I shouldn't do it"), interest in long-term well-being ("Getting arrested for assaulting this guy could cost me my job"), and social commitments ("My wife hates it when I assault people, and I don't want to disappoint her").

Importantly, although self-control research focuses in large part on behavior, self-control overriding is relevant also to thoughts and emotions. Thus, just as individuals can override an impulse to commit an assault, they can override impulses to get carried away by specific emotions (e.g., anger and indignation) or to dwell on specific thoughts (e.g., the nerve of the guy who did the disrespecting). This often involves *reframing* a situation to make it less thought consuming or salient ("That guy is nothing to me") or *redirecting* attention to other topics that are less tempting or stress inducing.

Regardless of whether the impulses in question involve behaviors, emotions, or thoughts, when individuals consciously override these impulses to adhere to higher-order standards, they are exercising self-control. Tangney, Baumeister, and Boone (2004, p. 272), for example, see self-control as "the self's capacity to inhibit its antisocial impulses and conform to the demands of group life." Similarly, Baumeister and his colleagues (2007, p. 351) speak of a capacity for "deliberate, conscious, effortful" actions that "restrain or override one response, thereby making a different response possible." And last, prominent criminological theorists Gottfredson and Hirschi refer to the tendency "to avoid acts whose long-term costs exceed short-term benefits" (Hirschi & Gottfredson, 2001, p. 83) and "to consider the full range of potential costs of a particular act" (Hirschi, 2004, p. 543). A key idea tying all these perspectives together is that self-control generally involves overriding *easy* responses to a situation (those that are immediately gratifying) and replacing them with *difficult* responses (those that adhere to higher-order standards involving values, social commitments, and long-term well-being).

Importantly, does this mean that people with high self-control avoid pleasurable things? It absolutely does *not* mean this. That point must be emphasized, because self-control sometimes is misunderstood as a joyless quality in which people simply *stop themselves from doing all the things they really want to do.* If that were in fact the essence of self-control, we suspect fewer people would consistently exercise self-control—who would want to live such a grim, pleasureless existence? Thankfully, this is a misunderstanding—self-control often is practiced with an explicit eye on pleasure. Thus, a person need not choose between having self-control and living a pleasurable life—both can be done, and there's a simple reason for why this is true: Life's pleasures often do not conflict with our higher-order standards. Virtually any temptation we can think of—involving such varied things as good food, sex, alcohol, thrilling experiences with friends, the acquisition of money and material possessions, and the free expression of one's ideas—can be indulged in ways that do not undermine basic ideals, morals, and long-term prospects. Thus, what seems to distinguish those with high self-control is not a disinterest in pleasure; instead, it is their tendency to pursue pleasure with a plan or with good instincts and habits born from their prior successes.

Taken together, this gives us a straightforward working definition of self-control: It is the practice of overriding immediate impulses to replace them with responses that adhere to higher-order standards that typically follow from values, social commitments, and interests in long-term well-being. This definition describes self-control as a *practice*, but we can easily make the leap to defining it in terms of an individual *quality* or *trait*—a person high in self-control has a strong, consistent tendency to engage in the practice of self-control. Importantly, we see this broad definition of self-control as capturing the basic meanings of the wide variety of self-control synonyms used across different areas of research, including "self-restraint," "self-regulation," "willpower," "delayed gratification," "future orientation," "impulsivity," and "risk-seeking" (the latter two qualities being marked by an *absence* of self-control).[1]

AN INTEGRATIVE APPROACH

This book is the sum of our efforts to answer big-picture questions regarding the causes, consequences, and development of self-control. For example, over the life course and across different arenas of life, what behaviors are significantly affected by self-control? Also, what key factors early in life affect whether a child develops self-control in the first place? And once a certain level of self-control emerges, does it remain stable throughout adolescence and adulthood? Or, conversely, do self-control levels fluctuate as the individual advances deeper into life, and if so, what are the life course events and experiences that give rise to such changes? And last, when self-control affects behavior, *how* does it do so—what is the causal process that explains how low self-control is translated into actual criminal, deviant, and harmful acts?

In tackling these questions and others, our approach is explicitly integrative in nature—it is designed to bring together streams of thought that often have been treated separately. This is done in two ways. The first involves a multidisciplinary approach that is true to the nature of modern-day self-control research. Scores of new books, articles, and chapters on self-control appear every month, and this research knows no academic boundaries—it spans a diverse list of disciplines, including criminology and criminal justice, psychology, sociology, social work, economics, behavioral and molecular genetics, cognitive neuroscience, and psychiatry. Each of these disciplines has its own research traditions and perspectives, and as noted earlier, different disciplines often have different terminology for our central concept. In each instance, however, they examine processes in which individuals try to control their emotions, thoughts, and actions to advance health, security, and well-being. We therefore draw from them all.

We should emphasize that this multidisciplinary, integrative approach is unique. Much self-control research has taken a narrower, discipline-specific approach; criminologists, for example, have comfortably stayed within their criminological schools of thought, while psychologists have adhered to a psychological approach. The problem, of course, is that all disciplines and their related perspectives have "blind spots"—things they miss because they are so absorbed by *other* things. This certainly has been true in our discipline of criminology, which traces its origins in large part to the field of sociology, with its emphasis on how cultural and social environmental forces shape social norms and behaviors among individuals and groups. Early criminological approaches to self-control were marked by an almost exclusive focus on the social environment; biological and genetic factors were neglected or entirely dismissed. Other disciplines, however, have impressively emphasized biological and genetic variables, but they suffer their own blind spots, and that, in fact, is our main point—any approach that is discipline specific will be incomplete.

With that in mind, the chapters that follow cover an incredible variety of studies—psychological studies of babies and toddlers interacting with their parents, macro-level sociological studies of concentrated urban poverty, behavioral genetics studies of twins and siblings raised together or apart, and cognitive neuroscience studies that use brain-imaging techniques to reveal patterns of electrical activity in the brain. By considering these types of studies and many others, we bring together the insights from all the areas of study that care about self-control.

Our approach is integrative in another respect. In addition to drawing broadly from multiple disciplines, we combine the insights of specific theoretical perspectives. As we emphasize in a later chapter, we have been most influenced by four specific perspectives: (a) a family-centered control theory approach prominent in criminology (Gottfredson and Hirschi, 1990; Hirschi, 1969), (b) a trait-based psychological approach (Caspi, Roberts, & Shiner, 2005; Tangney et al., 2004), (c) a biosocial approach that emphasizes self-control as an executive function of the brain with biological and genetic origins (Barkley, 1997; Beaver, Wright, & DeLisi, 2007; Steinberg, 2010a), and (d) a situational "strength" approach that sees self-control as a renewable and depletable personal resource (Baumeister & Tierney, 2011). These approaches have existed largely in isolation from one another; while at times they incorporate one another's ideas, they more commonly proceed as if the others barely existed. They are, in a sense, like Longfellow's "ships that pass in the night, . . . only a look and a voice, then darkness again and a silence."

Our view is that this need not be the case. As we discuss, these traditions are quite compatible, and each provides a valuable viewpoint for understanding some aspect of the self-control puzzle. True enough, there are genuine differences between them, but we see these differences as strengths rather than weaknesses—each perspective addresses its own niche, and putting their insights together provides a more compelling and thorough understanding of self-control. We therefore draw from them all liberally. Our goal is not to replace these approaches or subsume them into our own grandiose perspective; indeed, such things as personality psychology and the biosocial approach are themselves grand enough to be beyond any incorporation of that kind. Instead, our goal simply is to borrow their good ideas whenever doing so enables us to acquire better answers to the questions we raise.

A LIFE COURSE APPROACH

Our approach is marked by a heavy emphasis on the life course perspective that emphasizes the dynamic nature of development across various stages of the human life course (Elder, 1985; Laub, 2004; Sampson & Laub,

1993). In earlier decades, human behavior was often studied as a static, unchanging phenomenon—people either were criminals or they were not, or they possessed self-control or they did not. There was little appreciation for whether and how people changed as they advanced through different biological and social stages of life. More recently, however, the dynamic aspect of human behavior has taken center stage, and it has important implications for the way we study self-control.

From a life course perspective, self-control is not a quality that you either have or do not have—it is something that develops over time. Self-control has *trajectories* (or *pathways*) that can be marked by continuity (in which preexisting patterns persist) or change (in which there are turning points). And, most importantly, this dynamic, developmental nature of self-control must be viewed in conjunction with other major domains of life, including the biological, psychological, and social trajectories that are under way. As part of this life course approach, attention must be directed to key life events and transitions—like starting school, entering the labor force, and getting married—that may have implications for development.

In using this life course perspective, our discussion of the causes and consequences of low self-control will in some sense walk the individual through the different stages of the life course. We actually begin before birth by discussing how such things as genetics and prenatal experiences shape biological development in ways that are consequential for self-control. We naturally also emphasize the first decade of life—a period of intense biological development, but also a period in which individuals develop and hone their ability to socially interact with others, especially those in the family environment. We consider research with infants and toddlers that sheds light on the qualities and actions that become precursors for later displays of self-control.

And then we consider how self-control evolves as individuals age into the second decade of life—into the so-called "storm and stress" of adolescence. This period brings special attention to patterns of continuity and change. The events and developments of the first decade of life often set the stage for adolescence, and thus many adolescents will be marked by continuity in self-control; if they have successfully developed self-control as children (in ways that can reasonably be expected), they continue that pattern into adolescence. However, change during this period occurs as well, in part because of the major shifts that accompany adolescence. Adolescents are not only advancing biologically, but also experiencing major social shifts as their activities, social networks, and interests increasingly move them away from the family context and into contexts associated with peers, the school, and the community.

And of course, not all individuals experience these shifts similarly, therefore raising the possibility that there is a "re-shuffling of the self-control deck," so to speak—some who were doing quite well in self-control as children will struggle as adolescents, and vice versa. In studying these issues, we will incorporate the new science on the evolving adolescent brain (Steinberg, 2010a), because contrary to prior accepted wisdom, the adolescent brain is still very much in flux—brain development continues in significant ways through adolescence, and this has interesting implications for self-control.

And we do not stop with adolescence, because there are interesting self-control patterns in adulthood as well, especially early adulthood. This stage of life has been described as "demographically dense"—it involves more life-changing shifts in roles and identities than any other period in the life course (Caspi et al., 2005, p. 467). Early adulthood, after all, is often the period in which people graduate from college, enter the labor force, get married, and have children. However, these events allow for reversals also—employed and married individuals can lose their jobs or get divorced, and other individuals will get ensnared by complications in the areas of health, mental health, addiction, and even incarceration. For each of these life events (good or bad), one's level of self-control likely affects whether or not they occur, but in turn, these events often influence later self-control; key life transitions have a way of altering one's willingness and ability to exercise self-control. In covering these alternative possibilities, we hope to convey that a person's self-control should be understood as the product of a lifelong developmental process.

CONNECTING SELF-CONTROL
TO OTHER CAUSES OF BEHAVIOR

This book is based on the premise that self-control really matters for behavior. Yet, self-control is not the *only* important cause of behavior.

Criminology in particular has a wide array of theories that emphasize the causal effects of such things as social control in the family environment, negative experiences in school, social interactions in delinquent peer networks, and the social conditions of disadvantaged and disorganized communities. Therefore, it is useful here at the outset to ask this question: Where does self-control fit in the broader context of criminological theory?

There is no one way to answer that question, but a useful distinction can be made between *types-of-people* and *types-of-places* explanations for behavior. "People" explanations overwhelmingly emphasize the qualities of individuals as the determinants of behavior. Individuals commit criminal and deviant acts because of *who they are*—they possess biological or psychological attributes that make antisocial behavior likely no matter where they find themselves. In contrast, "place" explanations emphasize that individuals engage in crime and deviance as a result of *where they are*, and therefore what social environments, relationships, and subcultures they encounter. This is more of a blank-slate approach to human behavior—individuals behave and develop in ways that match the social influences around them. If they are in places that encourage crime, they commit crimes, but if not, they avoid crime. Prominent examples of place theories include Shaw and McKay's (1969) social disorganization theory (with its emphasis on neighborhood social control and neighborhood subcultures) and Merton's (1938) strain theory (with its attention to environments that emphasize monetary success goals but offer fewer opportunities for legally achieving those goals). Social learning theories (Akers, 1998) that emphasize reinforcements and punishments in primary social relations with parents and peers are yet another example of place-oriented explanations.

In reality, few theories are a pure version of either a people or place explanation, but they can be placed along a continuum, and theories of self-control definitely fall on the people side of that continuum. Indeed, in criminology, Gottfredson and Hirschi's (1990) self-control theory—which we will discuss in detail in the next chapter—is often cited as the prototypical types-of-people explanation. It sees self-control as an individual quality that develops early in life and becomes so powerful that it crowds out the effects of the place-oriented influences previously thought to matter (the family environment, peer groups, and the school and community contexts). Thus, in response to our original question—where self-control fits in the broader context of theories of crime and deviance—one clear response is that self-control has historically been seen as a types-of-people explanation that downplays the significance of types-of-places explanations.

We should, however, give fair warning—in the chapters that follow, we approach self-control in ways that substantially blur the lines between people and place explanations. This follows from a simple recognition: The more one studies self-control, the more it becomes clear that this prototypical types-of-people variable is inextricably intertwined with the types-of-places variables that are its presumed rivals in the world of criminological theory. Most notably, in the early years of life, the development of this individual quality depends on the type of place in which a child is raised—the family environment is especially consequential. Beyond childhood, the family environment continues to matter for self-control, but other places do as well, including the peer context, the school, and the community environment. Moreover, as we will discuss, the effects of low self-control on behavior are not uniform across different types of places—in some social contexts, low self-control produces especially high problems with crime and deviance, whereas in other places, the harmful effects of low self-control are repressed by social and cultural conditions that promote prosocial behavior. In such places, the deficit in self-control may persist, but the qualities of that place minimize its negative consequences.

Ultimately, therefore, we end up emphasizing causal variables from prominent place-oriented criminological theories that often have not figured greatly into prior discussions of self-control. We believe this approach will be increasingly common in the future. Simply stated, when you study self-control, you end up studying the many other important things to which it is connected.

ATTENTION TO PUBLIC POLICY

As the above sections indicate, our efforts involve a heavy emphasis on theory—we wish to advance a better theoretical understanding of the causes, consequences, and development of self-control over the life course. We are sensitive, however, to a critique often lodged against theoretical efforts of this kind: They approach a given phenomenon (such as low self-control) with a focus on its theoretical nuances and complexities rather than on how to fix the urgent real-world problems associated with that phenomenon. In short, intense concern over questions of theory leads to a disappointing neglect of questions of policy.

However, this need not be the case—a concern for theoretical advances is not the least bit incompatible with a concern for solutions to the real-world problems that follow from low self-control. Indeed, these two concerns should go hand in hand. Our thoughts on this are captured well by Greenstein's (2006, p. 5) view of the proper link between social scientific theory and public policy:

> If one is truly concerned with changing society, good theory is a necessity. Armed with good theory, we can design and implement interventions designed to change the world around us. If we really understand why an outcome occurs, we have the knowledge . . . to change that outcome.

With this in mind, we vow to "walk and chew gum at the same time," as the saying goes—we will focus on the critical theoretical issues while also emphasizing the implications they have for public policy efforts to reduce problems linked to low self-control. We will consider the key opportunities for social service, juvenile justice, and criminal justice intervention across key stages of the life course. For example, we will describe programs that invest in children and families in the prenatal and postnatal periods, as well as those that promote self-control among early childhood "troublemakers" and adult offenders alike. As we will discuss, extensive evidence-based policy efforts are well under way in these areas. We also will consider more global efforts to build cultural awareness of self-control and related cognitive abilities—a goal that many economists see as important for our nation's future productivity (Heckman & Masterov, 2007; Kocher, Rutzler, Sutter, & Trautmann, 2012).

CONNECTING THE SCIENCE OF SELF-CONTROL
TO THE STORIES WE READ ABOUT EVERY DAY

Our approach is heavily rooted in science and research, but we confess that an enjoyable part of writing this book has been our deep dives into popular culture and history to find compelling depictions of self-control in action. Simply stated, the news and entertainment media are replete with rich and informative illustrations of what goes well—or sometimes horribly awry—when it comes to self-control. We take many opportunities in the coming chapters to make the connection between the scientific principles we emphasize and these interesting examples.

We cover instances of extraordinary self-control, such as Aron Ralston (featured in the film *127 Hours*), who mustered the willpower to amputate his own hand to extricate himself from a dislodged boulder. There is also Ram Bahadur Bomjon, a devout young Buddhist in Nepal whose story has been featured in such varied Western media outlets as the BBC, *National Geographic*, and the magazine *GQ*—he has baffled the scientific community with his prolonged meditations in which he voluntarily goes without food or water for days, maintaining his meditative pose during the entire stretch. On the other side of the continuum, we consider extraordinary lapses in self-control, sometimes among powerful people whose lives are otherwise marked by extraordinary self-control.

We also get the chance to discuss television shows that have made self-control prominent in our society's cultural dialogue. These include, for example, one of the earliest reality TV programs: the Fox Network's 2001 show *Temptation Island* (see In Focus 1.1). More recently, MTV's reality show *16 and Pregnant* chronicled the lives of female teenagers experiencing one of the more life-altering results of self-control lapses: an unplanned pregnancy. The show has been described as "grim" and "brutally honest" about the challenges faced by these girls (Bellafante, 2009; National Public Radio, 2014). Interestingly, *16 and Pregnant* has attracted attention from scientists who see an interesting effect on its teenage viewers: It has increased their displays of self-control in avoiding unplanned pregnancies (Kearney & Levine, 2014). In seeing these various cultural and historical illustrations, we think readers will reach the same conclusion we have: Self-control stories are nearly everywhere you look.

IN FOCUS 1.1

Self-Control in Popular Culture: *Temptation Island*

One of the more outrageous reality shows on network TV was one of the first: Fox's short-lived *Temptation Island* (2001–2003). It put the relationships of real couples to the test by seeing if they could endure a steady dose of illicit romantic temptation. The selected couples were flown to a remote, tropical location where the male and female partners were separated from each other. However, they were given plenty of time with single, attractive members of the opposite sex, and the show included all sort of contrived opportunities for them to "date" those to whom they were attracted. Also, to invite maximum drama, the contestants were given vivid, detailed updates (sometimes with video footage) of exactly what their partner was doing (and with whom) on the other side of the island. The show garnered weak ratings, but it broke up plenty of relationships in its three seasons, and it also become infamous for the eye-rolling, cringe-worthy drama it induced each week. The staff at *Time* magazine (TIME Staff, 2009) cautioned viewers to approach the show not as reality or drama, but as "high comedy" that could be appreciated if you remembered that these "star-crossed lovers voluntarily jumped at the chance to ruin their long-term relationships for a free trip to Belize and some priceless exposure." The show illustrates how drama revolving around self-control dilemmas is often emphasized in popular culture. And this is the case not just in the United States—while *Temptation Island* lasted only three years in the U.S. television market, successful spin-offs emerged in more than 15 other countries. The French version (*L'Île de la tentation*) ran for eight seasons!

CONCLUSION

Self-control occupies an interesting place in modern society. As behavioral scientists, we approach it as a quality that explains individual differences in bad behavior. When looked at in a historical and cultural context, however, it is so much more. Self-control looms large, for example, in most world religions. In Christianity, it is central to the creation story in the Book of Genesis, as Adam and Eve, upon giving in to temptation, are exiled from the Garden of Eden. And at least five of Christianity's seven deadly sins (lust, gluttony, greed, sloth, and wrath) seem to directly implicate low self-control. Self-control is also the focus of epic works of art—including novels like *Lolita* and *The Scarlet Letter* and movies like *A Clockwork Orange*—that explore the dramatic human struggle between resisting and giving in to temptation. And in modern societies marked by an ethos of "self-help" and "personal transformation," self-control sits at the forefront of sought-after virtues, with popular titles promising insights on how to "develop unstoppable self-discipline" (Wyatt, 2014) and "rediscover your willpower instinct" (Perry, 2013).

And is it possible that shifts in self-control altered the course of human civilization? Acclaimed Harvard psychologist Steven Pinker (2011) says it has. Pinker makes the novel argument—one that he painstakingly supports with evidence—that we presently live in the *least violent* period of human history. Modern humans kill, torture, rape, and go to war against one another more than we should, but at a rate lower than that seen previously. Pinker says that a key contributor to this trend is a multiple-centuries-long "civilizing process" in which human societies have become more willing to "anticipate the consequences of acting on our impulses and to inhibit them accordingly," often in ways that encourage more humanitarian solutions to problems and conflicts. Pinker's compelling arguments underline a point that resonates throughout his book—that the concept of self-control reaches deeply into the arenas and chapters of the human story. We look forward to developing this idea in the pages that follow.

DISCUSSION QUESTIONS

1. What short-term pleasures are you sacrificing by taking the time to read this book chapter? How might your choice to do so relate to your self-control and your "future self?"

2. Recall a recent instance where you had the opportunity to give in to something tempting. Did you *override* the temptation, or give in? Do you think your self-control played a part in the decision you made, or was it something else?

3. Compare and contrast the ability of toddlers, teenagers, and adults to exercise self-control. How might the life course concepts of *stability* and *change* explain differences in ability between toddlers, teens, and adults?

4. Do you think people behave as they do because of *who they are* or because of *where they are*? Which perspective is self-control more compatible with? Could it be compatible with both?

5. Google "self-control in the news" and read one of the stories. How does it relate to the themes discussed in this chapter?

NOTE

1. In considering the definition of self-control, some scholars have considered the possibility that self-control comprises different facets or dimensions—perhaps there are narrower components that are part of an *overall* self-control construct. In criminology, debates about this have followed largely from Gottfredson and Hirschi's (1990) discussion of six "elements" of self-control. In our opinion, their discussion and the resulting debates have often obfuscated rather than clarified the meaning of self-control, and Hirschi (2004) seems to agree with this view. We purposefully avoid a rehashing of that literature, except to emphasize the potential uniqueness of risk-seeking, which sometimes is referred to as sensation-seeking. It involves a preference for intense, novel, and exciting stimuli that often, by their very nature, carry the possibility of immediate or long-term consequences. Individuals high in risk-seeking are those that would be bored by a life without danger (Eysenck & Zuckerman, 1978). They often are quick to embrace exciting or emotionally thrilling lines of action even if they undermine higher-order standards. Risk-seeking often goes hand in hand with the other self-control-related concepts and synonyms we have discussed. However, that will not always be true. Some individuals who are high in risk-seeking—which is expected of those low in self-control—may nevertheless be high in other traditional indicators of self-control, or vice versa (see Burt, Sweeten, & Simons, 2014).

TWO

THEORIES OF SELF-CONTROL
AND BEHAVIOR

————◆•◆•◆————

It was April 1961, and Leonid Rogozov found himself on the frozen southern tip of the Earth. A 27-year-old Russian surgeon, Rogozov had joined a Soviet expedition to the ice shelf on the coast of Antarctica. In doing so, he had interrupted a promising scholarly and medical career just before defending a dissertation on new methods for operating on cancer. Rogozov was part of a 12-person team that would build an inland base to serve future Russian explorations. Officially, he was the team's doctor; unofficially, he also was their meteorologist and occasional driver of ice-terrain vehicles.[1]

Rogozov was a scholar, not an explorer, so the challenges were daunting enough without the complications that would ensue. The team had traveled by sea for 36 days, and upon their arrival in Antarctica the polar winter was upon them, bringing bitter cold but also months of darkness punctuated with fierce, blinding snowstorms. The ship would not return for a year, and they had no contact with the outside world. The members of the team could rely only on themselves and what they had brought.

As he observed himself falling ill, Rogozov was sensitive to these constraints. Soon after arriving, he became fatigued and nauseated, and a mild fever became his norm. More telling, pain emerged in his upper abdomen and migrated to its lower right quadrant. As a trained surgeon,

Rogozov diagnosed his condition easily. "I have appendicitis," he wrote in his journal. Without an operation to remove it, the inflamed appendix would burst, spilling infectious materials into his abdominal cavity. His death would be certain. Transportation elsewhere was impossible, however, and he was the only physician on the exploration. Rogozov came to grips with what seemed his only option: "To operate on myself. It's almost impossible . . . but I can't just fold my arms and give up."

Following his instructions, the team assembled a makeshift operating room with a bed, two tables, a lamp, and the needed supplies. With materials brought for other purposes, they flooded the room with ultra-violet light and sterilized the instruments and bed linens. Rogozov trained several of the explorers, explaining how the operation would proceed. When it was time, he scrubbed himself clean and sat on the bed in a semi-reclining position. Using his direct line of vision and a mirror held above him, Rogozov injected himself with local anesthetics and used a scalpel to make an incision in his own abdomen. The surgery had begun. Working by feel, he probed his gut with his hands, identifying necessary cutting points. He took short breaks when he felt too dizzy or fatigued to go on, but then went back to work quickly. In his journal, he later described his approach and the doubts he had at critical moments:

> The bleeding is quite heavy, but I take my time—I try to work surely. Opening the peritoneum, I injured the blind gut and had to sew it up. Suddenly it flashed through my mind: there are more injuries here and I didn't notice them . . . I grow weaker and weaker, my head starts to spin. Every 4–5 minutes I rest for 20–25 seconds. Finally, here it is, the cursed appendage! With horror I notice the dark stain at its base. That means just a day longer and it would have burst. At the worst moment of removing the appendix, I flagged: my heart seized up and noticeably slowed; my hands felt like rubber. Well, I thought, it's going to end badly. (Rogozov & Bermel, 2009)

Miraculously, however, Rogozov completed the surgery successfully. It took him 1 hour and 45 minutes to do so. When he finished at nearly 4 in the morning, he instructed his team on how to clean and store the instruments and promptly administered himself sleeping tablets. Within a week, he removed the stitches he himself had sewn at the end of procedure. Within two weeks, he resumed his normal activities with the team.

When we describe Rogozov's story to students, many words are offered in reaction—"courageous," "incredible," even "crazy." Underlying them all is the obvious fact that Rogozov displayed extraordinary self-discipline. Indeed, in an article in *Psychology Today*, Wise (2010) labeled Rogozov's surgery "the most amazing feat of self-control ever"—it is one thing to conclude that performing an appendectomy on yourself is your best chance for survival, but quite another to actually do it. Even more striking is how *effective* Rogozov was despite being a firsthand witness to his own blood spilled across the room, his own opened abdominal cavity, and his perilously slim margin for error. An assistant observed that while others nearly fainted and could not watch, Rogozov himself was "calm and focused on his work." The surgeon later described his efforts to control his thoughts and attention:

> I didn't permit myself to think about anything other than the task at hand. It was necessary to steel myself . . . [W]hen I picked up the needle with the novocaine and gave myself the first injection, somehow I automatically switched into operating mode, and from that point on I didn't notice anything else.

Stories like these are not just fascinating—they are provocative. They raise questions about how such an extraordinary display of self-control is possible. What distinguished Rogozov from others? Was it something in his background or something he was born with? And were the signs of his self-control evident before that fateful surgery? Questions like these cut to the core of the science of self-control, directing attention to its meaning, causes, and effects.

This chapter reviews the major theoretical perspectives that grapple with these types of questions. Of course, these theories do not focus on emergency surgeries people perform on themselves; such events are sensational and rare. Instead, they center on common instances of high and low self-control, especially in choices people make regarding criminal, deviant, and harmful behaviors. In this chapter, we describe four major theoretical approaches. With each, our treatment is not exhaustive; instead, we emphasize the highlights and empirically supported insights that inspire new research and inform arguments we make in later chapters.

Our discussion starts with Gottfredson and Hirschi's (1990) self-control theory and its interesting history. In criminological dialogue on self-control, it has been the *Tyrannosaurus rex* of theories (DeLisi, 2011, p. 103), raucously and audaciously dominating the field. We discuss its arguments and related empirical evidence before moving to other major perspectives without ever fully taking our eyes off Gottfredson and Hirschi. These other perspectives are scientifically and historically impressive on their own—that much will be clear—but they also are interesting for how they illuminate and address gaps in Gottfredson and Hirschi's perspective. In the process of covering these other perspectives, we explore critical ideas that link self-control to long-standing psychological theories of personality and newly emerging research on the brain. We also consider the idea that self-control is a personal resource analogous to a muscle—its strength can be depleted from overuse but also replenished through rest and enhanced through practice. We begin, however, with a brief but spirited defense of the very idea of theory itself.

THE INEXTRICABLE
CONNECTION BETWEEN THEORY AND FACT

As college professors, we know that the mere mention of "theory" sometimes elicits groans. All professors have had students say they are "tired of discussing theory"—they want to discuss *the real world*. In their minds, theory is mere speculation, philosophy, and subjectivity—things that stand in contrast to *fact*. This view, however, reflects a mistaken understanding of theory, one we must confront before showing the important and interesting aspects of prior theory on self-control.

Scientists rightfully bristle at the suggestion that *theory* and *fact* are somehow detached from each other. In the world of science, no such separation should exist for long because theories are *explicitly designed to organize facts.* Sometimes they piece together facts already known; other times, they generate new facts by offering novel hypotheses. True enough, in these latter instances, theories involve speculating, but they do so with *testable* hypotheses. Researchers then gather the relevant data and conduct tests, and hypotheses are retained if they are supported by research. As this process unfolds, the theory comes to reflect the accumulated knowledge—the facts—gained during the research process.

This process does not always work perfectly or quickly. The limitations of scientists sometimes get in the way because we possess the same limitations that impede progress in all human endeavors. Problems emerge because of the difficult things we seek to explain. Human behavior, for example, is enormously complex. Also, most things that behavioral scientists study occur most vividly not in tightly controlled laboratories but in the real world (where perfect measurement and analysis are not possible). With all this in mind, we cannot claim that our theories capture the world *exactly as it exists.* Nevertheless, theories that are still standing after intense empirical scrutiny represent the best approximation of reality that can be gleaned from research. Thus, from the perspective of a scientist, a theory that is merely speculative, philosophical, or subjective simply needs to be put through the empirical rigors of the scientific process. As we discuss below, the perspectives we emphasize are great examples of this process at work—they are built on a foundation of rigorous, exacting studies.

EXPLAINING CRIME: GOTTFREDSON AND HIRSCHI'S SELF-CONTROL THEORY

Criminological discussions of self-control often begin and end with Gottfredson and Hirschi's self-control theory. Their perspective is firmly grounded in sociological theories of control (Durkheim, 1893) and early philosophical efforts like Hobbes's *Leviathan* with its emphasis on the "war of all against all." From this perspective, humans are endowed with a strong drive to self-interestedly pursue pleasure, and crime is quite normal. People are naturally inclined to take advantage of others if they can get away with it. This is why we steal, hit, embezzle, and lie—we are evolutionarily programmed to pursue self-interest, and force and fraud allow us, at times, to do so expediently.

A potent force, therefore, is needed to override this natural selfish impulse. In Hirschi's (1969) earliest theoretical efforts, this force was not self-control but *social control*, especially in the form of attachments and commitments to prosocial people, goals, and institutions. Being emotionally attached to family and strongly committed to school or a career offers incentives to follow the rules—bonded individuals do not want to disappoint valued others or undermine conventional pursuits. Thus, social bonds provide a *stake in conformity*, leading us to internalize law-abiding norms and repress antisocial impulses. The problem of inherent selfishness is solved to some degree; with strong bonds to conventional society, people avoid crime.

Hirschi's later work with Gottfredson did not starkly deviate from this perspective, but instead built upon it to place self-control at the forefront. This theoretical transition—one in which self-control replaced social control as the key force for repressing evil, selfishness, and antisociality—followed from observations about the nature of criminal acts. In *A General Theory of Crime*, Gottfredson and Hirschi (1990) argued that the specifics of criminal acts—for example, how they are committed, where they occur, and how much planning they involve—point to important insights. The typical burglary, robbery, or homicide involves little effort, planning, smarts, or skills. Indeed, most crimes are committed with convenience in mind—they occur close to where offenders live (burglars, for example, often walk to houses they target), and the strategies used are crude rather than complex. These crimes involve little forethought or planning. Many violent assaults, even those producing a homicide, are impulsive crimes of passion arising from petty disputes, often occurring in front of witnesses. Moreover, the rewards of these crimes are often fleeting and minimal compared to potential costs. They carry risks of jail, prison, or lethal retaliation from victims, but the typical payoff for robbery, for example, is a few hundred dollars or less. From Gottfredson and Hirschi's perspective, the benefits of crime are neither profound nor weighty, but instead are "benefits of the moment," often involving revenge or the mere removal of irritation (p. 33).

IN FOCUS 2.1

Dumb Criminal of the Week

Movies like *Ocean's Eleven* or television dramas like the USA Network's *White Collar* are entertaining precisely because they describe extraordinary rather than typical crimes. In *White Collar*, for example, the lead characters are FBI agents and consultants solving intelligently planned crimes involving such things as counterfeiting, art forgery, and corporate espionage. Nearly every crime is perfectly orchestrated, but the FBI has a secret weapon in Neal Caffrey (played by Matt Bomer). He is a brilliant forger, thief, and con man who was captured by the FBI for his own crimes and now serves as their indentured consultant. The show has garnered impressive reviews and ratings, but like much crime-related entertainment, it departs a great deal from the realities of crime and justice. In the real world of crime (even white-collar crime), offenses and offenders are typically not so impressive, and theories of self-control and crime are inspired in large part from that pattern. Most crimes involve rather crude techniques, are unplanned and even sometimes quite sloppily done, and are marked by minimal benefits but potentially extensive risks. Indeed, most offenders are opportunistic in nature—their crimes are committed with convenience rather than effectiveness or stealth in mind.

Some even have suggested that the approach taken in many crimes is, for lack of a better term, *dumb*. We mention this with caution—we study criminals every day and know the difficult life circumstances from which they often come, so we are reluctant to take a mocking or ridiculing tone. That said, their poor judgment is often unmistakable, and Slate.com's crime blog, which often crowns a "dumb criminal of the week," nicely illustrates this point (Peters, 2013). An entry in November 2013, for example, details the story of a Colorado burglar who committed a spree of 15 burglaries. He made a critical mistake: For each one, he was wearing a GPS ankle monitor that allowed his movements to be geographically tracked. (The monitor was court-mandated because of a prior burglary conviction.) Once police tied his location to the first burglary, they quickly connected him to all 15, and he found himself back in prison. Gottfredson and Hirschi would see this offender as perfectly capturing their arguments about the nature of crime and the typical offender.

From these patterns, Gottfredson and Hirschi make an important inference about those who commit crimes: They are low in self-control, and their crimes are instances in which they seek "immediate, easy, and short-term pleasure" without considering or being influenced by consequences (1990, p. 41). If they had more self-control, they would avoid crime, or just as important, would approach it with greater planning and diligence (a pattern rarely seen). Gottfredson and Hirschi expect these individuals to have the weak social bonds that Hirschi (1969) earlier described, but the defining and all-important quality of offenders is their low self-control. Everyone can spot the immediate pleasures and benefits of crime, but those with low self-control ignore the consequences and let their criminal inclinations run free. Thus, an individual's level of self-control should be the strongest predictor of criminal involvement.

Gottfredson and Hirschi also address this question: What causes an individual to have high or low self-control to begin with? The key for them is effective parenting during the first decade of life. All individuals start in a primitive state of lacking self-control, but parents instill self-control when they monitor behavior, recognize deviance when it occurs, and punish such behavior: "The person who cares for the child will watch his behavior, see him doing things he should not do, and correct him" (p. 97). This "correction" teaches children that deviance has consequences and that they must therefore regulate their actions. Gottfredson and Hirschi emphasize that parental socialization is most important—perhaps even exclusively important—in the first decade of life. This is the window of opportunity in which self-control must be taught, because beyond that period, children who have not learned self-control are unlikely to develop it later. As they enter adolescence, their low self-control will steer them toward circumstances and relationships that discourage self-control. They will, for example, select friends who are similarly low in self-control and do not care about doing well in school or following rules. The patterns that are established by age 10 therefore should persist into adolescence and ultimately adulthood. In short, there should be remarkable relative stability in self-control:

> The differences observed at ages 8 to 10 tend to persist . . . Good children [those with self-control] remain good. Not so good children remain a source of concern to their parents, teachers, and eventually to the criminal justice system. (Hirschi & Gottfredson, 2001, p. 91)

Two other aspects of Gottfredson and Hirschi's theory merit special attention. First, their theory is meant to explain more than just crime. More broadly, it can explain any harmful or deviant actions—many of which may be legal—in which individuals pursue immediate pleasures in disregard of the consequences of their actions. Most offenders "tend to pursue immediate pleasures that are *not* criminal" (p. 90). Their desire for immediate gratification draws them to many risky and costly actions, including smoking, drinking, using drugs, eating poorly, gambling, quitting school, cheating on spouses, skipping work, and driving dangerously (p. 91).

A final point from Gottfredson and Hirschi involves one of their more controversial claims. It has come to be known in criminology as "the spuriousness thesis" (Hay, Meldrum, & Piquero, 2013), or the "social selection" model (Wright, Caspi, Moffitt, & Silva, 1999). Gottfredson and Hirschi argued that many of the social experiences and relationships that criminologists *think* are causes of crime—including those related to the family environment, the peer group, schools, and the community—are not true causes but instead are spurious correlates of crime that result from low self-control. In social scientific research, "spurious" has a precise meaning—a spurious correlate is correlated with crime not because it causes crime, but instead because it is caused by the same things that cause crime. Thus, in applying this logic to self-control theory, presumed causes of crime like developing friendships with delinquents or having negative experiences at school are seen by Gottfredson and Hirschi not as causes of crime, but instead as variables that are correlated with crime only because they all result from the same thing: the level of self-control a person developed in the first decade of life.

As part of this argument, Gottfredson and Hirschi insist that most aspects of social functioning in adolescence and adulthood are highly reliant upon self-control. They emphasize, for example, that those low in self-control "do not tend to make good friends" (especially with law-abiding others) and have difficulty "satisfying the academic . . . requirements of school" (p. 163). These aspects of social bonding require diligence, thoughtfulness, and persistence—the very qualities missing in those with low self-control. Thus, those with low self-control can be expected to (a) seek out friends who are troublemakers, (b) perform poorly at school, and (c) commit criminal acts; however, these three variables are highly correlated not because any is causing the others, but because each results from low self-control.

These claims of spuriousness have attracted significant attention, and for good reason—they suggest that the social experiences and relationships that occur in adolescence and adulthood (and that are emphasized in much criminological research) are *causally unimportant* for crime. True enough, social experiences in the first decade of life—especially with parents—shape one's self-control, but once that has occurred, self-control becomes the critical factor determining behavior, with the other factors fading in importance. Gottfredson and Hirschi therefore argue that crime is caused by a process *much less complicated* than what we previously thought. Crime causation may, in fact, be quite simple. Low self-control may be the only important cause of crime.

EVALUATING GOTTFREDSON AND HIRSCHI'S SELF-CONTROL THEORY

These bold claims have made Gottfredson and Hirschi's theory arguably the most scrutinized theory in the history of criminology. It has been the focus of hundreds of empirical tests. We describe much of this empirical literature in other chapters, but a few broad patterns can be emphasized here. Importantly, many of self-control theory's claims have been supported. Most notably, self-control is among the most important predictors of crime, and its effects extend to many harmful or self-defeating acts that are noncriminal in nature (including involvement in accidents and poor educational outcomes).

In terms of the causes of low self-control, most research finds that parental socialization is a significant predictor (Burt, Simons, & Simons, 2006; Gibson, Ward, Wright, Beaver, & Delisi, 2010; Hay & Forrest, 2006; Meldrum, Young, & Weerman, 2012). Importantly, however, much research suggests *other* causes of self-control. Genetic variables matter and likely operate in part by transmitting from one generation to the next personality characteristics that are relevant to and overlap with behavioral science conceptions of self-control (Beaver et al., 2009). Also, factors that affect neurological development in the early years of life (even prenatally) are important because they affect the brain's ability to benefit from socialization. Social experiences—beyond parenting—also are important. Most notably, peer associations, the community environment, and experiences at school matter for self-control (Meldrum et al., 2012; Pratt, Turner, & Piquero, 2004). Aspects of physical health, including eating and sleeping habits, also are important.

On Gottfredson and Hirschi's claims of self-control stability, the research is supportive but not to an extreme. Self-control is fairly stable (a person's self-control tends to remain the same over time in both absolute and relative terms), and that stability may emerge even sooner than age 10—for many, it may be by age 5 or 6, or even earlier. Research uncovers many instances, however, in which self-control levels change unexpectedly during adolescence, and this sometimes involves individuals *losing* the self-control they earlier possessed. Thus, any suggestion that self-control is *fixed* in the first decade of life is unsupported—changes in self-control can and do occur (Hay & Forrest, 2006; Burt, Sweeten, & Simons, 2014).

And last, most research on Gottfredson and Hirschi's spuriousness thesis has been unsupportive. If the spuriousness thesis were correct, the effects of most criminological variables on crime would disappear once statistical models controlled for the correlation between these variables and self-control. On the contrary, such things as peer associations, the level of parental monitoring and supervision, performance at school, and attitudes about the moral acceptability of crime significantly affect crime in models that control for self-control. Self-control therefore is not the *only* cause of crime. From our perspective, however, it need not be. As we describe in later chapters, a better perspective seeks not to dismiss these other causes of behavior, but instead considers how they work together with self-control to affect involvement in crime, deviance, and other harmful behaviors.

In the end, Gottfredson and Hirschi have provided a powerful, parsimonious perspective that is empirically supported, even if not entirely so. Moreover, they have directed criminological attention to the impulsive and careless nature of most criminal acts—a pattern that is underappreciated in dominant theories, which often present offenders as more thoughtful or calculating than they likely are. This theory has also focused criminologists on the harmful *noncriminal* behaviors common among offenders. Perhaps most notably, this theory deserves credit for inspiring an extraordinary volume of research on the connection between low self-control and crime. Much of what criminologists know on this issue has emerged in research investigating the bold hypotheses arising from this theory.

IN FOCUS 2.2

Could You Amputate Your Own Arm?
(You might want to sit down before reading this.)

In 2003, 35-year-old Aron Ralston was hiking in southeastern Utah. As he climbed through a narrow chute at one point, a dislodged boulder tumbled down, crushing his right forearm and pinning it against the canyon wall. Ralston said he knew early on that cutting the bone and amputating his arm would be the only way to survive. However, doing so would be no easy task—his dull utility knife would not get the job done. Moreover, at least initially, he could not bring himself to do it. And this, of course, seems a normal human reaction. Enduring pain and discomfort to advance our own long-term well-being may be a normal part of exercising self-control, but the calculations clearly change when this requires amputating your own arm.

At many points, Ralston envisioned just allowing himself to die, but after managing to survive in this state for fully five days, he had an epiphany as he discovered that his decomposing arm bone was becoming flexible—if given enough torque, it would now snap like a piece of plastic. Using the weight of the boulder and his willingness to override the normal inclination to avoid breaking his own bones, he snapped the bone. He then cut through the remaining cartilage, tendons, and skin. Once started, the whole ordeal took about an hour. Miraculously, he then secured a tourniquet from his existing supplies and started his march out of the canyon that included, among other things, rappelling down a 60-foot mountainside. A few hours later, and with much help from others, he was resting in a hospital bed in Moab, Utah.

Is there something behavioral scientists can take from Ralston's extraordinary experience? We believe so. We see incidents like these as pointing to the idea that self-control is not a fixed trait that remains constant at all times. Instead, it responds to unique situations and circumstances that can trigger heroic displays of self-control; alternatively, a different set of situations and circumstances can lead to epic *lapses* in self-control, even among those with high self-control in the past. This is a theme we develop at various points in the book, including later in this chapter when we discuss a "strength" model of self-control (see Hannaford, 2011, for an excellent overview of Ralston's story and the resulting film *127 Hours*).

A PSYCHOLOGICAL,
TRAIT-BASED THEORY OF SELF-CONTROL

Around the time that Gottfredson and Hirschi's theory was first attracting attention, Caspi and his colleagues (1994) published a seminal article that provocatively asked, "Are some people crime prone? Is there a criminal personality?" In raising these questions, Caspi was not directly referencing self-control. He was, however, calling attention to a personality–crime link that had long been studied with trait-based personality models relating in large part to differences across individuals in how they regulate thoughts, emotions, and behavior. Before delving into this, however, we should provide some basics on personality research and its history.

Broadly speaking, *personality* refers to "characteristic patterns of thought, emotion, and behavior" (Funder, 2001, p. 198). Personality traits are thought to endure over time and manifest themselves consistently across different situations and experiences. Simply stated, we take our personality with us wherever we go and in whatever we do. We may not be able to *see* it—personality is an abstraction that cannot be touched or placed under a microscope—but it comes into play in all of our mental, physical, and social encounters. And yet, despite the seemingly obvious importance of personality, criminologists for some time avoided—or even rejected—the personality–crime connection. Miller and Lynam (2001, p. 765) point to this pattern in referring to "a long-standing mistrust by criminologists of personality." Delisi (2013, p. 270) points to this as well in specific reference to self-control: "There is a degree of awkwardness in the criminological literature [regarding] the relation of self-control to personality."

Why would criminologists be suspicious of the idea of personality? This resistance likely followed in part from disciplinary differences between early criminologists—many of whom were sociologists—and the psychologically based personality research. Sociologists often focus on how *characteristics of social environments* shape human behavior, whereas psychologists are more open to the importance of the *characteristics of individuals*. These different emphases sometimes explain the relative popularity of theoretical ideas.

Also, there were key limitations in the early empirical research on the personality–crime connection. Most notably, there were problems of tautology, otherwise known as circular reasoning. The early scales that measured different aspects of personality—including such things as *sociability*, *psychopathy*, and *aggressiveness*—were constructed to discriminate between offenders and nonoffenders, and many items contained specific reference to criminal activities. Not surprisingly, these items were quite effective at identifying criminal offenders. This is fine if such scales are used for the diagnostic purpose of identifying offenders, but to use them to *explain* the effects of personality on crime amounts to circular reasoning (Waldo & Dinitz, 1967). Cloninger (1996, pp. 76–77) describes this problem clearly:

> Mike is aggressive. How do we know? We have seen him beating up people. Why does he do it? His trait of aggressiveness causes him to beat up on people. The trait explains the behavior, and the behavior is the reason we infer the trait.

These problems are, however, quite fixable—scholars can overcome their disciplinary biases and also develop personality measures that are independent of the behaviors they should predict (e.g., crime). And regarding the latter, the research has come a long way in recent decades in identifying a small number of *master traits* that dominate the human personality landscape. The five-factor model has been especially studied and validated (Widiger & Costa, 2002). It identifies five master traits that all individuals can be scored upon (we all fit somewhere on their low-to-high continua): Agreeableness (trust, altruism), Conscientiousness (reliability, self-discipline), Neuroticism (emotional instability), Extraversion (sociability and positive emotionality), and Openness to Experience (curiosity, originality). These dimensions have emerged in an extraordinary volume of validation research conducted across at least 40 cultures, on five continents, and in dozens of languages (McCrae & Allik, 2002).

Many scholars see Conscientiousness and Agreeableness as the domains most relevant to self-control. Those high on Conscientiousness value such things as competence, order, self-discipline, and deliberation (instead of hastiness); in this way, Conscientiousness seems to effectively capture a willingness to monitor and regulate oneself to avoid actions that impose future costs. Those high on Agreeableness are trusting, honest, altruistic, and tender-minded. Simply stated, these are nice people who treat others well. At first glance, this seems different than having high self-control, but there is an inherent self-regulating aspect to Agreeableness: It requires "an ability to *inhibit* disagreeable tendencies" (Jensen-Campbell, Knack, Waldrip, & Campbell, 2007, p. 405). Being selfish and unfair is easy; *overriding* those tendencies is difficult, and the domain of Agreeableness captures a willingness to do so. With these logical connections, it is not surprising that several studies have found criminological measures of self-control to strongly correlate with personality measures of Agreeableness and Conscientiousness (O'Gorman & Baxter, 2002; Tobin, Graziano, & Vanman, 2000; Van Gelder & de Vries, 2012). These two master traits also are among the most important personality predictors of crime (Jones, Miller, & Lynam, 2012; Miller & Lynam, 2001).

The key question for our purposes is what exactly should we take from this research on the intersection of personality and self-control? What is its *value added*, to borrow an economic term, for understanding the effects of self-control on behavior? Some have suggested that the overlap between self-control on the one hand, and Agreeableness and Conscientiousness on the other, means that theories of self-control and crime can just absorb the prior research on the causes, consequences, and development of Conscientiousness and Agreeableness—all that is known about these two personality domains can now be seen as things we know about self-control. We are reluctant to take this approach—we are not sure that self-control really is equivalent to a combined Agreeableness/Conscientiousness domain. After all, self-control likely is relevant to other personality dimensions, not just these two. The master trait of Neuroticism, for example, includes problems with uncontrolled negative emotions, which certainly seems relevant to self-control. Also, Extraversion includes a facet of "excitement seeking" that is rash, foolhardy, or careless—sounds like something we would expect of those low in self-control. Thus, we agree with Van Gelder and de Vries (2012), who argue that self-control overlaps with but does not map directly onto any of the Big Five. We do believe that self-control is for all practical purposes a trait—a characteristic way of feeling, thinking, and acting—but it is better understood as its own trait (an "interstitial" one that draws from but goes beyond the Big Five).

With this in mind, we see personality research as valuable not because of the direct correspondence between self-control and previously established master traits, but because it provides a refined blueprint for *how* to study traits. Personality research has been conducted since at least the 1920s. That provides a fair amount of trial and error from which to learn. Modern personality theory is notably void of dogmatic, rigid positions (it has already worked those out), and in this regard, it is a nice counterpoint to some of the excesses of Gottfredson and Hirschi's theory. For example, in explaining differences between individuals in self-control, Gottfredson and Hirschi emphasize ineffective parenting as the only significant cause of variation and explicitly reject biological and genetic causes. This raises the familiar but empty debate of nature versus nurture. Personality theory has long since left that debate behind. Statements such as "Personality is shaped by both genetic and environmental influences" (Triandis & Suh, 2002, p. 13; see also Maccoby, 2000) are standard in this literature. Research in this area reveals that approximately 30% of individual differences in personality are attributable to genetic differences and a whole host of environmental variables shape key traits. This is a point we will emphasize: The sources of low self-control amount to a complicated, motley slew of genetic, biological, lifestyle, family, peer, and community variables. A comprehensive theory of self-control should consider them all.

Personality theory also is quite informative in its approach to stability and change. Recall that Gottfredson and Hirschi argued that relative changes in self-control are unlikely to occur over time—those low in self-control at age 10 (relative to other 10-year-olds) will be lower in self-control at later ages also. This rigid prediction has been a thorn in the side of Gottfredson and Hirschi's theory. Empirical tests reveal that relative shifts in self-control do occur (Burt et al., 2006; Burt et al., 2014; Hay & Forrest, 2006; Na & Paternoster, 2012); for some people, these shifts are extraordinary. This has created a theoretical problem in criminological approaches to self-control because our dominant theory offers no insight on what to do with such people. They are theorized *not to exist*, so there is no framework for understanding how they fit into the self-control puzzle.

This is where personality research comes into play. Life-span-development researchers have studied shifts in personality for decades, following children as they age through adolescence, young adulthood, and beyond and assessing how the typical individual changes and whether many individuals deviate from the typical pattern (see Roberts & Mroczek, 2008). The typical individual becomes more agreeable, conscientious, and emotionally stable over time, especially in the stretch from 20 to 40 years old. Young adulthood therefore is a period of unexpected personality development. These patterns are common across many individuals, so the personality differences between individuals that existed in adolescence often are maintained. This supports Gottfredson and Hirschi's contention that those low in self-control at one age likely will be low in self-control at later ages. However, in contrast to Gottfredson and Hirschi's thinking, personality research finds that many individuals deviate from the typical pattern (Roberts & Mroczek, 2008). As they age, some individuals become more agreeable (for example) at a greater rate than expected, while some become less agreeable. Personality theory absorbs this finding quite easily, arguing that shifts in personality often occur in response to changing investments and experiences in social roles tied to family, work, and the community. And individuals will not all move in lockstep with one another. Some will have happy, harmonious marriages, while others will not; some will see their professional careers thrive during their 30s and 40s, while others will not. These varied life experiences often translate into differences in the development of personality traits, and we expect this to be true of self-control as well.

BIOSOCIAL APPROACHES TO BEHAVIOR

A third perspective that greatly informs our understanding of self-control comes from biosocial approaches to human behavior. Perhaps no area of criminology has grown more extensively in recent decades. This area certainly overlaps with the personality approaches just discussed, but as we note, it forms a unique perspective on its own that is relevant to all aspects of behavioral science.

This approach is rooted in the simple idea that human behavior, across all situations and ages, results from a causal process in which the biological qualities of individuals combine with the social environments in which individuals operate. Wright and Beaver (2009, p. 163) describe this well: "From conception forward, the development of the human organism relies on the constant interplay between biological, genetic, and social influences." In short, this perspective eschews the nature-versus-nurture argument, emphasizing instead that any attempt to understand crime must consider nature *and* nurture and how they operate together. Central to this is a person-by-environment model in which the characteristics of the person (often of biological and genetic origins) interact with social environments to affect human behavior:

> According to this model, individuals vary with respect to their biological strengths and weaknesses . . . . These vulnerabilities influence the degree to which the individual is at risk for antisocial behavior. Rather than acting alone, however, these biological features operate by setting the stage for how adaptively an individual will respond to stressful experiences. In other words, a stressful environment is more likely to contribute to some form of behavioral or psychological problem when the individual experiencing it possesses a biological system that is somehow compromised. (Fishbein, 2001, p. 12–13)

The interaction that Fishbein describes often is revealed in biosocial behavioral research (Bakermans-Kranenburg & van Ijzendoorn, 2011; Beaver, Gibson, DeLisi, Vaughn, & Wright, 2012; Caspi et al., 2002; Conradt, Measelle, & Ablow, 2013). One illustration involves pioneering research on enzymes like monoamine oxidase A (MAOA). Such enzymes break down neurotransmitters that carry messages between the brain's billions of neurons. Neurotransmitters are the brain's way of communicating with itself to do anything. Thinking, speaking, listening, laughing, and crying—all of these actions involve important neurotransmitters like serotonin, dopamine, and norepinephrine (known commonly as *adrenaline*) that variously inhibit or "excite" human action, thoughts, and emotions. But these neurotransmitters require regulation. Too much or too little of any of them is problematic, and enzymes like MAOA assist in the regulation process. They sweep into the brain, "mopping up" the neurotransmitters in a metabolic process (Wright, Tibbetts, & Daigle, 2008, p. 131). Thus, insufficient MAOA activity allows neurotransmitters to, in a sense, run amok. It is linked especially to excessive levels of dopamine and norepinephrine, both of which contribute to aggression and reduced inhibition.

The effects of MAOA on behavior likely, however, are quite complicated, and this was considered in a groundbreaking study from Caspi and his colleagues (2002). They examined the effects of being abused and maltreated as a child on antisocial behavior as an adult. They expected this link to be especially strong for those individuals with insufficient MAOA, a genetic susceptibility that should limit one's ability to adapt to adversity. Their analysis of data from a male birth cohort in Dunedin, New Zealand, directly supported this hypothesis. By itself, low MAOA had no effect on antisocial behavior. However, it significantly moderated the effects of child maltreatment on adult anti-social behavior, such that the harmful effects of maltreatment were nearly three times greater among those with deficient MAOA activity. Moreover, this gene × environment interaction was central to under-standing the crime committed among this sample—individuals with both a low-functioning MAOA genotype and exposure to child mal-treatment constituted only 12% of the sample, but they accounted for 44% of its violent convictions.

Enzymes like MAOA and neurotransmitters like norepinephrine are relevant to crime, but do they matter for self-control in particular? They almost certainly do. This follows from the truism that any effects of self-control on behavior must reflect actions of the brain—*human behavior always involves the brain*. Thus, the neurological processes described above likely are linked to crime at least in part because they affect the brain's ability to regulate thoughts, actions, and emotions; that is, they affect the brain's ability to exercise self-control.

Beaver, Wright, and Delisi (2007) make this argument in treating self-control as an "executive function" of the prefrontal cortex (PFC) of the brain. The PFC is located directly behind the forehead. It is the product of more recent steps in human brain evolution, representing one of the last areas of the brain to mature (Walsh, 2009), and it is the portion of the brain most closely involved with higher-order thinking (including abstract reasoning and behavioral and emotional inhibition). It also is highly connected to other portions of the brain. This makes the PFC, in a sense, the *supervisor* of the brain that coordinates with its near and far reaches to enable—or stop—behavior. When things go wrong in the PFC, problems ensue, and low self-control certainly is one such problem. As Beaver and his colleagues (2007) point out, when executive functions of the PFC are described, it sounds like a list of acts that are directly associated with self-control. The PFC is directly implicated in such things as sustaining attention, formulating goals, planning for the future, self-monitoring, forming moral judgments, and inhibiting inappropriate actions.

Given the importance of the PFC, it is no surprise that biosocial criminologists have devoted extensive attention to things that may go wrong with it. This has produced an impressive list of interrelated and overlapping biological risk factors for crime and deviance (see Ellis, Beaver, & Wright, 2009; Raine & Liu, 1998). These risk factors should be associated with behavior problems, often by reflecting or producing impaired functioning of the PFC. The risks include such things as physiological underarousal (low resting heart rate), reduced glucose metabolism in the brain, respiratory sinus arrhythmia, birth complications and low birth weight, early developmental exposure to alcohol or toxins (like lead), and poor prenatal nutrition. Some of these risk factors are heritable, whereas others follow from social and environmental experiences. In either instance, they take on a biological life of their own and shape the brain's ability to successfully perform the executive functions required to exercise self-control.

One biosocial perspective that we draw upon later in the book involves exciting new research on the evolving adolescent brain (Casey, Getz, & Galvan, 2008; Steinberg, 2010a). Like much research on crime and deviance, we devote much attention to adolescence. In criminology, that is where much—but certainly not all—of the action is found, because adolescence is the life stage in which risky, rebellious, and rule-breaking behavior reaches its zenith for most individuals. Adolescents are just *different*. As Dobbs (2011) argues, this seemingly has always been true, and it has been noted by an impressive list of historical observers, including Aristotle (who compared the passions of adolescents to those of drunken men), Shakespeare (who wished that "there were no age between ten and three and twenty"), and the early-20th-century psychologist G. Stanley Hall (who drew attention to the "storm and stress" of adolescence).

Modern brain-imaging technology suggests part of the reason why adolescence is so different and why it is a period of heightened risky behavior. Specifically, this research indicates that contrary to prior accepted wisdom, the adolescent brain is still very much in flux—brain development continues in significant ways through at least the early 20s. And perhaps most important, development during this period is imbalanced, with some structures and functions leaping ahead of others, at least for a while.

Steinberg (2010b) describes this with his dual-systems model of adolescent risk-taking in which he argues that the neural system driving reward-seeking behavior zooms forward during adolescence in response to specific hormonal shifts. A second system, which is governed by the PFC and is responsible for controlling impulses, advances much more gradually. This creates a developmental imbalance of great consequence in adolescence: The adolescent brain's ability to detect the rewards of illicit, forbidden risks is rapidly advancing, but its ability to inhibit those impulses develops at a more leisurely pace. Thus, as individuals advance from early to middle adolescence (roughly age 15), there is a tendency (all else being equal) for reward-seeking to win over impulse control, and this contributes to the drop in observed self-control among some adolescents. Gopnik (2012, C1) cleverly describes this process with a quote we share every chance we get: "If you think of the teenage brain as a car, today's adolescents acquire an accelerator a long time before they can steer and brake."

Does this mean that all adolescents will have serious and repeated lapses in self-control? No, it does not; because individuals develop in different ways, this imbalance is experienced to varying degrees. Also, other biological, psychological, and social environmental factors come into play that amplify or diminish an adolescent's struggles with self-control. The dual-systems model is therefore useful not because it communicates a law of human behavior, but because it contributes a piece to the puzzle regarding adolescents' heightened problems with self-control.

This discussion also nicely captures the benefits of the biosocial perspective in general. It teaches us that in understanding the causes and consequences of low self-control, we must attend to a complex mix of biological, genetic, and environmental factors and the ways they interact with one another to affect behavior. Admittedly, biosocial researchers often have directed more attention to the "bio" dimension of "biosocial," but this is understandable given the historic neglect of biological variables in the behavioral sciences. If we are to understand how self-control develops early in life, evolves during adolescence and adulthood, and affects behavior at all points in between, we ultimately must attend to the complicated idea of person × environment interactions.

IN FOCUS 2.3

How and Why Did Self-Control Evolve in Our Species?

The theories in this chapter are largely concerned with *variation* (i.e., differences) in self-control—why do some individuals have more self-control than others, and do these differences explain differences in behavior? However, this raises an interesting related question: Why is it that *any of us* are capable of self-control to begin with? In short, how and why did the human evolutionary process produce a capacity for self-control?

Scientists have studied this issue in great detail to understand why humans are so much more cognitively sophisticated than other species (see Flinn, Geary, & Ward, 2005; Geary, 2005; Stout, Toth, Schick, & Chaminade, 2008). True enough, human brains are proportionately large, but the critical difference from other species—and from humans' earlier history—involves the complexity of the prefrontal cortex. It evolved to coordinate interactions between different brain centers in a way not seen before and not seen in other species. This enables the higher-order thinking in areas of intelligence, self-control, and self-awareness that is the unique trademark of humanity.

But what directly led to this evolution of the prefrontal cortex—what were the critical circumstances or experiences faced by the earliest human populations? Many theories have been offered. Some emphasize food, with human brains evolving in response to changes in diet and changing demands to secure specific foods. Others emphasize the emergence of bipedality among humans, with brains evolving to regulate the complex experiences and movements associated with walking. And still others highlight climate and weather conditions, emphasizing that harsh and variable climates triggered greater brain development to deal with unique demands. Each of these factors is relevant, but none has received steady empirical support—none explains the widespread brain evolution among humans and why it so far outpaced that seen for other species that faced comparable circumstances.

Researchers therefore have downplayed these explanations and focused on what appears to be *the* critical factor: Human brains evolved with such great sophistication in response to the demands of *dealing with other humans.* Once humans reached the point of being an ecologically dominant species— one that had figured out how to successfully navigate its physical environment—the selective pressures triggering evolution came increasingly not from extrinsic sources (e.g., food shortages, weather, or predation from other animals) but from interactions with other intelligent humans. As Alexander compellingly noted (1989, p. 469), the big transition occurred when humans became "their own principal hostile force of nature." Human interactions are complex and variable, and navigating them was no easy task. Flinn et al. (2005) describe this perfectly well, illustrating the critical way in which human social interaction triggered a biological evolution of epic proportions:

> The potential variety of human social puzzles is apparently infinite; no two social situations are precisely identical, nor are any two individuals ever in exactly the same social environment. Moreover, social relationships can change rapidly, requiring quick modification of strategy (p. 13). . . . Sophisticated social-cognitive and linguistic capacities were favored because such skills allowed individuals to anticipate and influence social interactions with other increasingly sophisticated humans (p. 35).

THE STRENGTH MODEL:
SELF-CONTROL AS A DEPLETABLE RESOURCE

The theories covered thus far have in many ways approached self-control as a trait—a characteristic way of thinking and behaving that is stable and that consistently distinguishes people from one another. In short, according to these theories, some people have high self-control whereas others do not, and these differences are evident across different social contexts and stages of the life course. The different theories vary in terms of how rigidly they adhere to these conceptualizations of self-control, but they all are largely in the same camp.

The self-control strength model advanced by Baumeister and his colleagues offers a different perspective. Baumeister agrees that self-control often functions as a trait, but he says it also can be seen as a *state*—a transient status that fluctuates from one situation to the next or across spans of hours, days, or weeks. This perspective directs attention to the shifts in self-control that occur *within individuals* across different situations and experiences. Baumeister is interested in this question: Why do individuals successfully display self-control at one point in time, but then suffer "self-control failure" at other points? For example, consider a struggling alcoholic who faithfully abstains for three consecutive days but then binges horribly on the fourth. What explains her apparent loss of self-control on that final day? True enough, this struggling alcoholic may have a low level of *trait* self-control (as the theories above would suggest), but what explains the fluctuations in her self-control over time?

Baumeister's perspective answers that question and gives insight into some of the ultimate causes of self-control (Baumeister, Heatherton, & Tice, 1994; Baumeister & Tierney, 2011; Baumeister, Vohs, & Tice, 2007). It argues that self-control should be seen, at least in part, as a personal resource that fluctuates over time within the individual. It is best understood with the analogy of a human muscle and its physical strength. Just like the strength of a muscle, self-control strength can be depleted over time from repeated exertions that tax self-control resources and increase the likelihood of self-control failure. Self-control resources can be replenished, however, through "rest" (an interruption of demanding stimuli); also, it can be strengthened through "practice" (simple tasks that focus individuals on their successful use of self-control).

Many studies support the basic tenets of this model (see Hagger, Wood, Stiff, & Chatzisarantis, 2010). These often have involved laboratory experiments in which people are randomly assigned to an experimental group that performs tasks requiring self-regulation (the control group is given a neutral task that does not tax self-control resources). Experimental subjects might be asked, for example, to watch an emotionally evocative film while trying to amplify or repress their emotional reactions. In doing so, they are being asked to *override* their normal emotional reaction and thus employ their self-control resources. Performance of these tasks often leads to within-individual reductions in self-control that exceed what is observed for control groups (Muraven, Tice, & Baumeister, 1998). Thus, the exercise of self-control produces at least a short-term increase in the odds of subsequent self-control failure—"dormant urges become unleashed after people have earlier engaged in self-regulation" (Vohs, Finkenauer, & Baumeister, 2011, p. 167). This perspective suggests that such things as aggression and substance use will increase in the wake of demanding and stressful experiences that require self-control (see Baumeister et al., 2007). Self-control strength is replenished, however, once rest and recovery occurs (Tyler & Burns, 2008). Also, easily accomplished daily exercises in self-control (like improving one's posture or using one's nondominant hand for simple tasks) leads to improvement in self-control tasks that are quite independent of the daily exercises. This suggests that the exercises do not simply improve specific skills, but instead produce across-the-board improvements in self-control (Baumeister, Gailliot, DeWall, & Oaten, 2006).

Recent research also adds a new twist on this perspective by indicating that self-control *strength* may actually be tied to a physical energy source. In short, something like *willpower* (a common synonym for self-control) may be more than a metaphor—the ability to use self-control relies on actual energy. The human brain consumes 20% of the body's calories despite constituting only 2% of its mass (Baumeister & Tierney, 2011). With the human brain taking such an energy-expending toll, researchers were naturally drawn to this question: Does depriving the brain of energy lead to short-term decreases in one's ability to self-regulate?

This question fortunately can be considered without actually starving someone; they merely must be in a state of normal, everyday hunger. This has been done in several innovative studies that examined the link between glucose and self-control. After food is consumed, glucose is metabolized in the bloodstream to fuel the brain's activities. Gailliot, Baumeister, and their colleagues (2007) used this process as the foundation for shedding light on the energy requirements of self-control, and they reached several remarkable conclusions in their study of undergraduates. Most notably, those asked to perform a self-control task experienced a significant drop in blood glucose levels, suggesting that self-control is in fact an energy-expensive activity. Moreover, those with low glucose levels after the self-control task also fared poorly on subsequent self-control tasks. However, drinking a glass of lemonade that contained sugar (and hence glucose) helped counteract these effects. Importantly, the lemonade was beneficial because of the glucose and not simply because it removed the irritation of being thirsty—the harmful effects of having to perform a self-control task were not eliminated among subjects who drank lemonade that contained a non-glucose sugar substitute. This research therefore suggests that inconsistent eating habits may also contribute to short-term, within-individual fluctuations in self-control.

IN FOCUS 2.4

The Harmful Effects of Being "Hangry"

Violent and aggressive behavior between married couples is an unfortunate reality, and a recent study points to a potential explanation for why mild forms of it may occur: Being *hangry*. Yes, that is correct—the popular phrase you may have heard (it even shows up in the "Urban Dictionary") for when people get *angry* because they are *hungry* is being studied by behavioral researchers. Specifically, Bushman, DeWall, Pond, and Hanus (2014) recently explored the relationship between blood glucose levels and aggressive behavior. One principal by-product of hunger is that it is associated with lower blood glucose levels, and according to resource depletion models of self-control, this lower blood glucose should lead to lower self-control, and thus greater aggression.

To test this possibility, Bushman and his colleagues collected data on married couples using unique, and somewhat humorous, methodologies. As one part of their study, they had 100 married couples measure their blood glucose levels every evening for 21 consecutive days at home. In addition, the researchers provided participants with voodoo dolls representing their spouse and 51 pins that could be pushed into the doll. At the end of each day, participants were instructed to place as many pins into the voodoo doll (up to the 51 pins provided) to indicate how angry they were with their spouse that day (done in private away from their spouse, of course). The researchers hypothesized that if glucose is a resource needed to exercise self-control, participants with lower blood glucose levels should be more likely to act aggressively by placing more pins into the voodoo dolls.

This is exactly what they found. In fact, those with the lowest blood sugar levels stuck more than twice as many pins in the voodoo dolls than those with the highest blood sugar levels. Moreover, these results held even when marital relationship quality and the sex of each participant were taken into account.

However, the researchers didn't stop there. At the end of the study, they also had participants engage in a computerized laboratory task (with 25 separate trials) that pitted husbands against wives. Following the established protocols, the winner of each of the 25 trials was allowed to "punish" their losing spouse by blasting them with loud noise through headphones (e.g., fingernails scratching a chalkboard, the noise of dental drills, and ambulance sirens) for anywhere from 0 seconds to 5 seconds and from a decibel level of 60 all the way up to 105 (about as loud as a fire alarm). Unbeknownst to participants, they actually competed against a computer and *not* their spouse, so no one's spouse was actually being punished. Instead, through random selection, the computer that each participant competed against was programmed to make them win the task for 12 out of the 25 trials. The researchers hypothesized that individuals with lower average blood glucose levels across the 21-day study period would be more likely to blast noise at their spouse at louder levels for longer periods of time. Just as with the voodoo dolls, the researchers' hypothesis was conclusively supported.

What do the results of this study mean for the model of self-control that views it as a depletable resource? Glucose levels appear to matter for behavior—in this case, aggressive acts of simulated torture. So, in the words of the 2010 Super Bowl ad featuring Betty White, the next time you feel yourself getting hangry (or suspect that your significant other might be), grab a Snickers, because, "You're not you when you're hungry."

New research on this perspective also ventures into the world of *sleep.* Behavioral scientists historically have ignored sleep, but this has changed in recent years as evidence accumulated on how sleep offers the central nervous system an opportunity for recuperation, the reinforcement of learning, and the consolidation of memory (Kopasz et al., 2010; Stix, 2013). Many individuals disrupt this process, however, by not getting enough sleep, and these problems are especially acute among adolescents (Centers for Disease Control and Prevention, 2013; National Sleep Foundation, 2013). This has negative implications for a wide range of outcomes, including delinquency (Clinkinbeard, Simi, Evans, & Anderson, 2011; Meldrum & Restivo, 2014; O'Brien & Mindell, 2005).

From the self-control strength perspective, sleep deprivation increases delinquency because the sleep needed to restore self-regulation resources is not achieved. Barber and Munz (2011, p. 315) describe this well: "Sleep may provide individuals with the opportunity to replenish self-regulatory resources. These resources get depleted during the normal course of the day . . . [Thus,] rest and recovery are required to return to optimal self-regulatory functioning." Their hypothesized link between sleep deprivation and self-control is supported in multiple studies (Abe, Hagihara, & Nobutomo, 2010; Barnes & Meldrum, 2014; Meldrum, Barnes, & Hay, 2013), therefore indicating that bouts of insufficient sleep can produce individual lapses in self-control.

One further point must be emphasized. These factors that affect short-term self-control *states* may also be relevant to long-term self-control *traits*. Such things as limited access to the energy that fuels self-control (glucose), sleep deprivation, and exposure to stress can be experienced not just on a short-term, temporary basis, but also in a more sustained fashion. For example, long-term exposure to stressful circumstances linked to an abusive family environment or chronic poverty may tax self-control resources in ways that affect not just immediate levels of self-control, but also long-term self-control development. The same could be true regarding chronic sleep deprivation. Under such circumstances, depleted self-control strength could become an enduring quality of an individual. We return to these possibilities in later chapters of the book.

CONCLUSION

The 1985 movie *The Breakfast Club* became a classic pop cultural statement about the high school experience. The movie revolved around five students who had broken school rules of some kind and had to spend a Saturday in detention. They were greeted testily that morning by their authoritarian vice principal, Mr. Vernon, who instructed them to stay in their seats and refrain from talking—for the entire day. Then, before leaving the room, he glanced at his watch and made a demand: "You have exactly 8 hours and 54 minutes to think about why you're here, to ponder the error of your ways." He then assigned a 1,000-word essay in which each student had to describe "who you think you are."

If this were a movie about writing an essay, nobody would have watched it. Instead, it grossed $45 million—a decent figure in 1985. The five students found entertaining ways to pass their time together despite the striking differences between them. The five came from vastly divergent social circles—there was the "criminal," the "athlete," the "brain," the "basket case," and the "princess." This group would never *voluntarily* spend their Saturday together, but over the course of the day they bonded—there was laughter and crying, fighting and kissing, and a little pot smoking. They discovered they were more similar than they thought, and their differences became a source of intrigue and appeal—something that tied them together. They became, in a sense, greater than the sum of their parts.

We think of the different self-control theories along these same lines. They are quite different, but this is appealing rather than problematic. The differences are clear. Some emphasize social environments as the causes of self-control, while others highlight biological and genetic forces. Some predict remarkable stability in self-control over time, but others are fascinated by self-control *changes.* Some conceive of self-control as a trait, whereas others focus on transient self-control *states.* And some see self-control as *the* cause of crime and deviance, while others explore connections between self-control and other aspects of life. Despite these differences, the unifying link is their mutual attention to self-control. And the differences across them are a strength—these theories are not duplicative and redundant. Instead, each addresses its own niche, and putting them together provides a compelling and thorough understanding of self-control—something greater than what any single one provides by itself. Like the students in *The Breakfast Club*, this group is much more than the sum of its parts. Each theory fills in gaps left by the others, and the connections between the different theories direct attention to novel possibilities. With this in mind, we draw from them all in the coming chapters to fully explore the causes, consequences, and policy applications of self-control.

DISCUSSION QUESTIONS

1. At one time or another, you have heard someone say, "I have a theory about that." Based on what you have learned in this chapter, how close did this "theory" come to what researchers would describe as a theory?

2. Think of a crime that was recently reported in the news. Was it a crime that required a lot of planning and forethought? How well does the simplicity or complexity of the crime fit with Gottfredson and Hirschi's view of criminal acts?

3. Do you agree with Gottfredson and Hirschi's argument that self-control is *the* explanation of all crime, at all time, in all places? What other factors might explain crime other than self-control?

4. Discuss what the phrase *person × environment* means as it applies to research on self-control. How is the biosocial perspective compatible or incompatible with Gottfredson and Hirschi's view of self-control?

5. Can you think of a daily hassle that might weaken your self-control *muscle?* What behaviors or habits could you engage in to strengthen this muscle to better deal with the hassle in the future?

NOTE

1. The details of this expedition were chronicled by Rogozov and Bermel (2009); the first author is the son of Leonid Rogozov.

THREE

WHAT ARE THE CONSEQUENCES OF LOW SELF-CONTROL?

————◆•◉•◆————

All of us occasionally make bad decisions. Perhaps we are enticed by temptation, oblivious to the complications that will ensue. Afterward, upon reflection, we may see how shortsighted and negligent we were.

Most of us, however, will never have an experience like that of a father in Sullivan County, Tennessee ("Buy this dad a brain," 2008). One day in October 2008, he drank 15 beers and combined that with liquor and cocaine. He then set off in the family van with a female friend and his three sons. He wisely decided not to drive; unwisely, however, he selected his 10-year old-son as the designated driver. The young boy traveled at speeds greater than 90 miles per hour, ultimately crashing the van and flipping it onto its roof. Miraculously, nobody was seriously hurt. When the police arrived, the father claimed he was driving but then later acknowledged otherwise. For obvious reasons, the father was arrested for endangering his own children. He was also cited for seat belt violations (despite the obvious dangers of the trip, he had failed to follow seat belt laws) and for having no auto insurance for the car that now was demolished. And his female friend attracted the attention of the police as well—when police arrived, they restrained her as she frantically tried to gulp down an eclectic mix of pills, including prescription pain killers, antianxiety medications, and a few other things. She would ultimately test positive for cocaine. The father was first taken to the hospital for treatment of his minor injuries and then sent to jail for processing on his many charges. In his mug shot, he can be seen wearing a T-shirt imploring others to "Buy this dad a beer."

This case is extreme, and in presenting it we run the risk of suggesting that self-control problems emerge only among those who appear hopelessly dysfunctional. That is not the case, as we will show—problems with low self-control often affect those who are ordinary in many ways. Nevertheless, there are instructive and even typical elements of this case. Most notably, if standard self-control measurement procedures had been available, they almost certainly would have revealed the father as having low self-control. His poor decisions are classic examples of low self-control in action, as he failed to consider—or was not deterred by—the easily anticipated negative consequences of his actions. This case also points to a basic reality of low self-control: Most commonly, it predicts *a wide variety* of problems rather than being limited to specific, narrow aspects of life. Thus, it is not surprising that the father's substance abuse was accompanied by such things as lying to a police officer, poor parenting, failure to follow seat belt and driving laws, and operating an uninsured car. Simply stated, the complications of low self-control are multiple rather than singular. And one last thing about this case is instructive: Those with low self-control often put themselves in social situations and relationships that reinforce their patterns of low self-control. Thus, it is not surprising that the father was spending time with a female friend similarly inattentive to the negative consequences of her actions.

With this example in mind, we seek in this chapter to describe the scientific evidence on the consequences of low self-control. Thus, while the previous chapter discussed theories *predicting* that low self-control should matter for behavior, this chapter describes research testing those predictions. Interestingly, the empirical story begins with a marshmallow, or more specifically, with the ability of some children to resist eating one. The classic "marshmallow study" in the field of psychology provided early insights into the behavioral science implications of self-control. We move from this study to describe the extensive research documenting important effects of self-control on criminal behavior. We then turn to consequences of low self-control that are *noncriminal* in nature (but nevertheless often quite serious), before concluding by discussing the key policy implications of this research.

THE MARSHMALLOW EXPERIMENTS

In the late 1960s and early 1970s, a fertile ground for pioneering behavioral science research was, of all places, a nursery school—the Bing Nursery School on the campus of Stanford University in Palo Alto, California. It was the site of numerous delayed gratification studies conducted by Walter Mischel and his colleagues, studies that came to be known as the *marshmallow experiments* because of their use of that sugary temptation that children crave.

Mischel's research group ran roughly 650 children (typically 4 to 5 years old) through studies that took a familiar sequence. Once comfortable in the experiment room, the child was shown two treats and asked to identify which he or she most preferred. In the iconic and most described version of this study, the experimenter presented children with the option of either one or two marshmallows. The children not surprisingly indicated that two marshmallows were better than one. They were instructed that after the experimenter left the room (leaving the child alone), he could be called back by the ringing of a bell, at which point the child would receive a single marshmallow. To get *two* marshmallows, however, the child had to wait for the experimenter to return on his own—the bell could not be used. The interesting question was this: Could the children postpone the gratification of one marshmallow to achieve the delayed but greater gratification of two? And if so, for how long? As an added twist, some children were randomly assigned to a condition in which the marshmallows were displayed on the very table at which they sat (for other children, the marshmallows were removed from the room).

Anybody even slightly curious about small children or human behavior in general would have enjoyed spying into the experiment room and observing the heroic self-regulation attempts of these children. (The good news: This experiment is conducted frequently, and the Internet is replete with marshmallow test video footage). Several striking patterns emerged from these studies, the first of which involves the variation in waiting times across children. Some children rang the bell quickly and gobbled up the single marshmallow. Others, however, showed remarkable self-restraint. In one of the original studies (Mischel & Ebbesen, 1970), 10 of 32 subjects waited for the maximum allowable time: 15 minutes. The authors noted, however, that in pilot studies preceding the formal experiment, no time limit was set and some children waited more than an hour. Mischel and Ebbesen were surprised, "considering the widespread belief that young children are incapable of sustained delay of gratification" (1970, p. 334). The clear conclusion was that as early as age 5, there are marked differences among individuals in self-control, with some being already capable of significant self-restraint.

A second pattern to emerge across many studies was that children who waited the longest often did so by distracting themselves and not thinking of the marshmallows (or whatever other treat was used). This was the case, for example, among subjects who were randomly assigned to the condition in which the temptations were taken out of the room, and therefore could not be seen. These children waited an average of more than 11 minutes before ringing the bell, but among those who had to *see* the preferred temptation, the average wait time was just under 5 minutes (Mischel & Ebbesen, 1970). But even among this second group, there were informative variations. Mischel and Ebbesen found that those who waited longest devised impressive ways to distract themselves from the visible temptation:

> Instead of focusing prolonged attention on the objects . . . , they avoided looking at them. Some children covered their eyes with their hands, rested their heads on their arms, and found other similar techniques for averting their eyes from the reward objects. Many . . . [generated] their own diversions: They talked to themselves, sang, invented games with their hands and feet, and even tried to fall asleep while waiting—as one child successfully did. (Mischel & Ebbesen, 1970, p. 335)

These children were *redirecting* themselves away from the temptation. This has been observed in other recent similar experiments, and one entertaining example comes from a test conducted by Kidd,

Palmeri, and Aslin (2013) at the University of Rochester. In this study, all children were exposed to the marshmallow resting on their table and, once again, many covered their eyes or found a way to remove it from visibility. This seemed to extend their waiting times. As part of this, one ingenious boy reminded us of an obvious but unappreciated fact: It is difficult to eat something you are presently sitting on. When he sat on his marshmallow, he sent a clear message to us all: If we sit on the food we crave, we will no longer want to eat it.

These examples of redirection are not just entertaining—they are important to the science of self-control. They reveal how self-control is not a *fixed* quality that is either *there* or *not there*. It involves habits or techniques—like redirection—that help facilitate the successful exercise of self-control and that almost certainly can be learned. Specifically, those who distracted themselves were using a behavioral tool of sorts that made the task easier. This is a theme we will return to at many points: Self-control is not merely an inherent quality, but also a set of tools, habits, and techniques that can be acquired.

This brings us to a final key finding from the marshmallow experiments: The ability to resist the temptation of a marshmallow as a child remarkably predicts behavioral outcomes later in life. In 1981 and 1982, Mischel, Shoda, and Peake (1988) recontacted 95 subjects from previous experiments. Now nearly 16 years old on average, they were assessed on various indicators of success and well-adjustedness. Those who had displayed longer waiting times more than 10 years earlier fared better in academics, getting along with peers, and coping with problems. They also scored better on various measures of ability to respond constructively to the challenges, opportunities, and stressors in one's social environment. Most notably, Mischel and his colleagues found that those who had waited longest as a 4 or 5 year old were more likely at age 16 to express their ideas well in language, to use and respond to reason, and to think ahead and concentrate. Correspondingly, they were less likely to "go to pieces under stress," see themselves as "unworthy," and struggle to make social contacts.

Similar results have emerged in follow-ups of former marshmallow test subjects who had reached their 20s and 30s. Ayduk and colleagues (2000), for example, found that greater waiting times during childhood were associated in some instances with lower drug use during adulthood.

More recently, Schlam, Wilson, Shoda, Mischel, and Ayduk (2013) reported that body mass index (BMI) scores 30 years later were higher among those who had demonstrated shorter waiting times as children. Thus, while research on self-control has come a long way in the past 40 years, the marshmallow studies conducted by Mischel and his colleagues provide an initial and compelling glimpse into the long-term and wide-reaching implications of self-control.

A QUICK NOTE ON THE
MEASUREMENT OF SELF-CONTROL

The behavioral sciences are replete with studies of the effects of self-control on behavior, and we describe this research below, but first we emphasize the issue of measurement. Strategies for measuring self-control have become more varied and complex than the simple marshmallow test. Although interesting and revealing, that approach is less useful in research outside the laboratory. Most self-control research now relies on *surveys* comprising items pertaining to different aspects of self-control faced by people in their daily lives; these items are scored together to produce overall scales of self-control.

To measure self-control in children, who are less able to provide reliable survey responses, surveys are conducted with parents. One common scale for measuring self-control in children (see Hay & Forest 2006; Pratt, Turner, & Piquero, 2004; Raffaelli, Crockett, & Shen, 2005) comes from the Behavior Problems Index, which measures internalizing and externalizing problem behavior among children and adolescents (Peterson & Zill, 1986). Mothers are given 32 examples of problem behavior (e.g., "very strong temper and loses it easily" or "impulsive, or acts without thinking") and then asked to indicate how often this is true of their child. In some instances, researchers use all 32 items to measure low self-control in children, whereas in other instances, they select a subset of items that most directly reflect low self-control.

To measure self-control in adolescents and adults, self-report surveys in which individuals describe their own qualities are common. A typical approach is captured by the Brief Self-Control Scale created by

Tangney, Baumeister, and Boone (2004). This measure asks subjects to assess 13 statements in terms of how much they reflect "how you typically are." Each statement relates in some way to one's willingness to control thoughts, emotions, and impulses to conform to the normal demands of life. Subjects provide answers on a five-point scale that ranges from *this is not at all like me* to *this is very much like me.* Illustrative statements include "I do certain things that are bad for me if they are fun" and "Sometimes I can't stop myself from doing something, even if I know it is wrong."

The Grasmick, Tittle, Bursik, and Arneklev (1993) self-control scale is a common measure, especially in criminology. This measure was created specifically to test Gottfredson and Hirschi's (1990) self-control theory. According to early statements of that theory, those with low self-control have six distinguishing qualities: They are impulsive, they have a strong temper, they are risk-takers, they are self-centered, they prefer simple tasks over difficult ones, and they prefer physical activities over mental or cognitive ones. Grasmick and his colleagues (1993) used four survey items to measure these six concepts, therefore creating a 24-item scale used in many studies (Longshore, Rand, & Stein, 1996; Piquero & Rosay, 1998).

Two points about these various approaches bear emphasizing. First, each has been subjected to extensive scrutiny to confirm that the survey items (a) are correlated with one another as expected, (b) are reliably assessed by different raters and at different points in time, and (c) predict behavior in the ways expected of valid measures of self-control. Any claims that these approaches *perfectly* measure self-control are not warranted—for behavioral science concepts, perfect measurement is not possible—but the evaluations of these measures have in fact been quite favorable. On the three criteria just noted, these measures perform well and therefore provide valid and reliable measures of self-control (Piquero & Rosay, 1998; Tangney et al., 2004). A related point is that because each measure provides a relatively accurate depiction of one's self-control, these measures are likely all correlated with one another; that is, individuals with high self-control on one of these scales will almost certainly score high on the others also.

A second point is that although the above measures are commonly used, other strong measures are absolutely available. Indeed, in a few select instances, researchers have used multiple-measure, multiple-source indicators of self-control that exceed the quality of those just described. Wright, Caspi, Moffitt, and Silva (1999), for example, combined nine variables drawn from eight different sources who could comment on the child's self-control: the child himself or herself, parents, two trained observers, and four teachers who had worked with the child at different ages. Most commonly, alternative survey measures have been similar but not identical to the three prominent measures described above (e.g., Burt, Simons, & Simons, 2006). The similarities follow from the fact that different researchers often select items from the same personality inventories, such as the California Psychological Inventory (Gough, 1975). In yet other instances, researchers measure self-control indirectly by assessing involvement in specific behaviors that seem like perfect illustrations of low self-control. Tittle, Ward, and Grasmick (2004), for example, measured *behavioral* self-control by asking subjects to report how often they drank alcohol, used seat belts when driving, and incurred debt. One problem with this behavioral approach, however, is that some of these behaviors are important *outcomes* in behavioral science research; thus, to examine the effects of self-control on these behaviors, researchers need a measure of self-control that is independent of the behaviors it is used to predict.

Taken together, this research reveals that valid, reliable estimates of an individual's self-control absolutely can be generated, and this can be done without marshmallows. Indeed, you can even assess your own level of self-control. In the process, you can test any hypotheses you have formed about where you stand on this important behavioral science variable. See In Focus 3.1 for the entire Brief Self-Control Scale and some notes on its scoring.

IN FOCUS 3.1

How Much Self-Control Do You Have?

Some of the best self-control measures take a straightforward approach in which subjects rate themselves on various statements. Tangney et al. (2004) took this exact approach in asking subjects to rate themselves on 36 statements. They found, however, that their 36-item scale was nearly perfectly correlated with a smaller scale—one that included just 13 items that formed a representative subset of the larger scale. These 13 items became the Brief Self-Control Scale used in many studies. With this scale, subjects rate themselves from 1 to 5 on each statement—1 indicates that a statement is *not at all* true of them and 5 indicates that it is *very much* true of them. Here are the 13 items:

Circle the correct number	1 = "not at all true of me," 5 = "very much true of me"
I am good at resisting temptation	1—2—3—4—5
I have a hard time breaking bad habits (R)	1—2—3—4—5
I am lazy (R)	1—2—3—4—5
I say inappropriate things (R)	1—2—3—4—5
I do certain things that are bad for me if they are fun (R)	1—2—3—4—5
I refuse things that are bad for me	1—2—3—4—5
I wish I had more self-discipline (R)	1—2—3—4—5
People would say that I have "iron" self-discipline	1—2—3—4—5
Pleasure and fun sometimes keep me from getting work done (R)	1—2—3—4—5
I have trouble concentrating (R)	1—2—3—4—5
I am able to work effectively toward long-term goals	1—2—3—4—5
Sometimes I can't stop myself from doing something, even if I know it is wrong (R)	1—2—3—4—5
I often act without thinking through the alternatives (R)	1—2—3—4—5

Using this scale to compute your own self-control level is easy. First, assess yourself on each of the statements above. Next, for each item with an R next to it, make an adjustment in which you *reverse the scoring*. Thus, switch your scores of 5 to 1, switch the 4s to 2s, keep scores of 3 the same, and so on. Why must you do this? As you may have noticed, the R items

(Continued)

(Continued)

are phrased such that answers of "very much true" indicate *low* rather than high self-control. Thus, their scores must be reversed so that high values on each item indicate high self-control. Once you make these corrections, add your values for all 13 items. Because each item can range from 1 to 5, your overall score will fall in the range of 13 to 65, and a higher score indicates higher self-control.

You might be wondering: Is there a way to "pass this test," so to speak? Yes, there sort of is. Tangney and her colleagues (2004) validated this measure in two studies of college students. They found that the average score was around 39 in both samples. (Interestingly enough, this is the exact midpoint of the scale—it often does not work out this way). If you scored above 39, congratulate yourself—you appear (at least at this moment) to have greater self-control than the average college student. And if you scored even higher, you should really congratulate yourself—48 or above puts you in about the top 15% of the distribution, and 57 or higher puts you in the top 2%.

There is, of course, also the low end of the continuum—less than 31 puts you in the bottom 15%, while less than 22 puts you in the bottom 2%. And scores below 20 are especially low—they indicate the level of self-control expected of a moderately smart dog. Actually, we're joking on that—to our knowledge, the Brief Self-Control Scale has been administered only to human populations.

RESEARCH ON LOW SELF-CONTROL AND CRIME

We now consider what research, with the measures just described, tells us about the consequences of low self-control. The idea that low self-control will lead to criminal acts makes good sense, and research strongly supports this notion across a wide range of prohibited behaviors, for individuals from a diverse set of backgrounds, and at different stages of the life course. Regarding delinquency committed by juveniles, low self-control influences the likelihood of substance use, violent behavior, and property offending (e.g., Burt et al., 2006; Cauffman, Steinberg, & Piquero, 2005; Hay, 2001; LaGrange & Silverman, 1999; Lynam, Moffitt, & Stouthamer-Loeber, 1993). Perrone, Sullivan, Pratt, and Margaryan (2004), for example, examined the link between low self-control and delinquency using data from the National Longitudinal

Study of Adolescent Health (Bearman, Jones, & Udry, 1997). The "Add Health" study is one of the most rigorous national studies on U.S. adolescents ever conducted. Initiated by researchers at the University of North Carolina, information was collected from tens of thousands of middle and high school students across the nation. The authors found that those lower in self-control were more likely to engage in substance use, lie to their parents, get into fights, and engage in disorderly conduct.

Benda (2005) reached a similar conclusion with data from a statewide sample of high school students from a midwestern state. He found effects of low self-control on alcohol consumption, drug use, crimes against persons, and property offenses, and these effects emerged even after controlling for over a dozen demographic and competing theoretical variables. This supports the idea that self-control has effects that are causal rather than spurious. In other words, self-control is statistically related to delinquency not just because it is correlated with demographic variables (like sex, race, or social class) that also are correlated with delinquency. Instead, self-control has effects that persist even when the effects of these other variables are statistically controlled. Taken together, these studies point to a clear conclusion: Low self-control predicts involvement in just about any illegal act you can think of that can be performed by a juvenile.

Indeed, research in this area finds important effects even when examining understudied populations or considering extreme forms of violence. Baron (2003), for example, collected data from approximately 400 homeless street youth in Vancouver, British Columbia. He found that homeless street youth low in self-control were more involved in property crime, violent crime, and drug use than those who also were homeless but had higher self-control. An important study from Chapple and Hope (2003), on the other hand, examined high school students (a common population to study), but considered the effects of low self-control on two novel and serious outcomes: violence within romantic relationships and gang-related violence. Low self-control significantly increased involvement in both.

While the bulk of research has analyzed data from the United States, some studies have considered effects of low self-control on delinquency elsewhere. Vazsonyi, Pickering, Junger, and Hessing (2001), for example, analyzed data on adolescents from four different countries: Hungary, the Netherlands, Switzerland, and the United States. Low self-control was positively related to delinquent behavior in each country, and generally speaking, the magnitude of the association did not vary across them. Effects of self-control have emerged in studies with adolescents from the Netherlands (Meldrum, Young, & Weerman, 2009) and Canada (Junger & Tremblay, 1999) also.

The research conducted on adults is similarly consistent (e.g., Burton, Cullen, Evans, Alarid, & Dunaway, 1998; Longshore, 1998; Tittle, Ward, & Grasmick, 2003): Self-control is strongly linked to involvement in a wide variety of illegal acts. This finding emerges when the adults in question are members of relatively advantaged subgroups—like college students (e.g., Piquero & Tibbetts, 1996)— but also when they are relatively *disadvantaged.* This was found, for example, in Longshore and his colleagues' study of drug-using adult offenders in the criminal justice system. Thus, even among samples consisting only of offenders, there were higher levels of crime among those with relatively lower self-control.

One especially influential study of self-control and adult crime was conducted by Wright and his colleagues (1999). Their study used data collected as part of the Dunedin Multidisciplinary Health and Development Study carried out in New Zealand (Silva & Stanton, 1996). The Dunedin Study is one of the most comprehensive long-term studies on human development ever conducted—researchers have been collecting data for 40 years on a cohort of individuals born in the early 1970s. As part of this, measures of self-control were obtained during childhood and adolescence from multiple sources (parents, teachers, clinicians); criminal behavior during adulthood was measured also. The analysis revealed that those with lower self-control in childhood were more likely to commit crimes many years later as adults. Follow-up analyses with the same data revealed that childhood self-control predicted official criminal conviction histories decades later, even after accounting for social class and IQ.

Last, in cross-national research, Rebellon, Straus, and Medeiros (2008) used data from the International Dating Violence Survey (IDVS) to examine effects of low self-control on adult crime across 32 nations. The countries included, among others, Belgium, Brazil, Greece, Lithuania, Portugal, Sweden, and the United States. The effect of low self-control on violence was significant in all 32 nations, and this was nearly the case for property offending also. Similar studies using other data sources have also reported a link between low self-control and crime in the Ukraine (Antonaccio & Tittle, 2008) and Japan (Vazsonyi, Wittekind, Belliston, & Van Loh, 2004).

These robust effects of self-control have also been confirmed in meta-analyses. A meta-analysis is a "study of studies" in which each prior study becomes an individual data point in an aggregate analysis that reveals an average effect across as many prior studies as possible. In one influential meta-analysis, Pratt and Cullen (2000, p. 952) concluded that low self-control is "one of the strongest known correlates of crime." Similarly, de Ridder, Lensvelt-Mulders, Finkenauer, Stok, and Baumeister (2012) reported on the results of a more recent meta-analytic review. They found that high self-control consistently reduced substance use, crime, and other forms of deviance among adolescents and adults alike. They ultimately concluded that "self-control is thus one of the most beneficial traits" that one can possess (p. 92).

THE EVERYDAY CONSEQUENCES OF LOW SELF-CONTROL

A growing number of studies consider *noncriminal* outcomes, and this research provides compelling evidence for effects of self-control that reach into nearly every aspect of daily life. This is perhaps unsurprising— by its very nature, low self-control involves poor decision-making. This should logically extend beyond crime to behaviors that, while perhaps legal, are harmful nonetheless. With this in mind, we review research on the likelihood of becoming a crime victim, experiencing academic and financial complications, struggling with interpersonal relationships, and suffering poor physical health and a reduced sense of psychological well-being.

Low Self-Control and Criminal Victimization

Research on the causes of criminal victimization grapples with this question: Do crime victims do things that make them easier targets for victimization? For some, a question like this may seem like blaming the victim, at least a bit. To be clear, though, scholars never argue that victims of crime *deserve* to be victims—this instead is a question of whether they possess qualities or habits that increase the likelihood of victimization. And there is, of course, a practical reason for considering this issue: The more we know about what causes victimization, the more we know about how to prevent it.

Much research in this area indicates that *committing* crimes is a major correlate of becoming a crime victim (see Jennings, Piquero, & Reingle, 2012, for a review), and, moreover, that low self-control places people at risk for both outcomes (e.g., Jennings, Higgins, Tewksbury, Gover, & Piquero, 2010). Research connecting self-control to victimization was advanced especially by Schreck (1999), who developed the theoretical rationale for why self-control should predict criminal victimization. He argued that in the same way that low self-control stops people from contemplating the negative consequences of their own criminal acts, it leads them to ignore vulnerabilities they face as victims. As a result, they place themselves in risky situations in which they are surrounded by dangerous others. For example, they stay out late at night in public settings, often in social proximity to other offenders. Also, low self-control increases their drug and alcohol use, which adds further vulnerability. Schreck (1999, p. 635) described it this way:

> It is not in anyone's self-interest to be a victim of crime, but low self-control behavior produces vulnerability as a by-product. Heavy drinkers, for example, are less able to defend themselves or guard their belongings. Criminal behavior, another indicator of low self-control, frequently involves untrustworthy associates who try to double-cross one another, especially if some of the conspirators take no precautions against betrayal.

In support of these arguments, a burgeoning number of studies find that different types of victimization are linked to low self-control (Pratt, Turanovic, Fox, & Wright, 2014). Whether based on samples of convicted offenders (Fox, Lane, & Akers, 2013; Piquero, MacDonald, Dobrin, Daigle, & Cullen, 2005; Stewart, Elifson, & Sterk, 2004), adolescents (Higgins, Jennings, Tewksbury, & Gibson, 2009; Schreck,

Wright, & Miller, 2002), college students (Schreck, 1999), or the general population (Gibson, 2012), research consistently finds that low self-control increases one's risk of violent victimization, even after accounting for criminal offending and other relevant factors. Indeed, Piquero and his colleagues (2005) found that those lower in self-control are at greater risk of becoming victims of not just assault and battery, but also homicide.

Studies further reveal an effect of low self-control on other types of victimization, including property victimization (e.g., Schreck, 1999; Schreck, Stewart, & Fisher, 2006) and consumer fraud. Holtfreter, Reisig, and Pratt (2008) addressed this issue with survey data from over 1,000 Floridians, finding that those low in self-control were more likely to engage in high-risk purchasing practices. They were more likely, for example, to make mail-order purchases from unknown vendors; as a result, they were more likely to become victims of financial fraud. Reisig, Pratt, and Holtfreter (2009), using a sample from the same data source, found that those lower in self-control were unlikely to adapt their online practices even if they felt they were at a higher risk of being victimized. It is difficult to avoid the conclusion that those with self-control are a bit gullible because they neglect the potential consequences of their consumer choices. When faced with an offer that is suspect or perhaps too good to be true, their response too often is "I'll take it!"

Low Self-Control, Academic Achievement, and Financial Success

In a modern industrial society in which financial and academic success depends on the long-term acquisition of advanced skills and knowledge, low self-control places one at a disadvantage. Gottfredson and Hirschi (1990, p. 96) predicted this pattern long ago in arguing that "the traits composing low self-control are not conducive to the achievement of long-term individual goals." Taking school as an example, they pointed to the simple reality that school requires individuals to "be quiet, physically inactive, and attentive . . . for long periods of time" (pp. 162–163). Those who lack self-control will struggle with this.

Much research supports these contentions regarding school, with studies that range in focus from achievement in elementary school to performance in college. Regarding the former, McClelland and Wanless (2012) found that Oregon children who scored lower on a self-control task in prekindergarten had poorer math and reading scores than others. Such findings extend to middle and high school as well. Duckworth and Seligman (2005), in following a sample of students over time, found that self-control during middle school predicted later academic outcomes, including grades, standardized test scores, and selection into a competitive high school. They found that those with high self-control did better in part simply because they spent more time doing homework. Speaking to the long-term implications of low self-control for academic achievement during adolescence, Mischel and his colleagues (1988)—well-known for their earlier-mentioned marshmallow studies—found that students who lacked self-control as preschoolers had poorer parent-reported ratings of academic achievement during adolescence and young adulthood. A similar conclusion was reached in a longitudinal study by Moffitt and her colleagues (2011) using the Dunedin data described earlier. They found that low childhood self-control increases the chances of dropping out of school.

For those fortunate enough to advance to college, self-control almost certainly plays a key role. That said, there are significant self-control differences among college students, and those with less self-control perform worse academically. For example, they have lower grade point averages (Tangney et al., 2004; Tibbetts & Myers, 1999) and are more likely to skip classes (Gibbs & Giever, 1995). Moreover, they experience greater academic-related anxiety and boredom but less enjoyment and pride in their academic work (King & Gaerlan, 2014).

Researchers have also considered the effects of self-control on financial difficulties in adulthood. Moffitt and her colleagues (2011) found that self-control measured during childhood was positively associated with financial practices employed decades later in adulthood. These practices included financial planning, the accumulation of savings, and the use of effective money management strategies. Also, those with lower self-control during childhood had more credit problems as adults. In line with this finding, experimental studies reveal a link between self-control and excessive consumer spending. Vohs and Faber (2007) found this to be true among individuals randomly assigned to perform tasks that required them to exercise self-control.

According to a self-control strength perspective, the use of self-control sometimes can deplete one's self-control resources and thus increase the chances of self-regulation failure in the future. This pattern was supported in the analysis from Vohs and Faber: Those whose self-control resources had been burdened felt stronger urges to make consumer purchases and were willing to spend more on various products. Last, we must emphasize a recent study from Werstein (2013), who explored the relationship between self-control and net financial worth. She collected detailed survey data on over 1,000 alumni of a midwestern university. Her analyses revealed that those with low self-control had significantly lower net worth, and this was the case even after statistically controlling for income, age, and the educational level of the study participants. Thus, low self-control is not just costly in the figurative sense—it literally costs a person a great deal of money.

Low Self-Control and Interpersonal Relationships

Developing and maintaining healthy relationships with others is critical to a happy life, and self-control plays a significant role in this process. For example, research with adolescents finds that those low in self-control are more likely to be rejected by their peers (e.g., Chapple, 2005; Mischel et al., 1988; Olson, 1989) and to bully others in both face-to-face and cyber contexts (Unnever & Cornell, 2003; Vazsonyi, Machackova, Sevcikova, Smahel, & Cerna, 2012). Low self-control is also related to key facets of friendship quality, probably because there is truth to the commonsense notion that those low in self-control lack qualities that we often expect of our friends. Finkel and Campbell (2001) found that individuals with low self-control were less likely to forgive others, while Tangney and her colleagues (2004) found that they were less empathetic about others' struggles. Similarly, Righetti and Finkenauer (2011) found that they are viewed as less trustworthy. These findings give us insight into the general conclusion that adults with low self-control are less likely to have close, meaningful friendships (Evans, Cullen, Burton, Dunaway, & Benson, 1997).

Studies also have considered the implications of low self-control for romantic relationships (e.g., Pronk, Karremans, & Wigboldus, 2011; Vohs, Finkenauer, & Baumeister, 2011). For example, Vohs and her colleagues (2011) uncovered substantial benefits for romantic couples in which both individuals have high self-control (as compared to those in which only one or neither has high self-control). Such couples reported greater relationship satisfaction, a greater willingness to forgive, less conflict within the relationship, and fewer feelings of being rejected. And then there is the issue of *cheating*. Extramarital affairs are a leading cause of divorce, but those who cheat are sometimes quite happily married (Pronk et al., 2011). Pronk and her colleagues therefore raised this question: "With the knowledge of what is at stake, why is it so hard to resist the temptation to cheat?" Their analysis revealed that self-control was a critical piece of the puzzle—adults scoring low on a measure of self-control expressed greater difficulty remaining faithful in romantic relationships and were more likely to flirt with others when given the opportunity. See In Focus 3.2 for more information on their experiment.

IN FOCUS 3.2

Depleted Self-Control and Flirting

Flirting is a fun, often innocent practice, but the calculus changes for those already in a romantic relationship—flirting with someone who is *not* your partner is frowned upon, especially by your partner. It suggests you might not be fully committed to the relationship, and it may point to problems ahead. It also may suggest that the one doing the unwarranted flirting is low in self-control. An ingenious study from Tila Pronk and her colleagues (Pronk et al., 2011) considered this possibility with 21 romantically involved men (all heterosexual). The subjects did not know that their willingness to flirt was being put to the test—they simply knew they were participating in a psychology experiment of some kind. Subjects went one at a time through the experiment, first performing a task designed to measure their self-control. The experimenter then informed them that the next stage of the process needed to be set up. In the meantime, the subject was to sit in a waiting room for 10 minutes. As you might imagine, they would not be alone—an attractive female "confederate" (a member of the study team) was also present. She was instructed to behave in a friendly but not overly interested way.

So, how did these men fare? Those with high self-control came out looking great; their counterparts with low self-control, on the other hand, were significantly more likely to flirt with the female confederate. The evidence for this was strong. Flirtatious behavior was measured in part by the female confederate's self-assessment, but video footage also was used. Four trained research assistants rated the videos independently; overwhelmingly, they reached similar conclusions to one another, and their assessments were highly correlated with the perceptions of the female confederates. Simply stated, when someone was flirting, it was obvious, and this was substantially more likely among those who scored low on the self-control test.

For those in romantic relationships, the practical implication is clear: Be on the lookout for obvious signs of low self-control in your partner. Systematic scrutiny now might prevent major hassles down the road.

Research has also examined the effects of self-control on the behavior of adults both as parents and as employees in the workplace. Research indicates, for example, that parents who lack self-control are less involved with their children. Using data from the Fragile Families and Child Wellbeing Study, Boutwell and Beaver (2010) found that mothers and fathers with less self-control are less likely to read to their children, show them affection, and play games with them. With regard to the workplace, Kiewitz and his colleagues (2012) collected survey data on employees and supervisors working at a large retail organization in the Philippines. The authors found that employees were more likely to report that the supervision style of their supervisors was abusive when their supervisors scored lower on a self-reported measure of self-control.

Taken together, this research reveals pronounced interpersonal effects of low self-control. In the major arenas of life in which interpersonal skills are needed—friendships, romantic relationships, relationships between parents and children, and interactions in the workplace—those with low self-control struggle more than their counterparts with high self-control.

Low Self-Control, Health, and Well-Being

Being physically and mentally healthy is one of life's great challenges, and important parts of it may be beyond our control—such things as genetics and misfortune come into play. We often have control, however, over many seemingly tiny decisions made each day about what to eat and drink, whether to exercise, and when to seek assistance from others. Self-control plays a key role in this process, and this starts well before adulthood. For example, high school students with high self-control exercise more often, are more likely to eat breakfast, are less likely to spend money on unhealthy foods, and have lower BMI scores than students with lower self-control (Junger & van Kampen, 2010). Indeed, the effects of self-control on BMI scores has been confirmed in many studies (Crescioni et al., 2011; Duckworth, Tsukayama, & Geier, 2010; Schlam et al., 2013; Tsukayama, Toomey, Faith, & Duckworth, 2010).

There also is direct evidence that possessing greater self-control can assist in weight loss. Crescioni and his colleagues (2011) found that among a sample of individuals participating in a 12-week weight loss program, those with more self-control at the start of the program lost more weight over the study period. A similar conclusion was reached by Leahey, Xu, Unick, and Wing (2013) when they evaluated the effectiveness of a six-month weight loss program. Physical exercise has also been repeatedly examined as an outcome of self-control. Wills, Isasi, Mendoza, and Ainette (2007) studied a large, multiethnic sample of ninth-grade students and found that students with more self-control exercised more, ate more fruits and vegetables, and consumed less saturated fat than those with less self-control. On the other side of the life course, using data from several hundred heart surgery patients in Germany who were in their 60s, Schroder and Schwarzer (2005) found that those with greater self-control exercised more, ate healthier, and were less likely to smoke.

Other health-related outcomes of self-control have been considered. Miller, Barnes, and Beaver (2011) found that adolescents who lacked self-control were more depressed and more likely to develop mental health issues as adults. They also had higher blood pressure and cholesterol during adulthood. Low self-control also increases the risk of acquiring sexually transmitted infections, gum disease, and other physical ailments (Boals, vanDellen, & Banks, 2011; Moffitt et al., 2011).

With this extensive evidence on self-control and mental and physical health, it is not surprising to find that recent research also indicates that those with higher self-control are *happier* (Boals et al., 2011; Hofmann, Luhmann, Fisher, Vohs, & Baumeister, 2013). Hofmann and his colleagues found that individuals with high self-control reported both greater momentary happiness (feeling happy at that exact moment) and greater life satisfaction (feeling good about one's life as a whole). They point to an interesting implication of this finding: It contradicts the "Puritan" hypothesis that a person with high self-control lives "a grim, joyless life marked [only] by dutiful self-discipline" (p. 266). High self-control instead promotes feelings of contentment and ease. Hofmann and his colleagues attributed the greater happiness among those with high self-control to how they balanced conflicting goals in ways that encouraged happiness and minimized stress. They reported fewer conflicting goals, but even when faced with desires that conflicted with their goals, individuals with high self-control reported higher levels of momentary happiness.

POLICY IMPLICATIONS AND POSSIBILITIES

Earlier in the book, we made a promise: We would describe self-control research not just in terms of what it tells us about the science of human behavior, but also with an emphasis on policy implications. This is a critical matter, given the compelling evidence presented in this chapter on the far-reaching implications of self-control. Consider all the horrible things that could be avoided—criminal victimizations, negligent accidents, substance use complications, and life hassles, among other things—if the self-control levels of citizens could be predictably enhanced. Similarly, consider the extraordinary gains that might be made in the areas of education, the economy, health, family life, and happiness if more citizens could override immediate and harmful impulses.

The key policy question is this: What if policies could be devised to systematically improve the self-control of our citizens and reduce the harmful effects of low self-control? Importantly, if this could be done, the gains would greatly improve the lives of those who normally would have low self-control. These individuals are, after all, their own worst enemies, often weighed down by hassles and dilemmas of their own making. However, the benefits would not end there—*all of us* would benefit. Low self-control is responsible for an extraordinary amount of human suffering among blameless victims. Also, the costs of low self-control spill over to everyone paying the taxes, insurance premiums, and higher prices that result from such things as crime, accidents, addiction and dependency, and lost productivity. Moffitt and her colleagues (Moffitt, Poulton, & Caspi, 2013, p. 357) have been sensitive to this point in their pioneering study of self-control for individuals followed from birth through age 38. They have highlighted the societal benefits that could pile up if self-control levels could be improved: "Our findings imply that innovative policies that put self-control center stage could reduce a panoply of costs that now heavily burden taxpayers and governments."

We are optimistic that the innovative policies that Moffitt and her colleagues describe are possible. Our optimism is fueled by impressive policy-oriented research on already-existing programs and policies. Thus, while the science of self-control improvement may be a new area of study, important new insights emerge every year. Our goal is to describe those insights for our readers. In this sense, rather than letting self-control theory and research sit idly by, we will *put it to work* to shed light on how it can advance the human condition.

In this chapter, we simply lay the groundwork for later discussions by describing the key mechanisms by which policies and programs can promote greater self-control among individuals. Then, in the coming chapters, we describe policy implications and possibilities that are relevant to each chapter's focus. For example, in Chapter 4, which focuses on the causes of self-control in the first decade of life, we discuss policy implications and possibilities relevant to a child's early acquisition of self-control. Across all these chapters, our goal is to identify strategic points for social service, juvenile justice, and criminal justice intervention and discuss specific programs shown to be successful (see In Focus 3.3 to see how such programs came to our attention). Chapter 9, the book's final chapter, then brings together these policy discussions into a cohesive agenda for implementing and advancing the policy science of self-control improvement.

IN FOCUS 3.3

Effective Programs:
How Do We Know What Works?

There is a long history in our society of governments, charitable organizations, and for-profit companies developing social programs to advance societal well-being by reducing social ills. Many programs focus on the behaviors prioritized in this book, including crime, delinquency, aggression, and substance use. These programs come in varied forms—some focus on improving families, while some are delivered in schools; some use therapy while others use incentives; some are short term in nature, while others are intensive over the long term. Across all these variations and many more, one conclusion is strikingly clear: Some programs effectively accomplish their goals and reduce problem behavior, while others do not. The challenge for social scientists and policymakers is to discern where different programs fit along that continuum.

Research that meets that challenge has taken off especially since the 1980s. Increased attention at that time was driven by the recognition that earlier program evaluation research was inadequate. Due to a wide array of methodological limitations, it could not clearly identify the effects of commonly used programs (Palmer, 1975). Since that time, there has been an explosion of increasingly sophisticated evaluation research that identifies model programs and best practices in prevention and rehabilitation programming. Many tools and techniques have aided these efforts, including the increasing availability of randomized experiments, more rigorous data collection, the development of meta-analytic techniques (which quantify the results across multiple evaluations of the same program), and the emergence of precise protocols for designating which programs are effective. And there are many historically influential books, articles, and reports that have pushed this process along (see Cullen, 2005). Taken together, this puts today's social scientists and policymakers in an advantageous position: When we speak of effective programs, there is a wealth of rigorous evaluation research backing these claims.

With that in mind, the specific programs and interventions that we emphasize in coming chapters—programs like the Nurse–Family Partnership, Functional Family Therapy, and the PATHS curriculum—are backed by solid evidence. In selecting programs to highlight, we relied on a number of organizations that have developed rigorous protocols for designating

(Continued)

(Continued)

programs as effective. These include the *Blueprints for Healthy Youth Development* designation created by the Institute of Behavioral Science at the University of Colorado, the *Crime Solutions* protocol from the National Institute of Justice, and the *Model Programs Guide* from the Office of Juvenile Justice and Delinquency Prevention. These designation efforts carefully scrutinize programs and apply their criteria, which involve such things as the methodological rigor of evaluation studies, the evidence of favorable effects, whether favorable effects of a program persist over time, and whether a program has the organizational capacity to facilitate its replication in other sites. Ultimately, they are able to tell us which programs are effective, which are not, and which programs may be promising. Thus, across all of our policy discussions, there is one common theme: When a program is described as effective, this cannot simply be because the program *seems* as if it is based on a good idea or *seems* as if it might work. Instead, there must be rigorous evidence.

For now, however, our key focus is on introducing three critical mechanisms for using policy to promote self-control. These mechanisms are *prevention, reversal,* and *suppression.* Simply stated, if we want to put a dent in our society's problems with self-control, it almost certainly must be done by capitalizing on these mechanisms, which will be emphasized in the policy discussions in later chapters. The most important of these is prevention. It involves efforts to stop self-control deficits from ever emerging in the first place. Prevention efforts necessarily will focus on the earliest stages of the life course, including the prenatal period, infancy, and childhood. As we discuss in the coming chapters, a whole host of factors emerge in these early years that place individuals on a self-control trajectory in which they either possess or lack the self-control they need. Prevention efforts are designed to get individuals started on a trajectory in which they optimally self-regulate. The prevention programs we discuss include such things as nurse home visitation programs during the prenatal period, preschool enrichment programs, and parenting-training programs that instruct parents on effective strategies for assisting their child's development. Prevention programs overwhelmingly target children who have not yet developed problems with self-control but who are at risk for this to occur.

Inevitably, however, some individuals will in fact develop problems with low self-control. This is where reversal comes in. Reversal relates strongly to the concept of rehabilitation—it involves individuals with low self-control reversing their position on the self-control continuum, advancing from a state of having little self-control to having high self-control, or at least having higher relative and absolute self-control than previously. Reversal efforts therefore focus on children, adolescents, and adults already exhibiting behavior problems. The reversal programs we emphasize in coming chapters often involve therapies used with adolescents and adults by social service and criminal justice agencies. Family therapy is critical to reversal efforts and is used with the recognition that the ultimate route to improving a struggling child or adolescent's level of self-control is to improve family functioning. Many especially promising approaches involve cognitive behavioral therapy for improving decision-making in aversive or tempting situations. As we discuss, cognitive behavioral therapy is commonly used with children, adolescents, and adults, and success can be accomplished across all these stages of the life course. This follows from a point we emphasized earlier in this chapter: Self-control is not just a fixed trait that someone either has or does not have. It also is a set of habits and techniques that can be learned.

This brings us to the final mechanism: suppression. The hard reality is that efforts at prevention and reversal can never be fully successful. Some individuals will fall through the cracks, developing problems with self-control early in life that continue over the life course and include lengthy criminal careers marked by a high frequency and seriousness of offending. What should be done to protect society against such individuals? Should we simply "lock them up and throw away the key"? This will at times be necessary, but too great a reliance on harsh criminal justice sanctions is arguably heartless and inhumane, and just as important, it is also quite costly and ineffective (Pratt, 2009). A more pragmatic approach is to continue reversal efforts wherever possible but also rely on suppression. Suppression efforts are not focused directly on improving self-control as much as on introducing protective factors that reduce the harmful consequences of low self-control. Thus, while the self-control deficit is not eliminated, protective factors that have been introduced strip the self-control deficit of its potency, potentially rendering it inconsequential (or *less* consequential) for crime, deviance, and harmful behavior.

Programs designed to suppress the harmful effects of low self-control can take many forms, with some enhancing formal and informal supervision of individuals to reduce opportunities for crime and deviance. Informal supervision can be provided, for example, through mentoring programs and after-school activities, while formal supervision might come from such things as electronic monitoring, probation, and case management programs. In other instances, the key protective factor that is introduced involves the encouragement of prosocial experiences and relationships, including educational assistance and access to extracurricular and community activities and commitments. Each of these things *could* lead to reversals of self-control deficits, but even if not, they nevertheless may suppress the harmful consequences of weak self-regulation—an individual's low self-control will be less likely to translate into actual acts of crime and deviance.

These three mechanisms—prevention, reversal, and suppression—are key tools in the self-control policy toolbox, but admittedly, prevention is arguably the most important. There are two critical reasons. First, by definition, preventing an individual's self-control deficit from ever emerging is preferable to reversing or suppressing it, because it allows our society to altogether bypass the crimes, accidents, and dysfunctions that would have followed from this deficit. Second, prevention in the early stages of life is far and away the most *efficient* approach. This argument has been made most notably by Nobel laureate economist James Heckman, who takes a broad, macro-level perspective on our society's overall well-being and economic productivity. He has emphasized the evidence showing that human skill formation is hierarchical in nature—foundational skills developed early in life become the prerequisites for the skills that are developed later and are essential for life success (Heckman, 2006; Heckman & Masterov, 2007). This has a key implication: There are key windows of opportunity early in life in which these skills are most productively taught. If society's efforts are successful during this window, the individual and society reap the gains of his or her diligence, conscientiousness, and productivity. Alternatively, if the window is missed, we suffer the long-term costs of the individual's deficits in such things as "basic intelligence, acquired skills, social skills, self-control, and persistence" (Heckman & Masterov, 2007, p. 466).

Heckman points out that later efforts to improve skills during adolescence still may be helpful and should be pursued. Nevertheless, because of the hierarchical nature of skill formation, they simply will be less efficient. Heckman (2006, p. 1902) therefore concludes that investing in prevention efforts for disadvantaged and at-risk young children represents "that rare public policy initiative that promotes fairness and social justice and at the same time promotes productivity in the economy and society at large."

CONCLUSION

Two decades ago, Baumeister, Heatherton, and Tice (1994, p. 12) noted that self-control is "a vital aspect of human adaptation to life." Their point was that from the beginning of human history, high self-control has been a fundamental tool for navigating life and advancing one's interests—a tool right up there with intelligence when it comes to facilitating human performance. In this sense, self-control is not a *narrow* talent with specific benefits—it instead is an all-purpose, multi-use tool that assists in virtually every human endeavor. Importantly, high self-control does not dictate *what* goals a person prioritizes; it simply increases the chances that they will accomplish whatever they pursue. In the words of Baumeister and his colleagues, "individuals benefit from self-control because over the long run they have a better chance of meeting their goals, fulfilling their plans, and adapting to their environment" (p. 12).

The findings presented in this chapter highlight that fundamental pattern. Many of the things critical to a comfortable and productive life follow from high self-control. As we have shown, those with high self-control are more likely to, among other things, refrain from crime, bypass problems with alcohol and drug use, reach high levels of education, earn high incomes, accumulate wealth, develop healthy and long-lasting interpersonal relationships, and be physically healthy. As part of this mix, they also are less likely to be victims of crime, to be interested in cheating on their spouse or partner, and to experience problems with debt. And, as we noted in the last section, they do well in perhaps the most important metric of them all—those with high self-control are, on average, quite *happy.* This tight clustering of positive outcomes—the tendency of those with high self-control to experience across-the-board life benefits—is one of the truly remarkable stories in modern behavioral science research. In this regard, we agree with Kruglanski and Kopetz's (2013, p. 297) assertion that self-control is "a supreme human facility, indispensable for the worthy life." This conclusion has a major practical implication: Innovative policies that encourage this supreme human facility can enhance our society's quality of life, productivity, and overall well-being.

DISCUSSION QUESTIONS

1. Think of someone you know who you think is low in self-control. Is this person's lack of self-control specific to a single domain of his or her life, or does it influence many different aspects of his or her life? How is this consistent or inconsistent with the overall theme of this chapter?

2. Do you think it is really possible to measure someone's self-control by asking him or her to respond to questions on a survey? What alternative methods might *you* propose to measure someone's self-control? What would be the strengths and weaknesses of your proposed method?

3. Most, but not all, of the studies linking self-control to delinquency and other outcomes have been based on samples of American adolescents. Why is it important for studies on the consequences of self-control to be conducted in other countries? What is the added benefit of expanding research on this subject to adolescents from other cultures and settings?

4. Using examples that you have thought of on your own, explain why a lack of self-control might increase someone's risk of being a crime victim. What changes could a person make to decrease this risk, and how might those changes reflect the exercising of self-control?

5. Health care continues to be a hotly debated issue among both the public and politicians. In what ways might self-control be related to more or less healthy decision-making by individuals? What role could trying to strengthen people's self-control play in developing programs and policies aimed at improving their health?

FOUR

INFANCY AND CHILDHOOD: WHAT ARE THE CAUSES OF SELF-CONTROL EARLY IN LIFE?

In June 2013, 16-year-old Ethan Couch was driving his father's pickup truck on a road near Fort Worth, Texas, with a bunch of his friends as passengers. He lost control of the truck, colliding with a parked car where four people were fixing a flat tire. All four were killed. Also, two of Couch's friends in the bed of the truck were tossed from it; one experienced internal injuries and broken bones, while the other incurred brain injuries so severe that he is now unable to move or talk; he can communicate only by blinking (Ford, 2014).

This was not just a tragic accident—it was a crime as well. Couch was three times over the legal blood-alcohol limit and was driving 70 miles per hour in a 40-mile-per-hour residential zone just after he and his friends stole two cases of beer from a Walmart store. Unfortunately, cases like this happen every year, but this one gained notoriety because of the unusual criminal justice proceedings that followed. The sentencing judge surprised many in deciding that the Texas teenager, who pleaded guilty to four counts of manslaughter, would serve no time in jail or prison. This decision occurred after testimony from an expert witness for Couch's legal defense who suggested that Couch was not fully accountable for his actions—he suffered from *affluenza*, a condition in which a person of wealth and privilege, who has been allowed to do whatever he wants, cannot appreciate and understand the consequences of his actions. In making these comments, the expert testified that Couch had been allowed to drink since he was 13 years old and that a year prior to the June crash, he had been found in a parked truck with an unconscious, undressed 14-year-old girl but had received no punishment from his parents for this (Walker, 2013).

Put in terms more familiar to our discussions in this book, the expert witness was arguing that Couch lacked self-control because his parents had done nothing to instill it; if they had, he could be fully accountable for his actions, but his parents had failed him (and the broader public) in this regard. This testimony may have worked to Couch's benefit. He was given 10 years' probation and required to complete a community-based rehabilitation program with no time in a juvenile or criminal justice facility. To be clear, the sentence stipulated that his parents must pay the estimated $450,000 price tag for his residential treatment, and he would not be allowed to drink alcohol, use drugs, or drive a car. Moreover, violations of these terms could put him behind bars. That said, as of now, he will spend no time in jail or prison even though prosecutors asked for the maximum of 20 years behind bars.

Putting aside debates about the fairness of this sentence, we raise this case because it highlights a certain conventional wisdom about self-control: If parents do nothing to instill self-control, children will not develop it, and the results can be catastrophic. Indeed, this argument goes well beyond conventional wisdom—it is central to various empirically supported theories of human development. These include Gottfredson and Hirschi's (1990) prominent theory of self-control described earlier. That theory sees individual variations in self-control as explained mostly by whether parents set clear rules and reinforce them with consistent monitoring and discipline. If parents do these things, children develop self-control through a learning process borne of their own trial-and-error experiences. But in some families, this does not happen, and by all accounts, that appears true for Ethan Couch. His parents failed to teach him—perhaps from a very early age—that deviance has consequences and that he must self-regulate.

But is it this simple? Almost certainly not. Human behavior typically is explained by a complicated set of causes, and Couch's story points to sources of low self-control beyond the actions and inactions of his parents. One question involves why Couch's parents were so seemingly remiss in setting rules. Their own self-control deficits may have been a problem—parenting itself requires a great deal of self-control. This points to interesting possibilities regarding the *intergenerational transmission of low self-control*, a process whereby parents with low self-control pass this quality on to their children through, for instance, genetic and biological mechanisms. Media reports on the Couch family suggest a process of this kind. Using county court records, ABC News found that Couch's parents had a history of criminal and other traffic-related violations dating back to 1989 ("Parents of Affluent Teen," 2013), with the most recent charge having come in August 2014, when Couch's father was arrested for impersonating a police officer (Crimesider Staff, 2014). If both Couch and his parents lacked self-control, might there be a genetic basis for self-control, as suggested by biosocial perspectives on self-control?

In this chapter, we consider these types of questions with a focus on the causes of self-control early in life. By "early in life," we especially mean the stretch leading up to early adolescence. We are asking this question: Why is it that some children get off to a good start on self-control while others get off to a decidedly bad start? This question historically has directed attention to the role of parenting and the family environment, especially during the critical period of late childhood and early adolescence. We review the major arguments and insights on that, but true to our focus, we dig back deeper in life, considering the earliest social interactions between parents and their children. When it comes to the link between parenting and self-control, that is where the story begins. If you want to know how parents have encouraged (or discouraged) self-control in any given adolescent, you first have to know what was occurring in the home when he or she was just a baby or toddler.

But as we just suggested, an exclusive focus on parenting and the home environment is incomplete—genetic and biological variables are critical pieces of the puzzle as well. We therefore focus on the idea of self-control heritability and the twin studies that have shed new light on this issue. We also consider neurobiological factors that follow from such things as prenatal exposure to toxins, birth complications, and exposure to intense or chronic stress. Each plays a role in shaping the emerging architecture of children's developing brains. This, in turn, shapes their ability to self-regulate when they reach ages at which self-regulation is expected.

If there is one theme that ties our discussion together, it is this: The etiology of self-control is *complicated.* No single academic discipline or research tradition can claim to have all the answers. Readers should rightfully be suspicious of any perspectives that claim they do.

THE ROLE OF PARENTS IN SHAPING SELF-CONTROL

In criminology, parental contributions to self-control have most notably been emphasized by Gottfredson and Hirschi (1990). They drew on past research (e.g., Glueck & Glueck, 1950; McCord & McCord, 1959), identifying significant associations between parenting practices and delinquency to build a framework for understanding the development of self-control. They began with this premise:

> Much parental action is geared toward suppression of impulsive behavior, toward making the child consider the long-range consequences of acts . . . Indeed, much parental behavior is directed toward teaching the child about the rights and feelings of others, and of how these rights and feelings ought to constrain the child's behavior. (pp. 96–97)

Given this, Gottfredson and Hirschi concluded that parents' ability to effectively socialize is the primary determinant of a child's self-control. Specifically, parents "must (1) monitor the child's behavior; (2) recognize deviant behavior when it occurs; and (3) punish such behavior . . . All that is required to activate the system is affection for or investment in the child" (p. 97). Though Gottfredson and Hirschi also discussed background factors like family size and whether the family has two parents or one, these factors are important only indirectly (by affecting whether the three conditions above are satisfied).

Early tests tended to support Gottfredson and Hirschi's claims about the links between parental rule-setting, supervision and discipline, and self-control (Feldman & Weinberger, 1994; Polakowski,

1994). This, by the way, supported earlier psychological research regarding the effects of parenting on a wide variety of child outcomes (Collins, Maccoby, Steinberg, Hetherington, & Bornstein, 2000; Maccoby & Martin, 1983). Polakowski (1994), for example, using data from the Cambridge Study in Delinquent Development, found that children whose parents were strong at rule-setting and monitoring at ages 8 to 10 had higher self-control at ages 12 to 14. Similar findings emerged in retrospective studies that asked college students to reflect on how they had been parented at earlier points in life (e.g., Cochran, Wood, Sellers, Wilkerson, & Chamlin, 1998; Gibbs, Giever, & Martin, 1998); recollections of effective monitoring and supervision were positively related with self-control.

Recent studies have confirmed these links in larger, more representative samples, offering greater confidence that results are generalizable to the broader population of children (Hope, Grasmick, & Pointon, 2003; Meldrum, 2008; Perrone, Sullivan, Pratt, & Margaryan, 2004; Unnever, Cullen, & Pratt, 2003). For example, Perrone and her colleagues (2004) analyzed data on over 13,000 middle and high school students who participated in the first wave of the National Longitudinal Study of Adolescent Health. This study revealed that a combined measure of parental attachment and parental recognition of deviant behavior, which they labeled *parental efficacy*, was positively related to self-control.

These studies indicate the importance of rule-setting, monitoring, and discipline, but there is one lurking question when it comes to the Gottfredson and Hirschi approach: Did they conceptualize the idea of effective parenting too *narrowly?* In short, did they emphasize some important parenting variables while excluding others that also are important? Some scholars (Burt, Simons, & Simons, 2006; Hay, 2001) have observed that the Gottfredson and Hirschi approach emphasizes *how much* control parents exert over their children—do they consistently set rules, monitor behavior, and punish transgressions? The related but unique question of *how* this control is exerted is less addressed. For example, is rule-setting, monitoring, and discipline done in ways that convey emotional warmth and affection for the child? Or alternatively, is the approach marked by hostility, suspicion of the child's motives, and a heavy reliance on coercion and threats?

Similarly, when discipline is needed, is it meted out in respectful and balanced ways or, alternatively, does it involve yelling, physical punishment, and intimidation? And as a child becomes more cognitively and socially mature, do parents adapt to these changes to emphasize higher-order principles involving fairness and reciprocity (rather than mere obedience and compliance)? All of these considerations fundamentally relate not to how much control parents exert but to the *parenting style* they use in doing so.

Baumrind's theory of authoritative parenting is an important example of a broad parenting perspective that attends to these issues. Baumrind's contention is that effective parenting is not controlling *or* warm, but instead is controlling *and* warm. Indeed, Baumrind (1996, p. 412) explicitly rejects what she calls "the false polarity between a child-rearing ideology of indulgence and one of tyranny in favor of one that balances control with warmth." In advancing this approach, she introduced the ideas of parental *demandingness* and *responsiveness*. The most effective parents are demanding of their children (when it comes to rule-setting, supervision, and discipline) but also responsive to their developmental needs in *how* demands are communicated, applied, and modified over time. In Baumrind's words (1991, pp. 61–62),

> Demandingness refers to the claims parents make on children to become integrated into the family whole, by their maturity demands, supervision, disciplinary efforts, and willingness to confront the child who disobeys. Responsiveness refers to the extent to which parents intentionally foster individuality, self-regulation, and self-assertion by being attuned, supportive, and acquiescent to children's special needs.

Ideally, parents should be both demanding and responsive. If so, they are using an *authoritative* parenting style, and their children should be more socially competent and well-adjusted than children exposed to other parenting styles that involve low levels of demandingness, responsiveness, or both. This includes parents who are demanding but not responsive (an *authoritarian* style), responsive but not demanding (a *permissive* style), or neither demanding nor responsive (a *rejecting-neglecting* style). Informatively, a large body of research indicates that children of authoritative parents fare better on a wide range of outcomes (see Gray & Steinberg, 1999; Larzelere, Morris, & Harrist, 2013). Additionally, variables that individually measure the specific practices central to authoritative parenting are associated with positive child and adolescent outcomes. These practices include such things as strong parent–child attachment and communication, praise of good behavior, encouragement of independent thinking, clear rule-setting, diligent supervision, and the use of discipline that is balanced, nonphysical, perceived as fair, and accompanied by clear reasoning and expectations.

Several studies have applied this approach to the study of self-control in particular. Hay (2001), for example, collected survey data on parent–child relationships from approximately 200 urban middle school students and found—in support of Gottfredson and Hirschi's view—that children had higher self-control when parents consistently monitored and disciplined. Self-control also went up significantly, however, when parents used discipline that was fair and nonphysical. Indeed, the strongest parenting predictor of self-control was whether children perceived their parents' discipline to be fair, thus indicating that *how* parents exercise parental control is quite important for self-control. Similarly, Colman, Hardy, Albert, Raffaelli, and Crockett (2006) collected data from a national sample of parents and children and found that two parenting practices at age 4 to 5 most predicted high self-control four years later at age 8 to 9: strong maternal warmth for the child and the use of nonphysical discipline. These two factors emerged as important even after accounting for differences among children in initial levels of self-control at age 4 to 5. Indeed, the effects of parenting held up in models that controlled for a host of other important factors, including the family's poverty status, demographic variables like the age and sex of the child, and the mother's level of intelligence and prior delinquency.

This finding has also emerged in contexts outside the United States. Vazsonyi and Belliston (2007), for example, found that increased parental support and monitoring predicted higher self-control among 9,000 adolescents from Hungary, Japan, the Netherlands, Switzerland, and the United States (see also Finkenauer, Engels, & Baumeister, 2005). Taken together, this research supports a central idea: Self-control is best learned when parents impose high behavioral standards (they set rules, monitor, and discipline) but do so in ways that are supportive, encouraging, and warm.

IN FOCUS 4.1

Spanking the Self-Control Out of Them

On the topic of best practices in parenting, perhaps no issue has received more attention than spanking. Many parents are appalled at the prospect of striking their own child, even in a measured way. They perhaps also suspect that their own use of violence undermines their ability to demand that the *child* must refrain from violence. Other parents, however, may feel that spanking is necessary to capture the immediate attention and compliance of the child. Moreover, they may assume that spanking is not such a serious thing: "I was spanked as a child, and I turned out okay." The key question, of course, is this: What does the actual research say? By and large, it indicates that spanking is more likely than not to make things worse—children who are spanked behave worse later in life than those who are not spanked, and this relationship holds even after accounting for differences in behavior that predict why some children are spanked and others are not (Gershoff, 2002; Smith, 2012). In connection to this, a series of new studies (summarized by Kovac, 2014) offers insight on at least part of the reason *why* spanking often backfires: Spanking children may actually reduce the volume of gray matter in their prefrontal cortex. The exact mechanism by which this occurs is not well understood, but less gray matter is thought to translate into less optimal brain functioning for higher-order thinking, including that involved with self-control. In reviewing this research, Kovac (2014) offers this regrettable possibility: "Behind all this science-speak is the sobering fact that corporal punishment is damaging to children. That gray matter we've been spanking out of them? It's the key to the brain's ability to learn self-control."

Research With Very Young Children

Many of the studies just cited were conducted with adolescents or near-adolescents. This has been typical in criminology. Because adolescence is the point in life when crime and deviance first emerge and become common, criminologists have studied those life stages with great intensity, trying to understand how parents interact and communicate with their adolescent children. The problem with this, however, is that when it comes to parenting, the story obviously starts before then.

Indeed, it starts *way* before then. There is good evidence, for example, that parent-child bonds are forged *before the baby even exits the womb.* Various experimental studies have found that the developing fetus recognizes the mother's voice and becomes attached to it—the mother's voice prompts an uptick in the fetal heart rate that is not observed for other voices and sounds (Lee & Kisilevsky, 2014). This explains why *fathers* sometimes speak to the midsections of their pregnant wives, asking absurd questions like "How's it going in there?" They are hoping that their baby, upon exiting the womb, will know who they are.

Once the child is born, the bonding process commences—ideally, with great intensity. In connection, there is much empirical support for psychological attachment theories (Bowlby, 1988; Bretherton, 1992) that emphasize the importance of parent–infant attachments in the initial hours, days, and weeks of life. This attachment provides the *secure base* that infants draw upon for support and soothing as they navigate their earliest days. This research has led to many insights, including the finding that early skin-to-skin contact between parents and infants improves infants' reactions to stress, ability to sleep, and brain development, including maturation of the prefrontal cortex (Feldman, Rosenthal, & Eidelman, 2014).

Does any of this have implications for self-control? It almost certainly does, but of course, the payoffs are not immediate—newborns are not capable of displaying self-control. However, when it comes to later self-control (and a host of many other favorable outcomes), there are two likely mechanisms by which early parent–child attachment is beneficial. First, early social experiences and relationships have significant implications for brain development, and make no mistake—*anything* that aids the developing brain is good for self-control. Self-control is by its nature cognitively and neurologically taxing, so healthy brain development is critical. A second mechanism, however, involves the ways in which early attachment gets the parent–child relationship off to a good start—greater attachment is the precursor to the effective parenting practices mentioned above. This includes strong control (demandingness) but also strong warmth and attentiveness (responsiveness). Simply stated, the habits, routines, and styles of social interaction that guide parent–child interaction in *later* years are first forged during infancy and toddlerhood. If parents and children start their journey in optimal fashion, they build a history of working together in ways that promote harmony and cooperation down the road.

IN FOCUS 4.2

The Lonely Beginnings of Orphans

Insights on the importance of early parent–child interactions have at times come from research focusing on one of the most unfortunate social circumstances for children: living in an orphanage. Such children often have no discernible mother or father figure to encourage secure attachment and offer consistent stimulation. The results of such benign neglect can be quite profound. This was observed most notably in research with children raised in Romanian orphanages that sprung up in response to the social upheaval following the overthrow of the Romanian government in 1989. Bleak government-run institutions housed thousands of Romanian orphans during a stretch in the 1980s. Neurological imaging studies of these orphans—like those done as part of the Bucharest Early Intervention Project—pointed to a startling conclusion: Various portions of the brain were less developed—not as thick—than what is typically seen (McLaughlin et al., 2013). Moreover, children raised in the orphanages exhibited lower levels of electrical brain activity than children raised in traditional family environments (Sheridan, Fox, Zeanah, McLaughlin, & Nelson, 2012). Charles Nelson, one of the authors of the study, offered a sobering analogy in describing the typical brain of the orphaned children: "Instead of a 100-watt light bulb, it was a 40-watt light bulb."

Research like this highlights a critical point for understanding any type of behavior that relies on higher-order cognitive thinking, self-control definitely being one of them: Social experiences and environments greatly shape the biological tools individuals one day will have at their disposal. As sobering as these findings are regarding the life prospects of orphans and other children deprived of early-in-life attachment and stimulation, the researchers involved in the Bucharest Early Intervention Project pointed to an additional finding that is encouraging: When children raised in the orphanage were removed and placed in foster care, their brain development and activity improved significantly relative to that of children who remained in the orphanages. This points to yet another important theme of our discussion. In the same way that deficits in cognitive development can emerge, they also can sometimes be reversed.

This facilitates the emergence of self-control, even if just in primitive forms, by the second year of life. This was illustrated in an early observational study from Power and Chapieski (1986). They studied mothers and their 14-month-old toddlers in their own homes and were especially interested in toddlers' willingness to avoid objects in the home that are "off limits" because they are dangerous or easily break-able. These are the objects that prompt parents to say, "Don't touch that—you'll poke your eye out!" Power and Chapieski asked mothers what they did when their children went after those objects. Some used physical punishment, like a slap or swat to the hand; others, however, used nonphysical approaches involving verbal communication, a disap-proving facial expression, or some other gentle reminder. The research-ers observed the mothers and toddlers in action, counting the number of times the toddler went for off-limits items. On average, they did so once every nine minutes, prompting the parent to get involved. As we might expect, the toddler did not always immediately comply, and the researchers noted an interesting pattern: Parents who used physical punishment gained compliance with just 51% of restrictions, much lower than the 69% compliance for parents who never resorted to phys-ical punishment. This supported the basic idea that parental control by itself was not the most effective approach—exercising that control in ways that are warm and nonphysical was also important.

This finding has been replicated in other studies that used larger samples and longitudinal research designs. Laible and her colleagues (Laible, Panfile, & Makariev, 2008; Laible & Thompson, 2002) have been attentive to how parents handle conflict situations with toddlers in the throes of the "terrible twos" stage of life. This is a point when chil-dren are developing a refined awareness of what they want; their skills for satisfying these wishes, however, are primitive and uncivilized. This creates an unusually high number of parent–child conflicts— sometimes up to 15 conflicts per hour—over such things as child com-pliance, issues of fact, and the parents' unwillingness to satisfy requests. These conflicts need not be negative events, however; on the contrary, Laible and her colleagues found that conflicts often trigger discussions that amount to "on-the-job training" for toddlers who are learning how to navigate their social world. The most effective parents explain and clarify their requests and explicitly avoid aggravating actions like insults and threats. Parents who approach conflicts in these ways have toddlers who score higher on such things as emotional understanding, social competence, and early conscience development, all of which are early-in-life manifestations of self-control. In this regard, responsive parenting can lead the terrible twos to be decidedly better than *terrible* (see also Gaertner, Spinrad, & Eisenberg, 2008).

These conclusions are reinforced by further observational studies that provide rich insight into the nuanced sequence of parent–child social interactions. Perhaps no researcher has spent more time watching and recording interactions among babies, toddlers, and their parents than Grazyna Kochanska (e.g., Kochanska & Kim, 2014; Kochanska & Murray, 2000). She and her colleagues have at times observed natural patterns of interaction—just letting the parents and children do what they normally do. At other points, they have introduced tasks that trigger specific problem-solving activities. Taking it all into account, Kochanska and her colleagues discovered a striking pattern: Some parents and children work extraordinarily well together. When they do, highly favorable outcomes emerge for the child. Kochanska sees these high-performing parent–child dyads as having a *mutually responsive orientation* that often emerges as early as late infancy (but perhaps sooner). It looks something like this:

- From the earliest point in life, the mother is responsive to the child's needs and communications—she attentively responds to the child's sounds, eye contact, and physical "bids."
- The child becomes secure in this responsiveness—he or she trusts that it can be counted on, and it becomes a vital tool for navigating life.
- The child becomes receptive and responsive to maternal care and socialization, and in growing older, develops an "eagerness to embrace maternal values and rules"—the child develops a "willingness to be socialized" (Kochanska & Murray, 2000, p. 417).
- A pattern of mutually rewarding cooperation and positive emotionality between the mother and child ensues—the child looks to the mother not just for what she can provide but also for what she needs.
- These things become, over time, enduring qualities of the mother–child dyad—in fact, the child extends this approach to other caregivers and social contexts.

Rigorous empirical studies reveal the favorable child outcomes possible from this process (Kochanska, 1997; Kochanska & Kim, 2014; Kochanska & Murray, 2000). As early as age 2, children who are part of a mutually responsive orientation are more likely to experience guilt after a transgression than those who are not; they also are more likely to show empathy and concern for someone who is distressed. Moreover, when left alone, they resist tempting but prohibited objects (including the kind that will poke their eyes out), and they persist longer in tasks requested by the mother (or an experimenter). In each instance, they are showing early-in-life indications of an ability to self-regulate. Moreover, the interactions that characterize these mother–child dyads are stable over many years and carry over into interactions at school in later years. Thus, a mutually responsive orientation with parents facilitates the early development of self-control and equips the child with social and interpersonal qualities that enable prosocial development in the future.

Parent Effects, Child Effects, and Reciprocality

One limitation of much prior parenting research is its tendency to treat parent–child interaction as a unilateral process in which the parent influences the child. This fails to recognize the pivotal role played by the *child*—the child is an active participant who has pronounced effects on the nature of parent–child social interactions. Indeed, there is good reason to expect that anytime a statistical relationship is observed between quality parenting and children's self-control, that relationship comprises two components. The first is a "parent effect," whereby parenting practices influence the development of self-control. This is precisely the pattern emphasized in the theory and research described in the preceding sections. A second component, however, involves a "child effect," whereby a child's early behavior or level of self-control—influenced perhaps by biology, genetics, or early features of the social environment—affects the type of parenting to which he or she is exposed. For example, a child with an agreeable temperament early in life is easier to work with and will invite positive forms of parenting, including strong attachment, consistent monitoring, and balanced, nonharsh forms of discipline. A difficult child, on the other hand, will provoke negative and harsh reactions from frustrated parents. Thus, simply stated, a parent effect is the influence of parenting on the child while a child effect is the influence of the qualities and behavior of the child on the type of parenting he or she receives.

Without question, this distinction between parent and child effects has received too little attention in self-control research. This lack has mostly consisted of the neglect of child effects. Two practices are most common. The first involves ignoring child effects altogether and assuming that any relationship between parenting and child outcomes follows from parents' influencing the child rather than vice versa. A second common practice is a notable step up from this, but still incomplete; it involves statistically controlling for characteristics of the child that affect the parenting he or she receives (child effects) when testing for the presence of parent effects. Such characteristics of the child include prior levels of delinquency, self-control, or antisocial behavior. Variables like these have been controlled for in studies that examine the effects of parenting on either self-control or delinquency (Burt et al., 2006; Hay & Forrest, 2006; Sampson & Laub, 1993; Wright, Caspi, Moffitt, & Silva, 1999). In taking this approach, these studies identify the presence of parent effects in models that at least statistically account for the sources of child effects.

As Meldrum, Young, Hay, and Flexon (2012) pointed out, however, there is a difference between controlling for child effects and actually estimating their magnitude. The authors sought to address this limitation in prior research. This was done by examining the relationship between maternal attachment (the mother's feelings of closeness to and warmth toward the child) and the child's self-control as children aged from 4 to 15 years old. An effect of maternal attachment on child self-control was interpreted as a parent effect, whereas an effect of child self-control on the degree of maternal attachment was seen as a child effect. As expected, there was an association between maternal attachment and self-control—mothers who were more attached to their children had children with greater self-control. Importantly, this occurred through both parent and child effects— maternal warmth encouraged greater child self-control in subsequent years, but children with greater self-control encouraged greater subsequent maternal warmth. In this analysis, the child effect was in fact modestly greater than the parent effect. Taken as a whole, this points to the highly reciprocal nature of parent–child interactions—the qualities of the child influence the type of parenting they receive, but parenting also influences the child's later qualities and behavior (see also Burke, Pardini, and Loeber, 2008).

Research like that from Meldrum and his colleagues is important for better understanding the joint existence of parent and child effects. Nevertheless, the reciprocal and mutual nature of parent–child interaction makes it difficult to cleanly distinguish the actions and contributions of the parent from those of the child. This is true even of sophisticated analytical approaches that seek to do just that. Although maternal attachment, for example, is taken as an indicator of a parent effect, it clearly relies on qualities of the child that encourage such attachment (a child effect). Similarly, a child's prosocial, cooperative temperament from early in life is seen as indicative of his or her innate characteristics (that contribute to a child effect), but this temperament follows in part from the physical and social context the parents shaped from early in the child's life (therefore suggesting an important parent effect). In short, the parent–child relationship is jointly constructed in ways that involve a complex interplay of the child's characteristics, the parent's characteristics, and their shared history in a unique developmental context.

Thus, the one thing we can say for certain is this—and in offering this conclusion, we refer back to Kochanska's work on parent–child mutuality: When a strong sense of parent–child cooperation and attachment emerges, a child's chance of developing self-control and other prosocial skills and behaviors greatly increases. Such cooperation necessarily involves a parent effect and a child effect working in conjunction with one another. In Kochanska's (2002, p. 192) words, when a parent and child "are responsive and attuned to each other, are mutually supportive, and enjoy being together, they form an internal model of their relationship as a cooperative enterprise." They go on to "develop an eager, receptive stance toward each other's influence and a compelling sense of obligation to willingly comply with the other." When this occurs, it enables the family to more easily accomplish its socialization goals, including the development of self-control among children. The parents obviously will want this, but as the process above emphasizes, the child will be quite receptive as well.

The Intergenerational Transmission of Self-Control

This attention to the ways in which parents and children jointly construct the family environment points to important considerations regarding the links between a parent's self-control and the child's self-control. There is good reason to expect parents and their children to have quite similar levels of self-control, and this points to a dynamic known as the *intergenerational transmission of self-control.* Boutwell and Beaver (2010) recently described some of the reasons for expecting a strong association between parent and child levels of self-control. Most notably, parental self-control affects the likelihood that parents will use effective socialization practices that involve attachment, supervision, and consistent nonharsh discipline. Additionally, however, much research indicates that self-control and related personality traits are heritable to some degree (we review this research below); if so, the genetic associations between parents and children should produce self-control similarities. Moreover, patterns of assortative mating (in which people tend to marry those with similar characteristics, including, perhaps, similar levels of self-control) reinforce the patterns just noted—marriages between those with similar levels of self-control increase the likelihood that genetic and environmental forces will promote self-control similarity between generations.

Boutwell and Beaver's (2010) analysis of data from over 5,000 U.S. families confirmed positive associations between self-control levels of mothers, fathers, and their 3-year-old children. Interestingly, though, they found that the effects of maternal self-control on the child's self-control were largely not explained by the parenting variables in their analysis. This suggests that other mechanisms—including those that involve genetic heritability or a more expansive set of parent–child variables—must be at work. Nofziger (2008) considered some of these same issues in examining whether maternal self-control predicted adolescent self-control and whether maternal supervision and disciplinary practices explained this relationship. Consistent with the findings of Boutwell and Beaver (2010), Nofziger found a direct influence of maternal self-control on adolescent self-control. Additionally, maternal supervision and discipline partially accounted for the influence of maternal self-control on adolescent self-control. Mothers with higher self-control were more likely, for example, to have clear expectations of their child, to deal with their tantrums, and to monitor their television watching.

Taken together, these studies indicate that self-control is transmitted across generations, a finding supported in personality research involving traits like Conscientiousness that are quite relevant to self-control (Caspi, Roberts, & Shiner, 2005). Part of this transmission likely involves the ways in which parental self-control affects the use of socialization practices that are consequential for the child's self-control. However, that is likely just part of the story—there also is the distinct likelihood that genetic and biological forces significantly explain the similarities in self-control across many generations. Momentarily, our attention turns to these types of variables.

IN FOCUS 4.3

The "Jukes" family

Discussions of the intergenerational transmission of crime and deviance often reference the infamous "Jukes" family from the rural backwaters of New York State (see Vergano, 2012, and Lombardo, 2012, for a review). In 1874, New York Prison Association volunteer inspector Richard Dugdale was examining familial relations among inmates. He discovered six related inmates who were being held in the same facility and whose family name was known locally for attracting scorn and reproach from reputable members of the community. In digging further, Dugdale identified 29 more males related to the original six, many of whom had been arrested and convicted of a variety of offenses, including burglary, larceny, forgery, cruelty to animals, assault, rape, and murder. Dugdale adopted the "Jukes" pseudonym to describe the family, and he traced it back many generations to "Ada Jukes," the supposed "mother of criminals" who got the criminal line of Jukeses started. Dugdale estimated that the family had cost society a total of $1.3 million in medical care, losses from crime, the costs of trial and imprisonment, and other relief measures (Dugdale, 1910, p. 70). This amounts to more than $20 million today (Christianson, 2003).

When Dugdale's work was published, it seemed to capture an idea that many embraced: Specific families were marked by a genetic "bad

(Continued)

(Continued)

seed" that they passed from one generation to the next. The Jukes story became especially infamous when it inspired commentaries, court decisions, and legislation advancing the practice of eugenics, whereby the genetic quality of the human population could be improved by forcing sterilizations upon those thought to be criminally disreputable. The practice of eugenics is, of course, abhorrent and inconsistent with basic ideals about human rights. Moreover, as many noted, the eugenics movement's embrace of the Jukes story was problematic from the beginning. Most notably, while eugenics advocates were quick to see the Jukeses as a "genetic morality tale" (Lombardo, 2012, p. 213), there was ample evidence in Dugdale's report of how poverty, social isolation, and other social environmental variables shaped the behavior of family members. Moreover, Dugdale's data indicated that the Jukeses were not a single clan but instead came from more than 40 families. Many of the offenders considered to be Jukeses were not in fact genetically related to one another, and many presumed members of the Jukes family went on to become exemplary citizens. It also bears emphasizing that, far from advocating eugenics policies, Dugdale himself showed a reformist's zeal for improving the social conditions faced by the poor.

Although the eugenics movement flourished for a time in many societies, support for it declined greatly in the wake of the world's experiences with the eugenics practices of Nazi Germany. Perhaps the most valuable legacy of the Jukes story—and its reanalysis over the decades—is its testament to the idea that while the intergenerational transmission of crime and deviance may genuinely occur, the approach to studying this phenomenon must be careful, rigorous, and subject to logical scrutiny. Moreover, any applications of this research must be evaluated and must adhere closely to fundamental principles not just of effective policy, but also of ethics and human rights.

Summary on Parenting and Self-Control

The studies described above span an extraordinary range of family-centered research. This includes initial supportive tests of Gottfredson and Hirschi's thesis that higher self-control results from rule-setting, monitoring, and discipline. Practices of this kind provide the reinforcements and punishments needed to convey that rule violations have consequences and self-regulation is necessary. We also examined research on Baumrind's notion of authoritative parenting, which directs attention to not just *how much* rule-setting, monitoring, and discipline parents exert, but also how they do so. This research confirms the improvements in self-control that occur when demandingness from parents is matched with a responsive approach built on high attachment, attention to the child's developmental needs, and the avoidance of harsh and coercive practices that undermine the quality of the relationship.

We also reviewed research on very young children and their parents that highlights the reciprocal nature of the socialization process. This is captured especially well in the empirically supported line of research on parent–child mutually responsive orientations (Kochanska, 2002). Parental responsiveness early in life leads the child to trust the parent, to count on this responsiveness, to be responsive in kind to parents' needs, and to embrace parental values. Under such circumstances, the child does not view parental socialization efforts as onerous or coercive; instead, they simply are part of a "shared working model of the relationship as a mutually cooperative enterprise" (Kochanska, 2002, p. 193). Not surprisingly, children whose families are marked by this type of social interaction score higher on various indicators of early self-control development.

Without question, the characteristics of parents *and* children help determine the presence—or absence—of this arrangement; in this sense, a mutually responsive orientation among parents and children reflects both parent effects and child effects, and this almost certainly encourages intergenerational similarities in self-control. The net result, however, is that parents, when working together with their children, can have a lasting impact on the child's development of self-control.

THE GENETIC UNDERPINNINGS OF SELF-CONTROL

A historic debate in the behavioral sciences pits the effects of social environments against the effects of genetics. In short, is behavior a function of individual *nature*, or is *nurture* the critical factor? In recent decades, behavioral scientists have come to see that debate as empty and uninformed. Human behavior is, almost by definition, a function of both nature and nurture, and this idea is captured well in prominent biosocial theorizing (e.g., Walsh, 2009).

The important role of genetics was slow to be recognized in criminological approaches to self-control, and this was reflected in Gottfredson and Hirschi's (1990) theory. As described earlier, it gave primacy to parenting and, in fact, singled out genetics as a causal force that should not even have a seat at the table, so to speak; for Gottfredson and Hirschi, genetic effects on self-control were estimated to be "near zero" (1990, p. 60). Those arguments were met with skepticism by many, especially those familiar with personality research in psychology suggesting that many master traits are heritable to some degree. As we discussed in Chapter 2, self-control may not map directly onto any of the existing Big Five traits, but it is quite traitlike (as a relatively stable pattern of thought, emotion, and behavior). If Big Five personality traits are partially heritable, should this not be true of self-control also?

Much research has set out to consider that question, revealing that genetics helps to explain variations in self-control—having low or high self-control follows in part from the genetic qualities people inherit from their biological parents. One unique challenge to identifying the presence of genetic and environmental effects involves the data needed to differentiate these effects. Traditional studies of child and adolescent outcomes have used data in which there is only one adolescent drawn from a family, therefore undermining efforts to account for genetic influence. Studies that examine heritability take a different approach by using data from sibling- or twin-pairs from the same families. The classic twin design examines differences and similarities in self-control among raised-together twin-pairs that differ in their degree of genetic relatedness. Specifically, such an analysis compares the correlations of raised-together monozygotic (MZ) "identical" twins (who have 100% genetic similarity) with those observed for raised-together dizygotic (DZ) fraternal twins (who have only a 50% genetic similarity). Because these twins are raised in the same environments, significantly higher similarities between the MZ twins are taken as evidence of genetic effects.

Using this research design, genetic effects are always found in studies of self-control; indeed, they often are quite strong. For example, Beaver and his colleagues (2009), in analyzing data on several hundred twin pairs from across the United States, found that approximately 50%

of the variability in self-control among twins was attributable to genetic influence. Quite similar conclusions were reached by Connolly and Beaver (2014) using data from a different national study of twin and nontwin siblings. These two studies are part of the greatly expanding attention to genetic explanation of individual variations in self-control (Beaver, Wright, & DeLisi, 2007). In most of this research, at least half of the variation in self-control is explained by heritability and the remaining variation in self-control is explained by a mix of *shared* and *nonshared* environmental influences. Shared environmental influences are those that are common between twins and that should encourage behavioral similarity, such as living in the same household and being exposed to similar parenting. Nonshared environmental influences, on the other hand, are those that twins experience differently and that should encourage behavioral differences, such as having different friends and being exposed, at times, to different forms of parenting. Most research in this area finds that among the environmental influences, it is the nonshared environment that matters most.

Admittedly, there are uncertainties in this research that hinge on assumptions underlying classic twin models (e.g., Charney, 2008; Collins et al., 2000; Meaney, 2001). There are questions, for example, about whether greater similarity among MZ twins is purely due to similar genetics rather than the tendency for identical twins to have more equivalent social environments and to receive more similar treatment from others (relative to what is observed for DZ twins and siblings). Closely related, some question whether genetic and environmental influences can be cleanly distinguished from one another given the uniformly accepted pattern of *gene–environment correlations*. People's genotypes affect the types of environment to which they are exposed, and this often magnifies behavioral differences between those who are genetically different. This occurs, for example, when a difficult child provokes harsh and hostile forms of parenting that increase problem behavior. Perhaps this reflects a genetic effect (because genetics "got the ball rolling," so to speak), but environmental influence was a contributing factor that may not be identified as such in classic twin studies.

An added complication comes from the emerging study of *epigenetics*, which focuses on the dynamic nature of the human genome.

Impressive research in recent years reveals that although a person's genes remain unchanged throughout life, the expression or activity of genes does change (Rutter, 2012). Think of it like this: Your DNA—your genetic code—provides a set of instructions for how your body should function and develop. That set of instructions stays the same, except that it gets "marked up"—as if with a highlighter or a pen that is used to underline certain things—in ways that direct more or less attention to certain aspects of these instructions. These mark-ups amount to epigenetic modifications in which genes are "switched" on or off. The process by which this occurs is still hazy, but there is growing evidence that epigenetic modifications can be inherited *or* shaped by external environmental forces, including the experience of nurturing relationships early in life (Walsh, 2009, p. 50). This points to an interesting and complicated possibility: Social experiences may actually shape the activity of our genetic qualities. This once again further obscures the distinction between genetic and environmental effects. Indeed, with these complexities in mind, many behavioral geneticists believe it is nearly impossible to cleanly demarcate effects of genes and the environment. In Meaney's (2001, p. 51) words, "Nature and nurture do not exist in a manner that can ever be considered independently quantifiable."

What should we therefore take from this research? While there are inherent limits on the ability to cleanly separate environmental and genetic effects, and while research must be interpreted with that in mind, we nevertheless see heritability studies as instrumental in identifying a critical role of genetics. Analytical models in any field of study are imperfect, but for heritability studies in particular, these imperfections do not undermine the compelling conclusion that genetics is a critical piece of the behavioral science puzzle in general and the self-control puzzle in particular. Simply stated, genes matter. These same twin studies often indicate, however, that the environment matters as well. That conclusion is supported by rigorous and sophisticated nontwin studies of parenting in recent decades (Hay & Forrest, 2006; Meldrum, Young, Hay, et al., 2012; Sampson & Laub, 1993; Wright et al., 1999). The important conclusion is that both genetic and environmental factors are critical in the development of self-control.

The Role of Specific Genes, Gene × Environment Interactions

Much research has gone beyond the question of whether genetics in general matters to also considering exactly *which* genes influence self-control and *how* this influence occurs. Central to this is the idea of gene × environment interactions (G×E) that was introduced in Chapter 2. From this perspective, genes and the environment affect behavior not independently, but instead through an interactive process—individuals vary with respect to their genetic vulnerabilities for antisocial behavior, and these vulnerabilities set the stage for how they will respond to adverse environmental experiences related to such things as bad parenting, antisocial peers, and struggles at school. An outcome of low self-control is especially likely when a genetic vulnerability operates together with social environmental adversity. Indeed, in the true statistical sense of the term *interactive*, the harmful effects of a genetic vulnerability will depend on the social environment, and vice versa. Specifically, a genetic vulnerability will especially decrease self-control among those exposed to an adverse environment. On the other hand, among those exposed to prosocial supportive environments, the harmful effects of the genetic vulnerability may be quite diminished.

Research from Kochanska, Philibert, and Barry (2009) illustrates this line of research nicely. They extended their interest in maternal–child attachment to consider whether its effects might be conditioned by the 5-HTTLPR genetic polymorphism that is important for transporting serotonin, an inhibitory neurotransmitter that is critical to the regulation of aggression, impulsivity, and depression. A high-risk version of this polymorphism involves a short allele inherited from one or both parents. Kochanska and her colleagues used cheek swabs to collect genetic data from toddlers and combined that with observational data on mother–child attachment. They also had data on self-regulation when children were 25, 38, and 52 months old. In support of a G×E, they found that the differences in self-regulation between those with low- and high-risk versions of 5-HTTLPR materialized only among those with poor parent–child attachment. For those with strong parent–child attachment, there were no differences in self-regulation between those with low- and high-risk versions of the polymorphism. The authors note that in this regard, "Early [attachment] security can be seen as a critical protective factor that can offset or buffer developmental risks conferred by genetics" (Kochanska et al., 2009, p. 1336).

Belsky and Beaver (2011) also recently examined G×E patterns pertaining to self-control in adolescence. Specifically, they considered whether effects of parental socialization on self-control depended on whether individuals possessed a *set* of genetic vulnerabilities (rather than just a single one). This study addressed the tendency in prior studies to examine genetic vulnerabilities one at a time in a way that does not fully capture subjects' overall genetic risk. To counter that, Beaver and Belsky (2012) used data on five different indicators of genetic *plasticity*—genetic qualities expected to make individuals more responsive to their social environments. The list of genetic indicators included, for example, the 5-HTTLPR polymorphism just noted and a measure of insufficient MAOA activity (which also indicates problems with neurotransmitter regulation). The analysis revealed that males with greater genetic plasticity (i.e., those who had more genetic vulnerabilities) were more responsive to the quality of parenting. The differences in self-regulation between those exposed to low- and high-quality parenting became progressively higher among those exposed to additional increments of genetic vulnerabilities. The effects of quality parenting were especially heightened for those exposed to four or five of the genetic vulnerabilities.

Studies like these (see also Bakermans-Kranenburg & van Ijzendoorn, 2011; Caspi et al., 2002; Conradt, Measelle, & Ablow, 2013) indicate that genetic and environmental factors do not *independently* explain differences in self-control—instead, the two sources of influence interact with one another. It is precisely for this reason that researchers in this area now explicitly disavow any notion of *nature versus nurture*, focusing instead on interactive models better described as *nature × nurture*.

NEUROBIOLOGICAL INFLUENCES ON SELF-CONTROL

All human behavior is coordinated by the brain, and this directs obvious attention to neurobiological processes and how our brain interprets both physical stimuli (e.g., feeling pain from touching a hot stove) and social stimuli (e.g., getting angry when someone is disrespectful). The manner in which we interpret and react to the world, then, is a result of cognitive processes that take place within the brain. With this in mind, an emerging perspective on self-control views it as an *executive function* of the brain controlled by the prefrontal cortex (PFC; Barkley, 1997; Beaver et al., 2007). We discussed the PFC in Chapter 2—it is located directly behind the forehead and is the region of the brain most closely involved with higher-order thinking (especially behavioral and emotional inhibition). It is also highly connected to other portions of the brain and closely coordinates with its other regions to initiate or inhibit all manners of behavior. When things go wrong in the PFC, problems often ensue.

In considering this possibility, researchers have had to tackle the challenge of measuring the existence of such problems. Recent research has used magnetic resonance imaging to directly observe abnormalities in brains structure and functioning, but much research still relies on a number of clever tests and tasks for children to complete that require attention, thought, and motor skills. Such tests seek to identify observable *neuropsychological deficits* that naturally should be linked to suboptimal PFC performance. These tests have children balancing, skipping, walking backward, and making connections between spoken words and pictures in a book (Dunn & Dunn, 1981; Meisels, Marsden, Wiske, & Henderson, 1997). Using tests such as these, researchers have identified clear links between neuropsychological deficits and self-control (Cauffman, Steinberg, & Piquero, 2005; Jackson & Beaver, 2013; Ratchford & Beaver, 2009).

Findings such as these direct obvious attention to what causes neuropsychological deficits—what leads things to go wrong with the PFC? One possibility involves heritable abnormalities—the genetic effects discussed earlier operate in part by affecting brain structure and PFC functioning (Toga & Thompson, 2005). Beyond this, however, physical and environmental experiences are also important. Researchers have been especially interested in prenatal exposure to harmful substances and toxins that cross through the placenta. The brain is sometimes adding up to 250,000 neurons per minute during this critical period of development, so there is much room for things to go awry. Harmful effects on the child's health, executive functioning, or later self-control have been observed from maternal use of cocaine (Gouin, Murphy, & Shah, 2011; Minnes et al., 2014), alcohol (Korkman, Kettunen, & Autti-Rämö, 2003), and tobacco (Turner, Livecchi, Beaver, & Booth, 2011; Wakschlag, Pickett, Cook, Benowitz, & Leventhal, 2002). As Beaver and his colleagues (2007, p. 1349) note, "these toxins act on the nervous system and can disrupt brain growth, they can cause a decrease in brain metabolic activity, and they can cause irreversible structural and functional damage to the prefrontal cortex."

Researchers have also been quite interested in the effects of lead, an organic metal heavily used in industry for centuries. Lead is, quite simply, everywhere around us, at least in small quantities—it is in the air, water, and soil, but also makes its way into homes (Narag, Pizarro, & Gibbs, 2009). For example, it can be found in household plumbing or in paint in homes built before 1970. The presence of lead within an individual can be detected in tests of blood, bone, or hair, with all measurement approaches indicating pronounced and harmful effects of lead poisoning. Importantly, lead poisoning especially hits the neurological system—magnetic resonance imaging tests reveal various abnormalities in the frontal lobe of lead-exposed brains (Bellinger, 2008; Trope, Lopez-Villegas, Cecil, & Lenkinski, 2001). Lead exposure then manifests itself in more obvious behavioral ways. Even after controlling for various confounders, lead-exposed youth have lower IQs, impaired reaction times, verbal and speech deficiencies, hyperactivity, problems with behavioral inhibition, psychopathy in childhood, and even adult crime (see Narag et al., 2009). All of this points to a specific causal pathway: lead exposure early in life affects PFC functioning, which in turn affects behavior and self-control.

Birth complications are yet another important source of a child's neuropsychological deficits. Such complications often relate to the level and purity of oxygen a baby receives during birth. In connection, Beaver and Wright (2005) found that anoxia (oxygen deprivation), eclampsia (seizures), cesarean delivery, respiration problems, meconium (the presence of stool in the lungs), and distress were related to parent and teacher ratings of self-control in kindergarten and first grade. Liu, Raine, Wuerker, Venables, and Mednick (2009) reached quite similar conclusions in an analysis of an overlapping but not identical set of birth complications. Researchers have also observed neuropsychological impairments that follow from birth prior to the 38-week mark and from low or extremely low birth weight (Anderson et al., 2011; Hack, Klein, & Taylor, 1995). Simply stated, complications in the birthing process and the extent of development at birth can have dramatic implications for early brain development and later self-control.

There is one final relevant factor that has been studied especially of late in the pediatrics community: the idea of *toxic stress* experienced early in life. Concern about this builds from the science showing that physiological responses to stress take a genuine toll. Stress hormones like cortisol surge, undermining the body's ability to regulate inflammation in cells and tissues. In a technical report prepared for the journal *Pediatrics*, Shonkoff and his colleagues (2012, p. e235) emphasize that this process leads to a "chronic 'wear and tear' effect on multiple organ systems, including the brain." They describe the many ways in which the developing structure and function of a child's brain is impaired in response to long-term stressors like child abuse, neglect, parental substance use or depression, and maternal stress during the prenatal period. Many of these things affect PFC functioning in particular (Shonkoff et al., 2012, pp. e235–e237)—the region of the brain so critical for inhibiting emotions, thoughts, and actions. The result is that children exposed to long-term or intense stress during critical periods of brain development will be at a neurological disadvantage—the architecture of their brains lowers the likelihood that they will be able to optimally self-regulate. This does not suggest that self-regulation will be impossible or necessarily uncommon—individuals exposed to toxic stress are not *incapable* of self-control. Instead, it simply means that, all else being equal, they will face a higher probability of suffering the myriad self-control complications we have described thus far.

POLICY IMPLICATIONS AND POSSIBILITIES

The findings presented in this chapter have extraordinary policy implications, and in considering this issue, two patterns stand out as important. First, there clearly is no "silver bullet" when it comes to understanding how one acquires, or fails to acquire, self-control.

Instead, a complex and interrelated set of environmental, biological, and genetic factors is the driving force. This means that policy efforts must focus on a wide variety of causal factors. Second, prior research consistently highlights the importance of the earliest stages of life, including the prenatal period. This points to the value of a prevention-heavy approach—an ideal policy approach will involve interventions that start early in life and offer a chance of preventing self-control deficits from ever emerging.

With these patterns in mind, we can highlight a number of promising policy avenues. The first of these involve interventions for disadvantaged families expecting a child. The struggles they face during the pregnancy and in the early years after birth will affect not just their present well-being, but also the developmental future of their child. The earlier that assistance is provided, the better, and the most notable program that takes this approach is the Nurse–Family Partnership developed by David Olds (Olds et al., 2007), which has been replicated elsewhere. First implemented in New York in the 1980s, this program consists of periodic visits with first-time mothers both during pregnancy and in the first couple of years of the child's life. During the prenatal visits, parents are provided with information on child nutrition and development, prenatal and postnatal care, and the importance of avoiding smoking and drinking during pregnancy. Then, once the child is born, the visits focus on such things as how to effectively interpret the child's signals and ensure that the child's safety and health care needs are addressed. All this training is designed both to prevent the emergence of neuropsychological deficits and to encourage positive social interactions between the parents and child.

Moreover, parents are assisted in handling the stresses of parenting a newborn child. Problems with depression and anxiety are addressed to advance parents' well-being and prevent abuse and neglect of the child. The nurse also consults with parents (and can refer them to other needed social services) on such things as reaching educational goals, finding adequate employment, and planning future pregnancies. One key theme operates throughout: When parents' lives are kept on track, the child's healthy development can be advanced.

Because the Nurse–Family Partnership has existed for some time, there is extensive research assessing its effects. Although these evaluations have never directly assessed program effects on self-control in particular, its focus on well-established predictors of self-control—especially the quality of early parent–child interactions and the prevention of neuropsychological deficits—suggests that beneficial program effects operate in part through the promotion of self-control. And the program's beneficial effects are in fact extensive—various randomized experimental studies reveal that children whose families have participated in this program fare better than similar children whose families have not been part of the program (see Olds et al., 1998; Olds, Henderson, Tatelbaum, & Chamberlin, 1986; Olds et al., 2007). In the first few years of the child's life, the program reduces parental substance use and abuse and neglect of the child. Then, by age 15, the children who have now grown into adolescents are significantly less involved in crime and antisocial behavior. Indeed, their arrest rate is more than 50% lower than that of similar children not taking part in the program. Farrington and Welsh's (2007) meta-analysis found similar results in summarizing the evaluations from nurse visitation programs in other sites—on average, program participants fared better. Such successes have led to the widespread adoption of this program in almost three dozen U.S. states and in over 400 cities (Rocque, Welsh, & Raine, 2012).

Other programs have similarly focused on improving the quality of parenting and parent–child interactions, but they have done so a little later in childhood, often when the child is between 5 and 10 years old. These programs are built on a simple idea: Although all parents *want* to parent well, how to do this is not always clear. Moreover, there are many opportunities for bad parenting habits to emerge, and parents and children sometimes develop a cycle of dysfunctional interactions that are essentially the opposite of Kochanska's mutually responsive orientation. Parent training therefore focuses on such things as how to effectively use rewards and punishments and how to discipline, supervise, and communicate in more positive and effective ways. Meta-analyses indicate that such programs are associated with significant improvements in parenting and reductions in children's antisocial behavior during the first decade of life (Farrington & Welsh, 2003; Serketich & Dumas, 1996). One specific program with strong evaluations results is Triple P—the Positive Parenting Program—which focuses explicitly on improving self-regulation among parents, who are then better equipped to instill self-regulation skills in their children (Sanders, Dittman, Farruggia, & Keown, 2014; Sanders & Mazzucchelli, 2013). A similar program that is highly endorsed and backed by proven results is the Incredible Years parent training program (Menting, Orobio de Castro, & Matthys, 2013).

Preschool and elementary enrichment programs are another notable area for prevention efforts. Such programs build on the idea that for high-risk children, schools can be a strong setting for developing the cognitive and language skills that form the foundation for later success in education and behavior. One classic example involves the Abecedarian Project (Masse & Barnett, 2002), which recruited 111 high-risk children who were mostly African American. Those randomly assigned to the experimental group received a whole host of resources that began in the first year of life and extended to age 8. Once the children started preschool, this included year-round, full-day nurturance and education from a highly trained teacher responsible for no more than five other children. That teacher would consult with the parents out of school and set targets for supplementary educational activities that would be done at home. The teacher also consulted with the family on other issues (e.g., parent employment or access to transportation) relevant to the child's development. Follow-up analyses at age 21 revealed that the experimental sample were significantly less likely to be marijuana users and to have become teenage parents; on the other hand, they were more likely to have attended college. Moreover, with respect to crime, the differences between the experimental and control groups (although not large enough to be statistically significant) were all in the desired direction. For example, 8% of the experimental group had been convicted of a felony, whereas 12% of the control group had. Similarly, 14% of the experimental group had been incarcerated by age 21, whereas 21% of the control group had.

Another successful school-based program is the PATHS curriculum. PATHS is an acronym for "Promoting Alternative Thinking Strategies," and it focuses explicitly on encouraging self-control among elementary school children (Weissberg & Greenberg, 1998). Using a teacher-led curriculum, children are instructed on and then engage in role-playing of strategies and skills for responding to temptations and situations that might provoke impulsive reactions. They are coached on such things as understanding the difference between feelings and behaviors, delaying gratification, controlling impulses, understanding the perspectives of others, and approaching problem-solving and decision-making, keeping in mind key steps that correspond to the lights on a traffic signal: "Stop, calm down" (red light), "Slow down, think" (yellow light), and then "Act, try my plan" (green light). These and other instructional methods are thought to increase higher-order control of the prefrontal cortex over lower-order impulses and strengthen communication between different hemispheres of the brain (Riggs, Greenberg, Kusché, & Pentz, 2006). Impressively, multiple evaluations of the PATHS curriculum find that it not only increases inhibitory control and verbal fluency, but also reduces internalizing and externalizing behavioral problems (Greenberg et al., 1995; Greenberg & Kusché, 1998; Kam, Greenberg, & Kusché, 2004; Riggs et al., 2006).

Taken together, these programs provide a multifaceted approach to preventing early self-control deficits, or perhaps even reversing some of the self-control problems that have already emerged but remain fixable. Nurse home visitation provides the earliest possibility of cutting down on problems with neuropsychological deficits and abusive and neglectful parenting in the first years of life. Parent-training programs like Triple P help parents develop greater knowledge and skills for constructively and prosocially influencing their child. Cognitive skills programs like the PATHS curriculum help foster in the child a greater capacity for and interest in exercising self-control. These types of programs hit upon the three contexts most critical to the child's development in the first decade of life: the environment of the womb during the prenatal period, the family environment in infancy and childhood, and the preschool and school environment that looms large once a child enters social institutions outside the home.

Many of these programs, especially nurse home visitation and early enrichment programs like the Abecedarian Project, are prevention programs in the purest sense. Alternatively, those more commonly used with children age 5 or older (including parent training and the school-based PATHS curriculum) might also accomplish reversal by helping to reduce problems with self-control deficits that already have emerged. In either case, however, a participating child leaves the program with greater self-control than he or she would otherwise have had. Given the differences across the programs, the differing ways in which they have been evaluated, and the fact that some have focused on correlates of self-control rather than self-control itself, it is difficult to specify exactly *how much* more self-control they are gaining. Nevertheless, the improvements appear to be notable, and evidence for this comes in part from a recent meta-analysis by Piquero, Jennings, and Farrington (2010), who summarized the results from 34 different self-control improvement programs targeting children age 10 or under. The 34 programs came in many forms that overlap with those just described: They were administered in school, family, and clinical settings; they used a wide variety of training methods; and some targeted high-risk samples whereas others were available to all. Piquero and his colleagues found that while not all programs significantly improved self-control, many did. In fact, the average improvement across them was statistically significant and relatively large across different measures of self-control that came from teachers, researchers, clinicians, and the children themselves. Piquero and his colleagues therefore reached this conclusion: "Unpacking these findings yields the overall conclusion that self-control is malleable, that self-control can be improved, and that reductions in delinquency follow from this self-control improvement" (p. 829).

Innovative and well-implemented programs, therefore, can absolutely lead to improvements in self-control. This leaves one final question: How much does society benefit from this? Cost–benefit analyses have sought to answer that question. They add up the total cost of administering these programs and then compare that to societal benefits that come in the form of reduced government spending (on such things as welfare, education, employment, and criminal justice) that follow from the better behavior of program participants. These analyses indicate that although prevention programs require a significant up-front expenditure, they more than pay for themselves over the long run. In short, the benefits that come from the better life trajectories of participants far exceed the costs of these programs. We can cite the Nurse–Family Partnership as one example (although we also refer readers to strong overviews of the cost-effectiveness of early prevention provided by Aos, Lieb, Mayfield, Miller, & Pennucci [2004]; Greenwood [2006]; and Welsh & Farrington [2007]). Nurse home visitation programs often cost about $3,000 to $4,000 per year for each family who participates. However, for every $1 spent on this program, governments experience roughly a $3-to-$4 reduction in costs (Greenwood et al., 2001). Early in the child's life, the reductions come most notably from the social services that keep the parents' lives on track (e.g., family-planning services that reduce later health care and welfare costs for unwanted pregnancies). Later in life, when the child has grown into an adolescent, significant benefits also accrue from reductions in crime—fewer crimes translate into lower costs for courts and corrections.

CONCLUSION

When it comes to understanding and explaining human behavior, there is a temptation to oversimplify, to make things less complicated than they really are. This is true sometimes even among brilliant and highly accomplished scholars. Regarding the causes of self-control, for example, they might claim that *it all comes down to parenting* or, alternatively, *it is all about genetics* (you either are born with self-control or you are not). This chapter has shown that the etiology of self-control is a great deal more complicated than that. It truly does not come down to one thing or another; instead, there are multiple factors at work, and this most notably includes how parents socialize their children, what biological qualities are inherited from parents, and how physical and social environments shape neurobiological development. And, of course, each of these big-picture factors is marked by nuances and complexities within it. Ultimately, they all come together in a complicated mix that produces self-control differences among children—some have superior self-control by age 10, some have seemingly very little self-control, and the others are scattered along the continuum between these two extremes.

Also, as we emphasized in our discussion of policy implications, exactly where a child falls on this continuum is not beyond our society's control. Instead, there are steps we can take to alter a child's self-control. In the first decade of life, this most notably involves early interventions with the family, including prenatal visits from nurses and parent training after the child is born. However, preschool and school enrichment programs also are beneficial, especially those that focus directly on self-control. Children who participate in well-designed, well-implemented self-control improvement programs do often fare better. Importantly, their success then spills over to all of us who live around them.

While we have filled in an important piece of the self-control puzzle in this chapter, we are just getting started. In a sense, we have connected many of the edge pieces that frame the self-control puzzle. As with any puzzle, this is a satisfying threshold to reach, but there is much more work to be done and many pieces to still consider. As we move into the next stages of the puzzle, our question is this: What happens *after* the age of 10? Do the differences that emerge then simply carry over into adolescence and adulthood? Or, alternatively, is there the prospect of changes, perhaps coming from unexpected events and transitions?

DISCUSSION QUESTIONS

1. Compare and contrast Gottfredson and Hirschi's (1990) view of effective parenting with Baumrind's (1991) view. In what ways could Gottfredson and Hirschi's view of effective parenting incorporate the ideas developed by Baumrind?

2. Why is it important to consider the influence children may have on the parenting they receive when studying the effects of parenting on self-control? In what ways might these two processes be mutually reinforcing? Use examples to support your argument.

3. In what ways could the self-control *of parents* contribute to self-control in their children? How might the quality of family environments differ in households where parents are either high or low in self-control?

4. How is the literature on the genetically based causes of self-control early in life consistent or inconsistent with Gottfredson and Hirschi's (1990) arguments? Do you think individual traits like self-control are heritable? Why or why not?

5. Discuss the role that the brain plays in the early development of self-control. What are some of the factors that can help or hinder brain development, and why would they ultimately be related to self-control?

⊰ FIVE ⊱

ADOLESCENCE AND ADULTHOOD: IS SELF-CONTROL STABLE OVER TIME?

————◆•◆•◆————

A s the previous chapter emphasized, how much self-control we develop early in life depends on pivotal factors related to early social interactions between parents and children, genetics, and neurobiological development, among other things. Without question, if high self-control is to emerge, a good start is critical—acquiring self-control early (relative to similarly aged others) is like starting a race with a head start and without the clock running. Under such circumstances, impressively hitting later milestones becomes much easier.

Indeed, those who develop self-control early tend to keep it and reap its rewards across the many arenas of life. This follows in part from its self-perpetuating nature. As we will discuss, those with high self-control often are selected and sorted into social arrangements that maintain or even enhance self-control. Also, the factors that got them off to such a great start often persist. For example, those who received terrific parenting in childhood often are treated to that same advantage in adolescence. But the converse also is true—those who get a rough start often have disadvantages that persist and pile up. Putting it all together, we see that the individual self-control differences established in childhood often are preserved or amplified in the years and decades that follow—those struggling with self-control in early adolescence continue to do so, while those with the greatest self-control thrive.

And yet, as you might imagine, that is not the whole story. Many individuals will fit the pattern of self-control stability just described, but there are exceptions. Some might be late bloomers—they successfully develop self-control over time but at a slower pace than others. This has them struggling with self-control deficits around age 6, 8, or 10, but by middle adolescence, they may have caught up with most others. There also are those who coast along just fine into the teen years but are then knocked off course. These individuals initially benefited from their head start, but the complex interplay of biological, psychological, and social changes during adolescence was too much. Both types of cases—the late bloomer and the late crasher—illustrate the same fact: A person's self-control is never set in stone. It is subject, instead, to subtle shifts, or even major transformations, as individuals biologically develop, encounter new social experiences, and drift into new habits and standards.

In this chapter and the next, we explore this idea of self-control stability and change. We begin by discussing research that addresses this question: As individuals advance into adolescence and adulthood, how much does their level of self-control change? How much does it remain stable?

We then focus in this chapter on patterns that involve *stability* in particular (we cover patterns of self-control *change* in the next chapter). Researchers have devoted significant attention to the idea of behavioral stability, much of it inspired by the adage that *past behavior is the best predictor of future behavior.* We describe the scholarship on this issue to offer explanations for the self-control stability often observed. In the process, we explore the idea that a person's self-control remains the same over time in part because self-control reflects a deeply rooted trait that is resistant to change. We also consider, however, that a person's self-control remains stable over time because the social environmental factors that shape it (including the quality of the family and community environments) often are themselves quite stable. And in joining these two ideas, we consider that a person's deeply rooted trait level of self-control—which may be developed quite early in life—shapes the choices they make about such things as who to choose as friends, how much to cooperate with parents, and whether to try hard in school. All these things have implications for *further* development of self-control.

STABILITY AND CHANGE IN SELF-CONTROL

As we age, how much do we change? One common perspective on behavior and personality is that we do not fundamentally change as we age—we are who we are, and that remains the same over time. This sentiment is captured well by William James, the noted philosopher and psychologist of the 1800s, who said that for most of us "the character has set like plaster and will never soften again" by a relatively early point in life (1890, p. 124). Suspicions of this kind have persisted through the present and are captured in a more recent quote that has floated around American culture, getting passed around on Facebook and Twitter and making an appearance on HBO's *True Blood* (one of the surprisingly large number of vampire dramas found on television in recent years). The quote is this: "People don't change, they just find new ways to lie."

Another view of human behavior, however, is that people *do* change over time, often in positive ways. From this perspective, we make cognitive and neurological advances as we age into adolescence and adulthood. There also are the benefits of experience—as we grow older, we are exposed to further socialization. This provides us a greater range of prior experiences from which to draw when we make important decisions. Taken together, this captures the *older but wiser* theory of human development.

In reality, there is truth to both perspectives, as we describe below. Before describing that research, however, an important but somewhat tedious distinction must be considered because it is critical for under-standing stability and change in self-control. This distinction is between *absolute* and *relative* stability (and correspondingly, absolute and rela-tive *change*). Absolute stability exists if people experience no individual changes in self-control as they age—their absolute level of self-control at one age is equal to their absolute level of self-control at another age. This can be considered in reference to the Brief Self-Control Scale (Tangney, Baumeister, & Boone, 2004) discussed in Chapter 3. This scale scores individuals between 13 and 65. If a woman scores 48 on this measure at both age 16 and age 26, she is marked by perfect absolute stability—she is staying the same in an absolute sense over time. The idea of *relative* stability, on the other hand, involves one's level of self-control when compared to similarly aged others. Relative stability occurs when one's self-control *ranking* in a sample remains the same over time. This occurs, for example, for a man whose score on the Brief Self-Control Scale is in the 50th percentile of a sample at both age 16 and age 26. In that 10-year span, he maintained perfect relative stability by staying in exactly the middle of the sample's distribution. If, however, there is movement from the 50th to the 40th percentile during this stretch, relative change has occurred—his level of self-control relative to the rest of the sample has changed (it went down).

In practice, absolute and relative stability often go hand in hand—large absolute improvements in self-control, for example, often correspond to large relative improvements within a given sample. However, this is not necessarily the case—if much of a sample improves over time in an absolute sense (and this may be true of self-control during certain stretches of the life course), then absolute improvements for an individual may not translate into relative improvements in the distribution. Indeed, if individual improvements in self-control are less than a sample's average improvement, *absolute increases* could correspond to *relative decreases* in self-control.

Having said all this, what can we learn from the research? In absolute and relative senses, does self-control stay the same or improve as people age? One approach to answering this question involves looking at an entire population, with all its differently aged individuals, and considering how levels of self-control vary across the different age groups. Are there interesting differences between adolescents, young adults, the middle-aged, and the elderly? Research on the Big Five personality trait of Conscientiousness indicates that there are. Roberts, Walton, and Viechtbauer (2006) drew from multiple studies to estimate absolute differences in Conscientiousness among individuals ranging from 15 to 70 years old. They found higher Conscientiousness among older individuals, thus supporting the contention that as individuals are exposed to further socialization and greater life experiences, they develop greater self-control. This pattern starts quite slowly in adolescence—Conscientiousness is only slightly higher among 20-year-olds than among 15-year-olds, but it is substantially higher among those who are 35 or older. Improvements continue from there and are quite steady through roughly age 65. Interestingly, a similar pattern is observed for traits like Agreeableness and Emotional Stability, both of which overlap with the concept of self-control. This shows that the effects of age are largely positive—as people age, they become (on average) more socially competent and mature. In Roberts and Mroczek's (2008, p. 33) words, "With age, people become more confident, warm, responsible, and calm."

We must emphasize, however, that cross-sectional age comparisons like these do not directly reflect *changes* in self-control that individuals experience as they age. There are two limiting factors. First, recall that these age curves come from large samples of individuals who differ in age and are mostly studied at a single point in time. Self-control differences between those of different ages might reflect the effects of aging, but they also might reflect the effects of unique historical experiences of the young and old individuals in the sample— the 35-year-olds just mentioned were born during a different historic and cultural era than the 20-year-olds, and their higher Conscientiousness could be explained by that. (If so, researchers refer to this as a *cohort* effect). Even if we set that possibility aside, however, there is a second complication: The differences we just described refer to *average* patterns for a sample (e.g., the average 35-year-old has higher Conscientiousness than the average 20-year-old). There is every reason to expect that these average patterns obscure a great deal of individual variation. Some individuals follow the average pattern quite closely, but others may diverge from it greatly, in both good ways and bad. Thus, we must move beyond the average pattern for a population to also consider unique individual variations.

To consider this, researchers need longitudinal panel data—we need data in which the same individuals are followed over time and measurements of self-control are collected at multiple points along the way. A number of criminological studies take this exact approach using direct measures of self-control (rather than measures of related personality constructs). They often use a method known as group-based trajectory modeling (Nagin, 1999). This method uses repeated measures of self-control across a span of time to identify the most common self-control trajectories for a sample. A major practical difference from the cross-sectional approach just described is that this method allows us to identify *multiple* self-control trajectories—not just the average one—for a given sample.

Most of this research has focused on children and adolescents. Hay and Forrest (2006), for example, studied stability and change in self-control from ages 7 to 15 for a national sample of about 3,500 children. Their analysis revealed *eight different common trajectories*, although some were much more common than others. These trajectories are shown in Figure 5.1. Each was given a hyphenated label indicating its initial level of self-control at age 7 and the nature of absolute change over time. For example, the High-Stable group started high in self-control and remained stable over time. Also, for each trajectory, the number in parentheses indicates the estimated percentage of children in that group. The different lines may appear to offer a chaotic picture, but a few themes can be readily discerned regarding both absolute and relative stability. Most notably, these trajectories point to high absolute and relative stability during this period, especially among the more than 50% of children who had high self-control by the start of the study period (i.e., those in the Very High-Stable and High-Stable groups). These groups had high self-control from the beginning, and this remained the case through age 15. Regarding absolute stability, they started with a score of 2.75 or higher (on a scale with a maximum of 3.00) and remained there through age 15. This corresponded to high *relative* stability—individuals in these two groups were mostly at the top of the self-control distribution throughout the entire study period.

There were another 25% (the Medium-Stable group) who had merely medium levels of self-control, but that also was marked by strong absolute stability—the members of this group were doing at least okay in self-control, and this was consistently true from age 7 to 15. On a relative basis, however, this group shows a bit of change—notice that the Medium-Stable trajectory is traversed by two smaller trajectories (at age 11 and then 13), indicating that its position in the distribution was not perfectly fixed.

Indeed, it is these smaller groups that showed interesting patterns of self-control change in both the absolute and relative sense. One group (Low-Increasing), representing about 5% of the sample, started

Figure 5.1 Trajectories of Self-Control (N = 3,793)

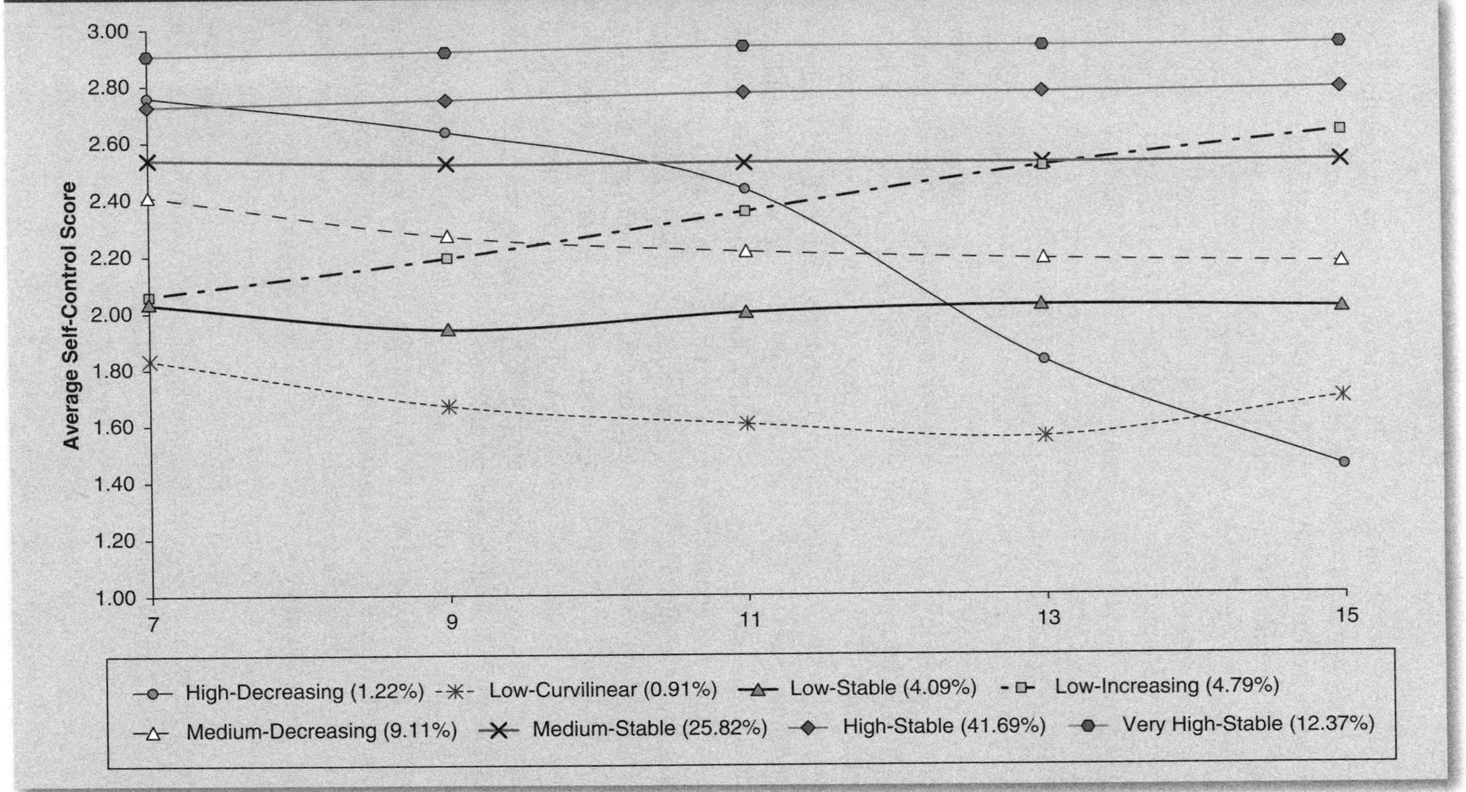

Average Self-Control Score
3.00
2.80
2.60
2.40
2.20
2.00
1.80
1.60
1.40
1.20
1.00
7
9
11
13
15
High-Decreasing (1.22%)
Low-Curvilinear (0.91%)
Low-Stable (4.09%)
Low-Increasing (4.79%)
Medium-Decreasing (9.11%)
Medium-Stable (25.82%)
High-Stable (41.69%)
Very High-Stable (12.37%)

SOURCE: Hay, C., & Forrest, W. (2006). The development of self-control: Examining self-control theory's stability thesis. *Criminology, 44,* 739–774.

with quite low self-control at age 7 but steadily improved over time. By age 15, they were nearly as high as the groups that started and ended with the highest self-control. On the other hand, the High-Decreasing group—estimated to be just over 1% of the sample—showed the opposite pattern. At age 7, they were excelling in self-control, but minor absolute decreases from age 7 to 11 (from about 2.75 to 2.40) were followed by dramatic absolute decreases from age 11 to 15 (from about 2.40 to 1.40). These absolute changes corresponded to relative change: This trajectory traversed the lines of almost every other one, and by age 15, this group had the lowest self-control in the sample.

Although the trajectories vary a bit from sample to sample, other trajectory studies have revealed similar results. For example, Higgins, Jennings, Tewksbury, and Gibson (2009) found that absolute and relative stability was the typical pattern among students from schools in six large to midsized U.S. cities. Change occurred as well, however, especially among one group (16% of the sample) that started high at age 12 but ended at moderate levels at age 16. Similarly, in studying a large sample of Kentucky students from age 13 to 16, Ray, Jones, Loughran, and Jennings (2013) found that about 70% started with at least medium or high self-control. Over the next three years, these adolescents maintained that level and stayed above most others in the sample, thus confirming the finding that absolute and relative stability in self-control is common, especially among those who start with reasonably high self-control by late childhood or early adolescence. The remaining 30%, however, experienced notable shifts in both an absolute and relative sense. Cases marked by better-than-expected self-control gains and unexpected self-control losses emerged in this study, just as they did in Hay and Forrest's (2006) sample.

Several studies have examined self-control stability and change with a slightly different approach, and more specifically with fewer data points. These studies often had access to just two waves of data with a relatively short time span (two years or less) between them. In such instances, a nuanced trajectory cannot be estimated; however, interesting insights are still possible. Computing the correlation between Time 1 and Time 2 self-control is quite informative—such correlations are referred to as *stability coefficients* because they indicate the extent to which the relative ranking of individuals is maintained over time. If self-control is stable, the Time 1/Time 2 correlation should be quite high; in principle, such correlations can be as high as 1.00, although random measurement error makes this a practical impossibility.

The studies on this question typically reveal correlations in the .40-to-.50 range over relatively short time periods (four years or less; Burt, Simons, & Simons, 2006; Raffaelli, Crockett, & Shen, 2005; Turner & Piquero, 2002; Winfree, Taylor, He, & Esbensen, 2006). This points to a strong but imperfect level of relative stability. Burt and colleagues (2006), for example, found a correlation of .48 between self-control measures taken two years apart in early adolescence. Underlying this correlation was a pattern in which about 65% of subjects remained in the same half of the distribution across the two time periods (e.g., those in the top half of the self-control distribution remained there two years later). Similar correlations have also been observed in personality research, and they become higher than .50 as individuals age deeper into adulthood (Roberts & DelVecchio, 2000).[1]

In taking this research as a whole, we offer this direct conclusion: Shifts in self-control do occur, but stability in self-control is quite common. Thus, people can change, and a nontrivial portion do just that, but in practice, stability is the more common pattern. With that conclusion in mind, any framework for understanding self-control over the life course must consider both stability and change, because there is plenty of both. In the remainder of this chapter, we focus on stability to consider why it occurs and how it shapes life as individuals navigate their way through childhood, adolescence, and early adulthood.

WHY DOES SELF-CONTROL OFTEN REMAIN STABLE?

The adage that past behavior is the best predictor of future behavior rings true, and as noted above, this often is the case for self-control in particular. In this section, we describe explanations for why self-control remains stable. We consider three central factors contributing to self-control stability. The first is that self-control remains stable because it is a manifestation of a *persisting individual trait*—because this trait persists within the individual over time, so too does a given level of self-control. The second explanation involves a comparable argument about *persisting social environments*—stability in self-control occurs because the early social environments that affect self-control tend to be stable themselves, therefore producing continuity in self-control. We consider this especially in connection to stability in parenting and peer associations during childhood and adolescence, but also in reference to the stability of poverty and economic disadvantage. And then our third explanation involves a life course theory dynamic known as *state dependence* that in some ways combines the first two ideas. These different explanations are sometimes seen as contradictory to one another, but as we discuss, each is almost certainly part of the puzzle for explaining the significant self-control stability that is observed.

IN FOCUS 5.1

The "Buddha Boy"

Few long-term displays of self-control are as remarkable, and as controversial, as the months-long meditation of the Nepalese teenager Ram Bahadur Bomjon, also known as the "Buddha Boy." According to various accounts, Bomjon set out to meditate undisturbed for a period of six years without food or water. Shortly after beginning his period of meditation in 2005, large crowds of followers, scientists, and journalists flocked to the site. Fences had to be erected and tight security enforced. While skeptics claimed that food and water was provided to Bomjon during the middle of the night, several film crews, including one from *National Geographic*, observed and taped him for lengthy periods, noting that the typical physical effects of dehydration and starvation were not happening to Bomjon. The frenzy surrounding Bomjon ultimately led him to leave the site to continue his meditations elsewhere, but the mystery surrounding his prolonged periods of meditation continues to stir debate as to the legitimacy of his feat.

Bomjon's story is intriguing for discussions of persistence and self-control, as it speaks to the human capacity to override basic impulses to eat, drink, or simply leave a seated position. So, the next time you find yourself fidgeting and antsy after having to sit in the same seat for an hour—maybe during a class, or, for those of us who are professors, during a tedious faculty meeting—consider the self-control it must have taken Bomjon to remain in the same position for days, weeks, and, if you believe the claims, perhaps months. For more information on the incredible story of Bomjon (who is now referred to by some followers as His Holiness Dharma Sangha), visit www.dharma-sangha.com.

PERSISTENT INDIVIDUAL TRAITS
AS CONTRIBUTORS TO SELF-CONTROL STABILITY

The presence of persistent individual traits is the most straightforward explanation for self-control stability. In criminology, this often is referred to as a *latent trait* perspective because of its emphasis on stable traits that are difficult to directly observe but that operate consistently over time. From this perspective, people who display low self-control at one point will continue to do so in the future simply because that is *who they are.* They possess deeply rooted, inherent characteristics that prevent them from regulating their emotions, thoughts, and actions. Nagin and Paternoster (2000, p. 119) refer to this characteristic as "an initial propensity or proneness . . . that has reverberations over time" and that "affects the probability of antisocial conduct early in life and at all subsequent points." Similarly, Wright and his colleagues (2008, p. 35) speak of a latent tendency that "resides within individuals"— something they refer to as *antisocial potential.* From their perspective, there is variation over time in how antisocial potential manifests itself, but the latent trait is always there, and it encourages behavioral stability over time and across different situations and realms of life, including the home, school, and work. Moffitt (1993, p. 679) speaks of this in reference to antisocial behavior in general (rather than self-control in particular), but her point on "cross-situational consistency" is the same: Those with the latent trait "lie at home, steal from shops, cheat at school, fight in bars, and embezzle at work."

The latent trait may be a function of genetic or biological forces from the earliest stages of life. Theorists like Wilson and Herrnstein (1985), Moffitt (1993), and Wright and his colleagues (2008) emphasize biological and genetic causes of the latent trait, including the neuropsychological deficits discussed in Chapter 4 that arise from such things as exposure to abuse, neglect, and harmful toxins in critical stages of development. Moffitt (1993), for example, emphasizes how neuropsychological deficits early in childhood interact with criminogenic social environments to produce a latent trait that persists over the life course. A latent trait could also follow from early social environmental experiences in which self-control habits and preferences become fixed. Gottfredson and Hirschi are the most prominent advocates of a self-control conceptualization in which the latent trait follows from social environmental experiences, especially those involving the quality of parenting. From their perspective, differences in parenting produce persistent individual differences in self-control that are unlikely to change:

> The differences observed at age 8 or 10 tend to persist . . .
> Good children remain good. Not so good children [those with the latent trait of low self-control] remain a source of concern to their parents, teachers, and eventually the criminal justice system. (Hirschi & Gottfredson, 2001, p. 90)

Regardless of how the latent trait emerges, the argument remains the same: Differences in self-control between individuals persist because of varying possession of a latent quality that becomes an inherent part of who people are. For those possessing the latent trait of low self-control, the idea of overriding—whereby an urge to behave impulsively is replaced with a line of action that better contributes to long-term well-being—is not a major part of their behavioral repertoire.

There is another important argument of this perspective, one that we emphasized in Chapter 2 when discussing Gottfredson and Hirschi's theory in particular: Because the latent trait explains stability in observed self-control over time, other events and relationships that might *appear* to affect self-control in fact do not. For example, we might observe that those with delinquent friends are especially likely to have low self-control. Perhaps delinquent friends lower one's self-control by encouraging impulsive behavior that prioritizes short-term thrills over long-term well-being. From a latent trait perspective, however, this argument is incorrect. The latent trait is responsible for both outcomes (having low self-control and having delinquent friends). Those with self-control deficits in childhood go on to have them in adolescence as well (because that is just who they are), and not surprisingly, they *self-select* into friendships with others who are similarly low in self-control. Indeed, they likely self-select into all sorts of antisocial arrangements, including problems at school during adolescence and rocky, unsuccessful romantic relationships in early adulthood. None of these circumstances, however, is critical to explaining their behavior. Over these different time periods and contexts, the latent trait is guiding it all.

PERSISTENT ENVIRONMENTAL CHARACTERISTICS: PARENTING AND PEERS

The argument of persistent environmental characteristics mirrors the latent trait approach. The main difference is its focus on the stability of *social environments* (rather than individual traits) as the source of self-control stability. Research on this possibility focuses especially on the stability of parenting. Parents who raise their children well during the early stages of life are expected to be similarly effective during adolescence. If so, stability in self-control may follow from stability in such things as parental attachment, involvement, monitoring, and discipline across the first two decades of an individual's life. To be clear, specific parenting techniques likely will vary across different stages of early life. For example, direct controls based on parents' power—including strict supervision or coercive punishments—that are common in early childhood often are phased out over time and replaced with parental appeals to principles of fairness, reciprocity, and specific values (Collins, Madsen, & Susman-Stillman, 2002; Steinberg & Silk, 2002). Nevertheless, the parents who are most effective during the early years should make the best adjustments during adolescence. If so, there will be significant relative stability in the quality of socialization.

Much research does in fact reveal notable relative stability in parenting. Stability coefficients for measures taken at different times can be computed for parenting variables in the same way they are for self-control. Meta-analyses often reveal correlations in the range of .40 to .50 (Holden & Miller, 1999)—a level of stability quite similar to what is observed for self-control. Kandel and Wu (1995), for example, in a study of children who aged from childhood to early and middle adolescence, found correlations of .45 and .46 for variables measuring the consistency of discipline and the closeness of the parent–child relationship (see also Loeber et al., 2000).

The stability of peer associations has also received attention. Of particular interest is the idea of "sticky" delinquent friends—when an adolescent begins hanging out with delinquents, those friendships have a way of sticking, much to the disappointment of parents. Warr (1993) looked at this phenomenon with five waves of data from adolescents who were initially 13 years old and 17 by the end of the study period.

Warr (1993) found that for various types of delinquency, many adolescents reported having no friends who committed the act during any year of the study; this was especially true for law violations involving marijuana and theft. This obviously is good news for parents who want their children to stay away from troublemaking friends, but Warr (1993, p. 31) also observed the sticky friends phenomenon in which "delinquent friends, once acquired, are not lost in subsequent years." Specifically, among those who *ever* reported having delinquent friends, the typical sequence involved delinquent friends emerging at one age and then being reported again *in every subsequent year of the study*. This stability in delinquent peer association has been replicated by others studying different samples (e.g., Jennings, Higgins, Akers, Khey, & Dobrow, 2013), and many studies indicate that having delinquent peers affects later self-control (Meldrum, Young, & Weerman, 2012). This suggests that stable self-control during adolescence follows in part from stability in the type of friends—delinquent or nondelinquent— with whom an adolescent spends time.

IN FOCUS 5.2

Is Self-Control Contagious?

Many studies point to how a person's self-control is influenced by his or her social networks. This raises an interesting possibility: On some level, is self-control *contagious*? Can it be transmitted from one person to another, paralleling what is seen with a virus? In an interesting series of experiments, vanDellen and Hoyle (2010) found that the metaphor of contagion is more relevant to the study of self-control than we previously thought. Across five separate experiments, they found that watching or even thinking about someone with good self-control made people more likely to exert self-control themselves. For example, in one study, subjects were randomly assigned to think about a friend with either good or bad self-control. Those assigned to think about the friend with strong self-control persisted for a longer time on a handgrip task used to measure self-control in laboratory studies. In a second study, participants were recruited to take part in a "taste test," but half of the subjects were given the role of observer. These observers were assigned to one of two conditions that involved small plates of chocolate chip cookies and carrots. In the experimental condition, observers witnessed an individual avoid the chocolate chip cookies and eat only the carrots (thus showing strong self-control), while in the control condition, this was reversed. VanDellen and Hoyle (2010) found that the observers in the experimental condition showed substantially greater self-control in a self-regulation task administered just a few minutes later.

This same basic pattern held in three other experiments—proximity to acts of self-control led to greater self-control among the subjects. One interesting aspect of this is that the experiments never involved the subject being socially pressured or coerced to use self-control. Instead, they simply were exposed—either by thought or in a face-to-face situation—to an act of self-control, and this by itself primed the participants to exercise self-control themselves. VanDellen and Hoyle emphasized that this pattern strongly goes against the notion that self-control is purely an individual struggle. How much we exercise self-control depends in part on how much self-control we are exposed to in our social networks, and, in that sense, self-control operates with an element of contagion.

PERSISTENT ENVIRONMENTAL
CHARACTERISTICS: THE STABILITY OF POVERTY

As others have impressively documented, poverty is highly consequential for child development, often because of its effects on such things as the emotional well-being of parents and the health and physical well-being of family members (Maholmes & King, 2012). Research indicates, for example, that family poverty increases a child's problem behavior in part by increasing his or her parents' stress, depression, and willingness to use harsh or physical forms of discipline (Rijlaarsdam et al., 2013). There are also important biological risks associated with chronic poverty during childhood. The neuropsychological deficits discussed in Chapter 4 that follow from such things as exposure to abuse and neglect, toxins like lead, and severe stress are all more likely under circumstances of intense and chronic poverty (Evans, Chen, Miller, & Seeman, 2012).

What makes this especially relevant to self-control stability is that for some children, exposure to poverty is a quite stable feature of their social environment—they were born into a poor family that remains poor over the course of their childhood and adolescence. This likelihood points to the fairly chronic nature of poverty in the United States. Indeed, for children who face poverty early in life, it often persists not simply during childhood but also into adulthood—the majority of children raised in households in the bottom 20% of income earners will be near the bottom of the income distribution as adults also (Pew Charitable Trusts, 2012).

Moreover, in adolescence—when individuals begin spending more time away from the household—poverty carries special risks associated with the neighborhood context. Chronically poor families often live in neighborhoods with high concentrated poverty, and this is especially true among racial and ethnic minorities—poor blacks and Hispanics are more likely than similarly poor whites to live in high-poverty neighborhoods (Massey & Denton, 1993). These neighborhoods have heightened problems of all kinds, including high unemployment, high population turnover, and weak social ties among neighbors. These factors in turn combine to produce greater levels of crime, drug use, and gang involvement (Sampson, 2013).

Ethnographic neighborhood research also documents cultural adaptations to these circumstances. Most notably, isolation from conventional institutions and opportunities can produce an oppositional street subculture that rejects mainstream values, instead prioritizing toughness and the maintenance of respect from others (Anderson, 1999). In these social contexts, individuals often must respond violently to any challenges and provocation. As Stewart and Simons (2006, p. 6) note, "the street code and the respect it demands is so entrenched among the hard-core, street-oriented individuals that they are willing to risk dying violently rather than being 'dissed' or victimized by another."

To be clear, the power or prevalence of these cultural beliefs should not be overstated—in even the poorest neighborhoods, street-code values are interwoven with conventional values emphasizing hard work, self-reliance, and staying out of trouble (Anderson, 1999; Benoit, Randolph, Dunlap, & Johnson, 2003). That being said, it is easy to imagine how self-control development would be undermined by residence in a high-poverty neighborhood in which street-code values are common. Self-control involves overriding dangerous, harmful impulses, whereas the street code embraces such impulses, no matter how much they detract from future well-being. Indeed, a common theme in this literature is that hard-core street youth do not envision a bright future worthy of protecting (Drummond, Bolland, & Harris, 2011; Piquero, 2014). Thus, regulating one's impulses in the present perhaps carries little payoff for the future. In support of this, several studies find that residence in poor, socially disorganized neighborhoods reduces self-control even after statistically controlling for the quality of parenting (Pratt, Turner, & Piquero, 2004; Teasdale & Silver, 2009). These patterns indicate that stable problems with self-control could follow in part from enduring poverty and consistent exposure to environments that discourage long-term considerations.

STATE DEPENDENCE AS A CONTRIBUTOR TO SELF-CONTROL STABILITY

Two explanations for self-control stability have been considered thus far. First, a latent individual trait may persist and manifest itself similarly over time. Second, features of the social environment may persist over time, steadily pushing one in the same behavioral direction (independent of any individual trait). Importantly, however, these two ideas are not incompatible with one another—they may be true at the same time, and there may be an interesting connection between them. This possibility is central to the idea of *state dependence*, a commonly invoked concept in life course and developmental approaches to behavior (Nagin & Paternoster, 1991; Sampson & Laub, 1993).

A state dependence perspective begins with the recognition that some children will have low self-control and behave poorly from the earliest point in which such patterns can be detected. Such children may be especially restless and difficult to soothe as toddlers and inattentive and aggressive as young children. Perhaps this involves a latent trait, or it may simply reflect powerful effects of an existing social environment. In either case, some children stand out by virtue of their impulsive antisocial behavior. The defining quality of a state dependence view is that this bad behavior is expected to have a *causal effect* on the likelihood of bad behavior in later years—bad behavior at one point actually produces bad behavior at a later point.

How might that occur? The basic idea is that through patterns of social exclusion and self-selection, an individual's behavior fundamentally shapes the social environment to which he or she is exposed. Those who behave poorly are treated differently by the people and institutions in their lives—their bad behavior provokes stigmatizing reactions and exclusion from prosocial opportunities. Moreover, poorly behaving children may actively exclude themselves from prosocial relationships and experiences.

This can be seen in reference to a hypothetical 10-year-old boy who shows all the signs of low self-control: he cannot stay quiet or sit still when he is supposed to, he loses his temper and throws tantrums when not getting his way, and he pushes other children to secure an object or get to the front of a line. Such a child will be treated differently by others. Parents and teachers will be frustrated by him and will more commonly use coercive or harsh forms of discipline that are counterproductive over the long term. Moreover, they will be less likely to become emotionally attached to him and therefore will invest less in his future. Other children—especially those who know how to regulate their own emotions and behavior—will be turned off as well. They will avoid playing with him, will not become friends with him, and may even ostracize him. Parents, teachers, and children alike may socially label him—they may define him as *the problem kid* or *the stupid kid* and treat him accordingly, and he may accept this self-identity and behave in ways that match it (Jussim & Harber, 2005; Rosenthal & Jacobson, 1968). All this contributes to a vicious cycle in which problems with self-control and social functioning persist, perhaps even growing worse. Moffitt (1993, p. 682) describes this process aptly: "It may well be that early behavioral difficulties contribute to the development of persistent antisocial behavior by evoking responses from the interpersonal social environment, responses that exacerbate the child's tendencies." Caspi, Elder, and Bem (1987, p. 308) comment similarly: "The child acts; the environment reacts; and the child reacts back in mutually interlocking evocative interaction."

This pattern is likely to persist into adolescence and adulthood, with this child's low self-control (and the behavior it produces) affecting much along the way. He is unlikely to develop strong commitments to school—his grades will be low, he may not graduate from high school, and he will forego college. The people he becomes friends with will be similarly impulsive and uninterested in school. Together, they may get involved in drugs, alcohol, and some degree of property and violent offending, behaviors that could give rise to contacts with the criminal justice system and further undermine his future. His low self-control and resulting behavior will also have implications for his relationship with his parents. That relationship may not have been strong to begin with—problems in the family environment likely contributed to his initial self-control deficits—but it likely will grow worse as the possibilities for parent–child conflict multiply during the teenage years. And in early adulthood, he likely will bypass two things that might have pushed him to a better path: steady participation in the labor force and the development of a long-term romantic relationship with a prosocial partner.

In this sense, his problems with low self-control are like a snowball rolling down a hill, gaining speed but also surface area as it accumulates more snow with each rotation. Consistent with this analogy, Sampson and Laub (1997, p. 21) describe state dependence as a process of *cumulative disadvantage* in which "deficits and disadvantages pile up" to produce "environmental traps" that restrict future options and encourage involvement in deviant subcultures. Similarly, Nagin and Paternoster (1991; 2000, p. 118), who have done much to clarify the implications of state dependence for criminal behavior, describe it this way:

> It is a process of contagion in which an offender's current activities make their life circumstances worse, accelerating the probability of future crime. For example, committing crimes can weaken or destroy one's involvement in a network of conventional relationships (spouse, children, relatives, neighbors) that could have provided even partial restraint on criminal tendencies. Criminal acts committed now can also increase one's risk of future crime by leading one into closer affiliation with other offenders.

In Nagin and Paternoster's quote, each reference to crime and offending could easily be replaced with a reference to low self-control.

The state dependence logic is the same regardless of which problematic outcome is emphasized—involvement in problem behavior is often stable because such behavior tends to increase exposure to antisocial roles and relationships that encourage further problems.

There is, however, one other interesting and important twist to the state dependence idea: In the same way that antisocial roles and relationships encourage low self-control, the unexpected emergence of *prosocial* roles and relationships can jump an individual to a *different* self-control trajectory. Thus, just as things can get worse, they also can get better. Such things as new friendships with prosocial others, entry into college or the military, the start of a career, or a good marriage can "increase social capital and investment in [pro]social relations and institutions" (Sampson & Laub, 1993, p. 21). These beneficial social experiences are less likely among those low in self-control, but they still may occur (Hay, Meldrum, & Piquero, 2013), and when they do, positive changes may ensue. We pursue this idea further in the next chapter, which focuses on self-control changes that have often been observed.

AN IMPLICIT IDEA: HUMAN AGENCY

The state dependence perspective includes an idea that is implicit in the discussion above but that merits explicit focus. This is the idea of human agency, which Laub (2006, p. 244) has defined as "the purposeful execution of choice and individual will." Simply stated, human agency involves the idea that people are not merely passive entities governed by powerful forces beyond their control (such as a deeply rooted latent trait or adverse social environments). Instead, there is a degree of *choice* whereby we actively help create our own future. Indeed, individuals play a big role in *creating their own environments*. This idea is very much seen in the preceding paragraphs—those with low self-control make *choices* about such things as who to spend time with (e.g., delinquents or nondelinquents), whether to commit to education, and whether to cooperate with parents, and these choices in turn shape the types of experiences and relationships that characterize their lives.

Human agency comes into play in interesting ways for self-control, although we must speculate to some degree—quantifiable assessments of an abstract notion like human agency will always be difficult. That said, we believe that human agency often—but certainly not always—enhances the absolute and relative stability in self-control that is observed over time. This happens when individuals make choices and develop identities and commitments that reinforce their existing self-control tendencies. As a result, those with low self-control often remain low, those with high self-control often remain high, and the differences between the two groups are reinforced over time.

This role of human agency first arises when individuals become cognitively capable of purposefully and consciously embracing certain lifestyles. Under such circumstances, some individuals may actively adopt the principles of self-regulation. Being a thoughtful and deliberative decision maker (i.e., having high self-control) becomes a personal ethos that guides their self-identity and daily choices. These are individuals that "look before they leap," so to speak, and they do so with conscious self-awareness. Should they prepare for an exam or blow it off? Should they exercise today or skip their workout? Should they drive home after drinking too much? Each question seems like a separate discrete choice, but through this process of human agency, there is something that ties them all together: a personal commitment to self-control, whereby a person sees himself or herself as the type of person who controls desires for immediate gratification, assesses actions in terms of the benefits they offer *and* the costs they impose, and then behaves in ways that protect long-term well-being.

Those with low self-control would be drawn to a different self-identity and approach to decision-making. Instead of seeing themselves as conscientious deliberators, they may actively appreciate the excitement and thrills of taking unnecessary risks, rebelling against convention, and testing the boundaries of behavior. Especially for adolescents, such actions may be seen as a "liberating departure from the typical status of youths in which their behavior is constrained by adults" (Meldrum & Hay, 2012, p. 694). Rebellon and Manasse (2004) make this point in noting that adolescent peer subcultures may reinforce this identity by rewarding those who are willing to take risks, rebel against authority, and test the boundaries of allowable behavior.

Thus, in the same way that some may embrace a personal ethos of high self-control, others may do the opposite. In so doing, they prioritize thrills over prudence, courage over caution, and quick action over careful deliberation. In this sense, human agency is exerted—the peers they select, the ways they spend their time, and the goals they pursue (or ignore) all come to reflect their own personal will and the identity they have embraced.

Two relevant lines of thought suggest that human agency comes into play in this way. The first involves Tittle, Ward, and Grasmick's (2004) insightful distinction between one's self-control *ability* and *interest*. The concept of self-control ability captures the traditional approach in which self-control is seen as a traitlike *capacity* that is fairly stable over time. Self-control interest, on the other hand, is more a matter of *preference* that can vary over time and across situations as individuals decide whether they are interested in using self-control. As part of this, some individuals will not exercise the self-control ability they possess simply because they lack an interest in doing so. Others may be the opposite— their strong interest in self-control leads them to make full use of any self-control ability they have. The analysis from Tittle and his colleagues (2004) supported this contention: Measures of self-control interest independently predicted involvement in crime (net of any correlations with self-control ability). This finding has key relevance for understanding the links between human agency and self-control: One's observed level of self-control at least partially reflects the self-control interest that guides daily choices about whether to avoid costly temptations and whether to place oneself in social contexts in which temptations abound.

Silver and Ulmer (2012) also emphasize human agency in their discussion of *future selves*. They argue that research on self-control has not properly highlighted the ways in which self-regulation decisions are informed by people's "conceptions of themselves in the future" (p. 701). From this perspective, a given course of action is appealing if it helps one achieve a desired future self. If that desired future self is oriented around a respectable and prosocial identity, then behaving impulsively is unappealing and perhaps even unthinkable. On the other hand, for those embracing a future self that is built around thrills, risk-seeking, and immediate gratification, it is the consistent exercise of self-control that is unappealing and unthinkable.

Moreover, and consistent with the emphasis on human agency, these differences are not just episodic in nature—they guide how people organize their lives. Silver and Ulmer (2012) emphasize that conceptions of future selves encourage the development of "commitment portfolios" by which people become committed to (a) specific courses of action, (b) moral rules that justify those actions, and (c) social relationships that reinforce those actions. This is reflected, for example, in a person whose future self rejects a personal ethos of self-control—as part of this, he or she may become committed to recreational drug use and may embrace moral values that justify this use (perhaps relating to the importance of personal liberties), and their friendships and romantic relationships may encourage further recreational drug use in the future.

Once again, the resonating idea behind all of this is human agency—humans are not merely puppets that are manipulated and determined by internal traits or external social environments. Instead, there is the possibility of personal reflection and choice as humans critically evaluate and construct the conditions of their lives (Emirbayer & Mische, 1998; Hitlin & Elder, 2007). As argued above, this role of human agency will often encourage self-control stability, as individuals develop identities, interests, habits, values, and relationships that reinforce their self-control tendencies. We do not suggest, however, that this is always the case. Quite the opposite, human agency may often be a catalyst for change—reflections on one's life will sometimes encourage a fundamentally different course of action. In this sense, human agency is not just about continuing a given trajectory—it also sometimes involves constructing a new one.

IN FOCUS 5.3

Human Agency, Self-Control, and the Four-Minute Mile

Athletics provide a great forum for seeing self-control in action. A fascinating example of the intersection between human agency and self-control comes from the human quest to run a mile in less than four minutes.[2] Few activities require greater self-control than pushing your body to maintain a

(Continued)

(Continued)

fast running pace after the body has seemingly edged up against its maximum capacity for exertion. In the mid-1900s, that maximum capacity in the mile rested right around the 4:00-minute mark. In 1942, the record stood at 4:06.4, but it was broken six times over the next few years, and by 1945, the record was 4:01.4.

Fully nine years later in 1954, however, mile runners worldwide had gotten no closer to a sub-4:00 mile, despite a zealous pursuit of a breakthrough. A trio of runners were most visible in this pursuit: Australia's John Landy, England's Roger Bannister, and America's Wes Santee. The case of Landy is particularly interesting. Between 1952 and 1954, he ran between 4:02 and 4:03 fully *six* times, but he could never go lower. In one race in December 1953, Landy was indeed on pace for a sub-4:00 mile, but he seized up a bit in the final 200 meters and finished at 4:02 again. After the race, he famously declared to reporters, "I feel I could go on for 10 years, but I don't think it's worth it. Frankly, I think the four-minute mile is beyond my capabilities. Two seconds may not sound [like] much, but to me it's like trying to break through a brick wall." This was an astounding declaration—one of the most accomplished middle-distance runners in human history was essentially giving up, conceding that he could not imagine running two seconds faster.

Five months after Landy's sobering declaration, Roger Bannister stepped on to a track at Iffley Road in Oxford, England, and ran the mile in 3:59.4. The human quest for a sub-4:00 mile had been achieved, and Bannister earned himself a permanent place as one of the great athletes in history. But where did this leave Landy? His pursuit of the four-minute mile was decidedly not yet over, despite his earlier claims. Bannister's landmark performance had a powerful motivating effect on Landy, one that we see as comparable to a surge in Landy's self-control interest. Bannister had shown Landy that humans *were* capable of a sub-4:00 mile. Bannister had also struggled to get over the 4:00 mark, but he had broken through. Why couldn't Landy as well? The "brick wall" had been broken—Landy needed to persevere for four laps in a way he never had before and bound over the wall himself.

Little more than a month later, at a race in Finland, Landy smashed Bannister's record with a 3:57.9 mile. After an unsuccessful three-year quest to shave two seconds off his time, Landy improved by *four seconds in the span of just six months*. Landy's breakthrough almost certainly cannot be explained in purely physiological terms (Tucker & Dugas, 2009). Instead, it followed in part by the removal of a mental barrier, a barrier that we see as a self-imposed limit on his self-control. That limit was built upon Landy's belief that a sub-four mile was not accomplishable. Once the limit was removed, a record-setting performance followed.

EMPIRICAL EVIDENCE ON
EXPLANATIONS FOR STABILITY

The three explanations for behavioral stability offered above—a persisting latent trait, persisting social environmental factors, and the integrative idea of state dependence—have been assessed empirically. The idea of persisting social environmental factors (regarding such things as parenting, peers, and poverty) is widely accepted (some of this research was described above). Much research has focused instead on comparing the accuracy of the latent trait and state dependence perspectives. These two have been pitted against one another in large part because of a key contrast on the question of whether social roles and relationships are potent causes of self-control and behavior over the life course. The latent trait perspective is interpreted as saying they are not—once the latent trait emerges (as indicated perhaps by early self-control deficits), it drives all subsequent outcomes. Any statistical relationships between social roles and relationships (like peer relationships or problems at school) and later self-control and behavior are spurious—these things are correlated because they all follow from the same cause (the latent trait/early self-control deficits). The state dependence perspective, on the other hand, predicts that these social roles and relationships *do* have causal significance—they help causally explain the relationship between early self-control deficits and later self-control and behavior. Specifically, early problems with self-control lead individuals to self-select into antisocial roles and relationships, and once they do, those antisocial influences have causal significance of their own—they encourage further problems with self-control and behavior.

So, what does the research indicate? On balance, the research supports a mixed version of a state dependence perspective—one that acknowledges the importance of a latent trait but also allows for an important effect of adolescent and adult social roles and relationships. This general conclusion is supported across a wide variety of studies. An especially influential study from Wright, Caspi, Moffitt, and Silva (1999) used data from a birth cohort in New Zealand. They had comprehensive, multimethod measures of self-control for childhood (ages 3 to 11) and adolescence (ages 15 to 18); they also had measures of social roles and relationships and criminal behavior during adolescence and young adulthood. They found an unmistakable pattern: Low self-control in childhood led to antisocial roles and relationships in adolescence (e.g., poor relationships with family, weak commitment to school, and association with delinquent peers). These things, in turn, led to criminal behavior in young adulthood, even after statistically controlling for the self-control deficits in childhood that got everything going to begin with. This pattern is consistent with a state dependence view on the importance of social roles and relationships.

Other findings from Wright and his colleagues (1999), however, show the value of a latent trait perspective that emphasizes the enduring importance of early levels of self-control. Most notably, there was relative stability in self-control that existed independently of the effects of social roles and relationships—self-control deficits in childhood were followed by self-control deficits in adolescence, and this was followed by crime in young adulthood. This life course continuity in self-control and resulting behavior from very early in life points to the powerful influence of a latent trait (even if it is not so powerful as to crowd out the effects of social roles and relationships later on).

Similar findings have been reached in other studies with independent measures of self-control, social roles and relationships, and criminal behavior (Hay et al., 2013; Longshore, Chang, & Messina, 2005; Nagin & Paternoster, 1994). Low self-control increases the chances that adolescents associate with delinquent peers, are weakly committed to school, and get along poorly with parents; these things, in turn, have an independent effect on delinquency even after accounting for initial levels of self-control. Self-control typically has effects of its own, however, and self-control often is quite stable over the study period, even after accounting for the social roles and relationships noted above.[3]

Taken together, this line of theorizing and the related research give a clear picture of why individual self-control remains relatively stable from childhood into adolescence and then young adulthood. Part of the explanation is that children's initial level of self-control is linked to a stable latent trait. Because of a complicated mix of genetic, biological, and social environmental forces, having low (or high) self-control becomes a fairly enduring part of who that individual is, and it sticks with that person as he or she advances through the different stages of life. Another important contributor, however, is the process of state dependence, whereby self-control remains stable because early levels of self-control lead to social roles and relationships that reinforce the earlier patterns. For example, those with low self-control become friends with delinquents, dismiss the value of educational success, and develop stormy relationships with parents as they enter adolescence—all of these are likely to further erode their self-control. Those with initially high self-control, on the other hand, will do the opposite in these key arenas of life. The net effect is that initial levels of self-control will often lead to consistency in the antisocial or prosocial nature of the experiences, roles, and relationships to which an individual is exposed. This in turn encourages a high level of self-control stability in which the differences between individuals are maintained over time.

POLICY IMPLICATIONS AND POSSIBILITIES

This chapter has focused on the significant stability in self-control observed from childhood into adolescence and then adulthood. On the face of it, this seems to offer few prospects for policy—children with high self-control remain that way, those with low self-control do the same, and policy efforts will make little difference. Quite the opposite is true, however; we see three notable policy implications that follow from the research described here.

The first is that we must remember that although stability in self-control is quite high, it is far from perfect—self-control changes *do* occur, and major shifts over the life course may occur among as much as 15% to 20% of the population. These self-control reversals are the focus of the next chapter, and we will discuss the policies and programs that can bring about reversals among children who enter adolescence with less-than-optimal levels of self-control.

A second major implication of self-control stability is that it underscores our earlier emphasis on early childhood prevention. Without question, the best policy approach involves preventing self-control deficits from ever emerging in the first place. If this can be done, self-control stability over the life course will be working to society's benefit rather than its detriment. This directs our attention back to the programs that establish good outcomes in the early stages of life, such as home visitation programs like the Nurse–Family Partnership, family training programs like Triple P or Incredible Years, and preschool and school enrichment programs like the Abecedarian Project or the PATHS curriculum.

A third major policy implication involves those adolescents who enter adolescence seemingly doing just fine. We might be tempted to think that these individuals can be left alone—through processes of state dependence and human agency, they will naturally gravitate toward prosocial experiences that reinforce existing self-control levels. Thus, these are the cases in which self-control stability will naturally work in our favor. Although this may often happen, the threat of change is always there, and this follows in part from the "storm and stress" possibilities of adolescence that we discuss in the next chapter. The key message is this: If we want self-control stability to work to society's benefit, we must take concrete steps to *encourage* self-control in adolescence, even among those high in self-control to begin with.

The promising programs in this regard are often school-based life skills programs that are universal in scope; rather than targeting only those adolescents already showing signs of behavior problems, they target the broader adolescent population. Thus, while they may promote reversals among those entering adolescence with self-control deficits, they can also encourage self-control stability among those relatively high in self-control. Two programs in particular have generated impressive evaluation results and focus on skills relevant to self-control. The first of these is Life Skills Training (Botvin, Griffin, & Nichols, 2006), a classroom-based middle-school program that uses 30 sessions taught over a span of three years. The program is designed to reduce substance use and risky behavior by promoting social skills and self-regulation habits (e.g., setting personal goals and self-monitoring one's progress, assessing problem situations, considering the consequences of different actions) that can lead to better decision-making. The Positive Action program is quite similar (Lewis et al., 2013). It is implemented on a schoolwide basis to encourage a school culture that reinforces prosocial values and behavior. In the middle school years, it includes roughly 80 lessons that last about 15 to 20 minutes each and that provide guidance on a wide variety of skills relevant to self-control, including problem-solving in difficult situations, using good self-management skills (setting standards and self-monitoring), and making decisions based on a future orientation.

CONCLUSION

Do people stay the same over time, or do they change? The major theme of this chapter has been that when it comes to self-control, there is a good amount of both continuity and change. Studies using a wide variety of samples and research designs indicate that a person's absolute and relative levels of self-control remain fairly stable through adolescence and adulthood, but changes occur also. After describing these results, we presented the major explanations for the stability that is often seen: (a) a *persistent individual trait* explanation in which self-control remains stable because it reflects a deeply rooted quality that is an enduring part of who that person is; (b) a *persisting social environments* explanation in which the social environments that influence self-control are themselves quite stable over time, and (c) a *state dependence* explanation that combines the first two in key respects. Research generally supports a state dependence perspective in which persisting individual traits affect later outcomes, in part by influencing the types of social environments and relationships a person experiences.

For many individuals, this will involve a reinforcing cycle of behavior, one in which self-control tendencies from the first decade of life give rise to social experiences, roles, and relationships that reinforce those initial tendencies. For those coming out of childhood with high self-control, this cycle increases the chances of smooth and prosocial transitions to adolescence and adulthood. On the other hand, for those with initially low self-control, this will be a vicious cycle fraught with problem behavior, life hassles, and unexpected complications. We should not, however, overstate the predictability of these patterns. As we discussed, there are policy tools at our disposal— effective programs can intervene to encourage the use of self-control skills. Moreover, as we convey in the next chapter, opportunities for self-control change still abound, even for those who get off to a rough start in childhood and adolescence—a person's self-control is never set in stone.

DISCUSSION QUESTIONS

1. What is meant by the phrase *past behavior is the best predictor of future behavior?* How can this be extended to a focus on self-control?

2. Consider three friends: Jim, Jake, and Josh. In the third grade, Jim has a self-control score of 15, Jake has a score of 20, and Josh has a score of 25. By the time the three boys reach eighth grade, Jim has a score of 30, Jake has a score of score of 25, and Josh has a score of 20. How many of these boys have experienced *absolute* increases in self-control? What about absolute decreases? Has each of the three boys experienced *relative* stability in self-control?

3. Describe the idea of state dependence and how it encourages self-control stability.

4. What is human agency, and how might it contribute to self-control stability?

5. What is the difference between self-control *ability* and *interest?* Describe some hypothetical situations in which someone who is high in self-control may nonetheless be uninterested in exercising it.

NOTES

1. Some researchers argue that stability is even more common than these figures suggest. According to this view, measurement complications make it difficult to observe the full extent of stability. When subjects complete self-control surveys, they may at times not pay attention to the questions as much as they should; moreover, they may sometimes answer in biased ways, depending on random circumstances. Also, a parent's assessment of a child's self-control could be especially influenced by a single recent event that has exaggerated importance in their minds. With these things occurring, observed shifts in self-control over time could follow from measurement error. Another complicating issue is that the manifestations of low self-control can vary across different ages. For example, whining and throwing tantrums may be common among 6-year-olds, whereas substance use and risky sexual activity are impulsive behaviors that become possible only in adolescence. If measures of self-control are not adapted over time, children and adolescents may appear to show changes in self-control that instead reflect *heterotypic stability*, which occurs when traits express themselves in different forms over time (Wright, Tibbetts, & Daigle, 2008). We concur that these factors come into play, but as we emphasize in the next chapter, we also believe that shifts in self-control do occur—studies with impressive methodological rigor indicate as much.

2. Our discussion draws in large part from Tucker and Dugas's (2009) excellent retelling of this history in *The Runner's Body*.

3. Many other studies have reached similar conclusions with different datasets, often with quite sophisticated analyses that try to account for the effects of an initial latent trait that is not expected to be directly observable. This is quite the analytical challenge—if we cannot observe and measure the latent trait, how can we statistically account for its effects? A common approach tracks individuals over time to see if the changes in social roles and relationships that they experience correspond to shifts in their own behavior (Bushway, Brame, & Paternoster, 1999). For example, if they experience an increase in association with delinquent peers, does this lead to corresponding decreases in self-control and increases in crime? In analyses like this, each individual serves as his or her own control—examining individual changes over time controls for time-stable latent traits that affected their initial circumstances and behavior (Bushway et al., 1999). Studies of this kind often indicate that shifts in social roles and relationships in adolescence and adulthood are associated with shifts in observed behavior even after accounting for observed and unobserved individual differences (i.e., differential exposure to a latent trait; Horney, Osgood, & Marshall, 1995; Nagin & Paternoster, 1991, 2000).

SIX

WHAT LEADS TO
SELF-CONTROL CHANGE?

———————•✦•———————

"**B**reaking bad" has become a salient idea in American popular culture, fueled by the AMC Network's acclaimed series set in Albuquerque, New Mexico. The show chronicled the fictional experiences of Walter White, an unremarkable high school chemistry teacher diagnosed with inoperable lung cancer. The series begins with Walter worrying about how his family will get by if he dies. His knowledge of chemistry, his connection to a hardened former student, and healthy doses of serendipity and desperation push Walter toward a novel possibility: He could make big money in the production and distribution of methamphetamine—enough to pay for expensive medical treatments to stave off his cancer, but also to provide for his family in the event of his death. And from there, the excitement commences.

Walter's life does in fact get extended, thus allowing him to fall ever deeper into the meth world. Along the way, he experiences the extraordinary personal transformation promised by the show's title, changing from the sympathetic, well-intended protagonist of early episodes into a reckless villain in later ones. He protects his interests ferociously and in ways not reconcilable with his initial good intentions—he orchestrates murders, enacts revenge against his associates, and even poisons a young boy. Along the way, he gives viewers ample opportunities to cringe and recoil over his bad acts as they softly whisper to themselves,

"Did he really just do that?" But sympathy for Walter likely persists—we know deep down that being forced to make it big as a meth king could bring out the worst in any of us.

Far from just entertaining, *Breaking Bad* is instructive for our purposes. It illustrates in dramatic fashion a point we previously made: Although stability is the norm, a person's self-control is never set in stone. New events, circumstances, and identities can intervene and alter one's self-control ability and interest. In Walter's case, his interest in self-regulation nosedived, perhaps from his feeling that he had nothing to lose—he was facing his own death and his family's financial ruin. Under such circumstances, normal practices of self-regulation become irrelevant. Also, once fully entangled in the meth world—with its threatening array of criminals and malevolents—Walter encountered predicaments that invited further antisocial and violent behavior. Acts that would have been unimaginable in years prior became normal as new standards emerged. Indeed, as part of his evolution, Walter even embraced the violence. Bryan Cranston, the actor who played Walter, summed it up this way in advance of Season 4: "Walt's figured out it's better to be a pursuer than the pursued. He's well on his way to badass" status (Ginsberg, 2011).

The transformation portrayed in *Breaking Bad* is extreme and fictional, and as you might expect, the research we review in the following sections does not chronicle how mild-mannered, professionals turn into lawless gangsters. But in connection to *Breaking Bad*, we direct our attention squarely to the idea of *change*. When it comes to self-control, people sometimes do change. Moreover, there are scientific and public policy insights that come from understanding why and how such changes occur.

We focus especially on changes that occur in adolescence and then adulthood. By that point, the early-in-life factors we have discussed—genetics, neurobiological development, and social interactions with parents—have already significantly shaped the child's self-control. Moreover, through the processes of self-selection and state dependence described in Chapter 5, the adolescent is likely enmeshed in social roles, relationships, and experiences that correspond to and reinforce that initial level of self-control. Change, however, is possible, and we focus especially on three sources of change. The first involves adolescence and its powerful mix of biological, psychological, social, and lifestyle shifts that can—for some individuals—profoundly affect self-control ability and interest. Considering this issue will have us delving into the neuroscience of the evolving adolescent brain. The second source of change involves shifts in one's social environments and relationships— in the family and peer contexts, for example—in which unexpected events and circumstances jump someone onto a different self-control trajectory. As part of this, we come back to the topic of human agency, considering the possibility that through sheer force of will, some individuals redefine themselves in ways that involve major shifts in self-control. In viewing our third source of change, we shorten our time horizon—rather than looking at shifts that occur over the course of years or decades, we consider short-term fluctuations in self-control that are especially linked to patterns of sleeping, eating, and substance use. And then to conclude it all, we consider the implications that these sources of self-control change have for public policy efforts to reduce problems associated with low self-control.

THE PERVASIVENESS OF CHANGE

Few behavioral scientists have written more about the idea of behavioral change than John Laub and Robert Sampson (Laub & Sampson, 1993, 2003; Sampson & Laub, 1993). Across their many influential books and articles, they have theorized about and empirically verified a surprising amount of behavioral change. They have framed this work with an emphasis on *turning points*, which they define as "alteration[s] or deflection[s] in a long-term pathway" (Sampson & Laub, 2005, p. 16). Simply stated, a turning point occurs when an individual deviates from the behavioral pathway upon which he or she has been traveling for some time. This sometimes involve *breaking bad*, but *breaking good* is also possible. Indeed, because problems with crime and low self-control often spike during adolescence, the typical turning point in late adolescence and early adulthood has individuals increasing their self-control and decreasing their involvement in crime and antisocial behavior. Regardless of which direction someone is breaking, Laub and Sampson's (1993) point is clear: "Life is dynamic; change is clearly possible" (p. 309).

In Chapter 5, we reviewed notable studies on self-control stability and change, and a few themes on change merit emphasis here. Most notably, recall that although self-control stability is quite common, patterns of change have emerged in virtually every study that has considered the issue (Burt, Simons, & Simons, 2006; Na & Paternoster, 2012; Turner & Piquero, 2002). This is true even though many studies have examined self-control over fairly short periods (3 to 4 years) in childhood and adolescence that are less likely to reveal self-control shifts. Studies with lengthier follow-ups generally reveal greater shifts in absolute and relative self-control. The study from Hay and Forrest (2006) is a good example. Self-control at age 7 had a correlation of .64 with self-control measured two year later at age 9, but its correlation with self-control at later ages dropped continuously (going to .52 for age 13 and .43 for age 15). Winfree, Taylor, He, and Esbensen (2006) reached a similar conclusion—one-year stability coefficients were typically around .60 or above, whereas four-year stability coefficients were around .40 or below. Burt and her colleagues (2006) conducted a quartile analysis that intuitively revealed the individual changes underlying these middling-level stability coefficients. They found that across two waves of data, 15% of their sample moved fully across the self-control distribution by shifting from its bottom one fourth to its top one fourth, or vice versa.[1]

Studies of self-control-related personality traits like Conscientiousness have yielded similar results (Roberts & Delvecchio, 2000; Roberts, Wood, & Caspi, 2008). This research is especially informative in two ways. First, it has rigorously considered whether differences across individuals in self-control development are large enough to be deemed *real* differences. This is critical, given that absolute and relative changes from one observation to the next could just be minor fluctuations or mere measurement error. To consider this possibility, researchers developed the Reliable Change Index, which compares the amount of personality change that is observed to the amount that could be expected to occur just from chance and measurement error. Using this approach, along with various growth curve modeling approaches, Roberts and his colleagues (2008, p. 382) concluded that there is "unambiguous evidence" that real individual differences in personality trait change exist.

A second interesting aspect of personality studies is that some have followed individuals over unusually long stretches of time—sometimes as much as 40 or 50 years. Such studies typically reveal stability coefficients around .20 (Roberts et al., 2008). The fact that these correlations are not closer to .00 is perhaps impressive—50 years is a long time. That said, these correlations reveal genuine change in personality traits over the life course. As Roberts and his colleagues (2008, p. 379) note, "we might not recognize the 70-year-old from what we knew when he or she was 20."

Thus, as people traverse the varied terrain of childhood, adolescence, and adulthood, they do not move in lockstep with one another—some maintain a consistent level of self-control, some show unexpected improvements, and others are marked by decline. And along the way, the self-control rank ordering among individuals is "reshuffled" to some degree—those starting at a medium or high position sometimes are passed by others, and vice versa. A key question therefore emerges: What explains these relative and absolute changes in self-control?

THE TRANSFORMATIONS OF ADOLESCENCE

In contemplating self-control changes over the life course, a good place to begin is adolescence—the transitional period between childhood and adulthood known for its intense "storm and stress" (Hall, 1904). True enough, adolescence does involve a powerful mix of biological, psychological, and social changes, but defining exactly what it is and when it begins and ends is far from easy. This is because adolescence is a classic example of a *socially constructed* concept—adolescence is not a concrete thing that we can place under a microscope or put on a scale. Instead, it is an invented social idea with a meaning that is arbitrary to some degree and that varies over time and across cultures. Simply stated, adolescence is what we define it to be, and those definitions change over time.

For example, in earlier periods of human history—and this is especially documented for preindustrial agrarian societies—there was little existence or need for the transitional period of adolescence. At that time, the teenage years saw youths—especially males—make a rapid transition from childhood to adulthood, quickly moving into adult roles and responsibilities, especially those involving labor associated with their family's agrarian subsistence (see Gillis, 1974, and Kett, 1977, for impressive historic overviews that inform our discussion). However, as societies moved from a rural, farm-based model to one rooted increasingly in urban industrialization, a conception of adolescence began to emerge. In providing the first academic treatment of the topic, Hall (1904) reflected on the changing cultural values of the time in suggesting that the rapid transition to adulthood was not such a good thing. Those exiting from childhood would be better served, he argued, by a transitional period that prolonged childhood to protect teens from the problems, temptations, and vices of adulthood (all of which were becoming more obvious in growing urban centers). These concerns were matched by technological and economic shifts that increased the need for education. As the needed years of schooling went up, youth involvement in adult labor went down. Indeed, child labor and compulsory education laws rapidly spread in the United States from 1900 to 1930. This mix of cultural and economic changes had profound effects for teenagers, "prolong[ing] their period of social dependency" (Kett, 2003, p. 356) and ushering in a new concern for the care, protection, and tutelage of those nearing adulthood. And *voilà*—a new stage of life was born.

One might argue that rather than creating a new stage of life, these changes merely extended an existing stage: childhood. This, however, ignores the fundamental biology of it all—the clear thing differentiating adolescents from children is biological sexual maturation. Puberty typically marks the beginning of adolescence, and its early stages have the endocrine system flooding the body with sex hormones (primarily estrogen for females, primarily testosterone for males). This begins by age 8 to 11 for females and one to two years later for males. The initial changes are not readily visible, but they will be soon enough, with both males and females rapidly gaining height, weight, and muscle mass (especially for males), along with advances in the various indicators of sexual maturity (Wright, Tibbetts, & Daigle, 2008, pp. 232–239). The end result is that by the middle teen years, most adolescents are—in reproductive terms— essentially adults. They have not yet graduated to adult roles and responsibilities, but they are decidedly *not* children, and in this sense, adolescents are suspended in a purgatory of sorts. A key question for us is this: What are the implications of this reality for self-control?

The Adolescent Maturity Gap

One distinct possibility is that, all else being equal, the onset of adolescence *discourages self-control*, at least for a stretch of time. Moffitt (1993) points to this possibility in her influential discussion of the *maturity gap*. She emphasizes two master trends of advanced industrial societies: First, improved nutrition and health care have reduced the age at which biological maturity is reached; second, modernization of work has delayed the age of employment and prolonged the period of social dependence. These two trends create the maturity gap, a "5- to 10-year role vacuum" (p. 686) in which adolescents are biologically capable of being adults but are denied adult status in most ways—they are discouraged from engaging in sexual relations, and they are not allowed to work or get a driver's license until age 16, vote until age 18, or legally drink alcohol until age 21. Moreover, they are financially and socially dependent upon their parents through, in most cases, at least age 18 and have less input than they would like on important decisions in their lives.

Caught in this situation, adolescents seek a remedy. Importantly, risky and rebellious antisocial behavior is not merely a convenient or feasible remedy—it is quite an effective one. The basic source of adolescent frustration is unwanted control from adults who undermine the adolescent's desire for autonomy and independence. What better way is there to demonstrate that one is beyond that control than to *defy* it? As Moffitt (1993, p. 688) argues, "antisocial behavior is an effective means of knifing-off childhood apron strings and of proving that they can act independently to conquer new challenges." She goes on: "Every curfew violated, car stolen, drug taken, and baby conceived is a statement of personal independence" (p. 688).

A key implication, therefore, is that when adolescents are fully in the throes of the maturity gap, their *interest* in self-control likely declines. Indeed, they may perfectly fit the pattern Tittle, Ward, and Grasmick (2004, p. 146) mention in distinguishing self-control interest and capacity: "Some people will have a strong capacity for self-control but may not always want to exercise it." For adolescents, actively practicing self-control—thoughtfully deliberating on different courses of action and acting with an eye toward long-term interests rather than immediate gratification—may have negative connotations. Indeed, far from being seen as appealing, the adolescent who is especially strong in self-control may be seen by other teens as timid, docile, uninteresting, and bland—by adhering so closely to a deliberative and conscientious path, he or she may seem very much under the control of adults, and therefore lacking the exact qualities that adolescents so want to possess: independence and autonomy.

All of this seems quite bleak. Indeed, for those thinking of starting a family one day, this is not exactly a ringing endorsement—*start a family, love your kids, invest everything in their well-being, and when they become teens, they'll hate you as the oppressive tyrant blocking their freedom.* Importantly, however, and contrary to the claims of some parents, it typically is not so bad. First, according to Moffitt's perspective, this should all be short-lived. As individuals progress through adolescence, tangible adult opportunities and freedoms arise in the areas of education, work, romantic relationships, and the power to make decisions. As this occurs, the maturity gap recedes—the gap between biological and social maturity lessens, and late adolescents can envision their adult future and the incentives for protecting investments in that future. All else being equal, this should encourage greater interest in self-control. Personality research bears this out to some degree—as individuals are making their way out of adolescence, self-control-relevant traits like Agreeableness and Conscientiousness are starting to increase by leaps and bounds (Roberts & Mroczek, 2008).

A second important caveat is that many adolescents do not experience such an intense maturity gap with all its negative implications. Indeed, a primary critique of the storm-and-stress perspective is that many adolescents and their parents navigate this period quite smoothly. True enough, there is a spike during adolescence in parent–child conflict; also, adolescents' feelings of warmth and closeness with their parents decline during this period (Smetana, Campione-Barr, & Metzger, 2006; Steinberg & Silk, 2002). However, these shifts are often moderate and in line with what is expected as adolescents go through processes of *individuation* and *distancing* in developing social identities that go beyond their connection to parents (Scharf & Mayseless, 2007). Indeed, Smetana and her colleagues (2006) estimate that severe alienation from parents, active rejection of adult authority, and excessive rebellion are enduring problems among as little as 5% to 15% of adolescents.

This points to a basic reality: The brand of adolescent turmoil that lowers self-control interest is not experienced evenly across the adolescent population. Some will get a big dose of it, others will experience it only moderately, and some may skip it altogether. And this has implications for self-control interest and observed levels of self-control change for the adolescent population. Specifically, processes involving Moffitt's maturity gap likely lead to differing levels of absolute self-control change across individuals, and this translates into *relative* self-control change for a given population—some adolescents see their place in the self-control distribution go down as their self-control takes a nosedive, whereas others move up in the distribution when they bypass the storm and stress of adolescence. We later return to this idea of varied outcomes to consider *why* individuals differ so much in how they experience the period of adolescence.

The Neuroscience of the Evolving Adolescent Brain

Recent decades have seen ever greater attention to the neurological nature of adolescent change (Albert, Chein, & Steinberg, 2013; Casey, Getz, & Galvan, 2008; Steinberg, 2010b). This research nicely complements the work just described on the psychological and attitudinal shifts experienced by adolescents—all the while that those shifts are occurring, notable changes are also under way in an adolescent's brain. Modern brain-imaging technology has fueled new insights in this area, revealing that significant brain development continues through at least the early 20s. Most important for our purposes is the unmistakable relevance of this for self-control.

Developmental psychologist Laurence Steinberg has been a leading researcher on these issues, and his dual-systems model of development organizes much of what we know. That perspective begins with the idea that neurological development during the adolescent years is quite imbalanced, with some structures and functions leaping ahead of others, at least for a while. Specifically, Steinberg (2010b) emphasizes two neurobiological networks in the teenage brain: (1) the *socioemotional network* responsible for reward-seeking behavior and (2) the *cognitive control network* responsible for controlling impulses in favor of long-term goals. The socioemotional network that drives reward-seeking zooms forward during adolescence, largely as a result of surges in dopamine that are linked to puberty. This surge greatly enhances the positive sensations associated with reward-seeking behaviors, a pattern observed in several experimental studies (see Casey et al., 2008). Simply stated, the adolescent brain is programmed to better detect the rewards of illicit, forbidden risks. And adolescents often, of course, are surrounded by *other adolescents* experiencing the same neurological shifts. This is an environment in which risk itself comes to be valued.

Far from being entirely dysfunctional, these shifts have been evolutionarily necessary—they encourage the risk-seeking that has been an adaptive part of maturation over the course of human existence. The chief complication, however, is that the cognitive control network responsible for controlling impulses advances much more gradually. This network is governed in large part by changes in the prefrontal cortex (PFC), including synaptic pruning and myelination, that increase the speed and efficiency with which the PFC connects with and coordinates other parts of the brain. As this process advances, the cognitive control network strengthens, allowing the PFC to better play the regulatory role described above, especially with inhibiting impulses. When this process runs its course, an advanced cognitive control network provides a suitable self-control counterbalance to the surges in reward-seeking that come from an advancing socioemotional network.

But again, this does not happen immediately—improvements in the cognitive control network are gradual rather than extreme, advancing in a fairly linear fashion through late adolescence and early adulthood (Steinberg, 2010b). Thus, as individuals advance from early to middle adolescence (roughly age 15), there is a tendency (all else being equal) for reward-seeking to win over impulse control, and this encourages momentary or sustained lapses in self-control among adolescents. Their neurological ability to exercise self-control actually is *increasing* during this period, but it is doing so at a slower rate than what is seen for their neurological ability to detect the rewards of various allures and temptations. Gopnik (2012, C1) cleverly describes this process: "If you think of the teenage brain as a car, today's adolescents acquire an accelerator a long time before they can steer and brake."

We alluded above to the role of peers, and this is a central part of the story. Various experiments indicate that adolescents' sensitivity to reward-seeking opportunities is greatly enhanced by the presence of peers. Gardner and Steinberg (2005) discovered this with an experiment they dubbed the Chicken Game that was designed to assess risky driving in the context of a computerized game. Subjects were asked to advance a vehicle along a course as far as possible within a specified amount of time; as part of this, they had to avoid walls that could appear on the course at any time and lead to a crash. Initial analyses indicated that early adolescents (about age 14), late adolescents (about age 19), and adults (about age 37) took similar amounts of risks when they played the game in isolation. However, when a same-aged peer was also in the room, notable differences in risky driving emerged—the rate of risky driving increased by 100% (a complete doubling) for the early adolescents and by 50% for the late adolescents. Among adults, peer context had no effect on the extent of risky driving.

Neuroimaging studies provide further insight into these dynamics, revealing that adolescents truly are different. Those studies examine electrical activity in the brain, and they point to an interesting conclusion: When adolescents are placed in situations in which the social judgments of peers are in question, portions of their brains light up like Christmas trees in ways not seen in the brains of children and adults (Burnett, Sebastian, Cohen Kadosh, & Blakemore, 2011; Somerville, 2013). More specifically, these studies reveal that adolescents experience heightened neural activity in response to social stimuli manipulated in a laboratory setting. This can include anything from exposure to varied facial expressions to scenarios that introduce social feedback and social evaluations. Steinberg sees this as central to understanding greater risk-seeking behavior among adolescents. It is not just that the reward centers of the brain are outpacing the cognitive control centers; instead, on top of this, these reward centers are hypersensitive to social rewards in particular. Thus, the presence of peers amplifies the salience of risky rewards in the minds of adolescents. And perhaps somewhat strangely, these processes come into play indiscriminately—adolescent decision-making is undermined even in experiments in which the peers in question are anonymous and not physically present (Albert et al., 2013, p. 116; Paternoster, McGloin, Nguyen, & Thomas, 2013).

Taken together, this research indicates a few basic realities of the adolescent experience. Their brains are quickly developing a fine-tuned ability to detect rewards in their environments. This is especially true for social rewards in particular, but the structures and function of the brain most responsible for *regulating* these impulses to seize those rewards advance at a much more leisurely pace. For most individuals, these systems come into balance with one another in early adulthood. In the meantime, this disequilibrium contributes to the increase in risky behavior observed among adolescents.

The Varied Experience of Adolescence

The sections above have emphasized fundamental shifts that leave adolescents both less interested in and less capable of self-control—the maturity gap and related processes increase desires to take risks and prove one's power and autonomy, and neurological developments leave the brain temporarily less equipped to resist risky temptations. And yet, there is an empirical reality that must be confronted: Although some adolescents spiral out of control, experiencing severe and sustained lapses in self-control, most do not. What explains these varied experiences of adolescence? A number of important factors likely come into play. First, regarding biological shifts, individuals develop in different ways—there is no single version of adolescence. Many studies suggest that early onset of puberty leads to increased delinquency and substance use (Cance, Ennet, Morgan-Lopez, Foshee, & Talley, 2013; Felson & Haynie, 2002), perhaps because it intensifies the maturity gap. The same may be true regarding Steinberg's dual-systems model—the relevant imbalances in neurological development will be experienced to varying degrees by different adolescents.

It also is critically important to recognize the significance of social context and social relationships. Biological development does not occur in a vacuum; instead, it plays out in a social context marked by varying interactions and associations with family, peers, and the school. Recall Chapter 4's discussion of Kochanska's model of a mutually responsive orientation between parents and children (Kochanska & Kim, 2014). This involves an established pattern in which parents are attentive to their child's changing developmental needs and children are accustomed to cooperating with parents to achieve joint goals. Under such circumstances, parents likely find ways to smoothly navigate their son's or daughter's experience of adolescence, shifting from "patterns of influence and interaction that are asymmetrical and unequal to ones in which parents and their adolescent children are on a more equal footing" (Steinberg & Silk, 2002, pp. 113–114). Behavioral boundaries are gradually adjusted, psychological autonomy is encouraged, and adolescents are granted a greater say in the events that affect them. Most importantly, the parent–adolescent lines of communication remain open so that the challenges and risks associated with adolescence can be discussed. For many families, these shifts may occur in steady, somewhat unremarkable ways—the cooperation and reciprocity established in the relationship at earlier points carry over into adolescence.

We know, however, that this will not always occur—some parent–child dyads that were doing just fine in the preadolescent period will struggle once adolescence commences. Steinberg and Silk (2002) estimate that in cases of severe adolescent maladjustment, about 20% had little in the way of parent–child problems in childhood. Moreover, for some of the parent–child dyads that were struggling even before adolescence, the turmoil of adolescence may intensify the differences between these individuals and others; simply stated, a child that was moderately lower in self-control than others may evolve into an adolescent who is *substantially* lower in self-control than others. All of this adds up to the same result: The intersection of adolescence and dynamics in the family context may lead to a modest reshuffling of the self-control distribution that has individuals' places in that distribution changing over time.

The peer context is also consequential. As both perspectives above emphasize, adolescent-triggered problems with low self-control and antisocial behavior are pushed along by exposure to peer associations that encourage risky sensation-seeking and experimentation with deviance. It bears emphasizing, however, that not all adolescents have equal access to this peer subculture. Moffitt (1993) emphasized this explicitly, noting that any arrangement that affects access to antisocial peers can variously amplify or diminish the behavioral problems associated with adolescence. For example, some adolescents are naturally gregarious and make friends easily, whereas others are more socially reserved and make fewer friends. Some adolescents have parents who ignore which peers they are spending time with and where they are, whereas others have parents who closely monitor their peer associations and discourage friendships with those thought to be troublemakers. Some adolescents care little about school and have lengthy stretches of free time to spend with peers, whereas others devote a great deal of time away from school to studying. Also, geographic factors likely matter as well—some youths will live in close proximity to many other adolescents (some of whom may have antisocial leanings), whereas others will not. In each of these instances, there is varying access to peer friendships, and this may account for differences in the experience of adolescence.

UNEXPECTED SHIFTS IN SOCIAL ENVIRONMENTS AND RELATIONSHIPS

In many ways, the complications of adolescence that we have been discussing are expected. However, as individuals make their way through adolescence and then adulthood, the *unexpected* can occur as well, and this has implications for self-control and behavior.

Unexpected events may happen in a countless number of ways and manners. In some instances, they may be beyond the control of the individual and may even involve instances of good or bad luck— Sampson and Laub (1993, p. 318) emphasize this in noting that there is "an element of luck, randomness, or chance operating throughout the course of life." Also, in some cases, these unexpected events may be sudden and extreme. These would include the fictional case of *Breaking Bad*'s Walter White as well as the nonfictional case of Phineas Gage, a 19th-century railroad supervisor dubbed history's "most famous neuroscience patient" (see In Focus 6.1). His abrupt drop in self-control followed an explosion that sent a railroad spike straight through his prefrontal cortex (it cannot get much more unexpected than that). "Exogenous shocks" are also possible; these involve historical events such as wars, economic depressions, and natural disasters that fundamentally reorganize individual lives (Sampson & Laub, 1995, p. 150).

IN FOCUS 6.1

Phineas Gage: "Neuroscience's Most Famous Patient"

Changes in self-control sometimes come from dramatic occurrences that affect brain functioning, and this is vividly seen in the historic case of Phineas Gage. As a railroad worker for the Rutland and Burlington Railroad Company, Gage was exemplary in many ways. The 25-year-old was rarely sick, extremely muscular, and he had "an iron will as well as an iron frame" (Harlow, 1869, p. 4). It was the 1840s, and he had risen to the position of foreman and was responsible for leading a team of workers who drilled into rock and laid railroad ties. He was widely regarded as smart, persistent, energetic, and shrewd. Little did he know, however, that he was about to become "neuroscience's most famous patient" (Twomey, 2010).

On September 13, 1848, Gage was working with his crew drilling holes into rock, followed by a process known as "tamping it in." This involved setting the powder and fuse in the hole, pouring in sand, and lighting the charge so the ground could be cleared for the railroad ties. As Gage sat above a hole, preparing it for his crew, he became distracted and turned his head just before an explosion sent the tamping iron—43 inches long and weighing 13 pounds—straight through his skull (Harlow, 1869, p. 5). It entered his cheek below his eye and exited completely through the top of his skull. The force knocked Gage to the ground, where his crew helplessly watched him convulse.

Immediate death seems the most likely outcome of this event, but miraculously, Gage did not die. He maintained consciousness, spoke to his doctor (expressing hope that he was "not much hurt"), and even walked (with assistance) to the bed, where his doctor attended to his burns and wounds (Harlow, 1869, p. 6). Succumbing to the immensity of his injuries, Gage then spent the next two months in bed during a stretch punctuated by delirious fever, moments of stunning clarity, and even a brief coma. But he came out of it all. A mere 64 days after an iron bar was sent through his skull, Phineas Gage was walking the streets of the city and preparing to return to his home.

To the astonishment of all involved, Gage suffered no motor or speech impairments from the injury, and his memory was intact as well. This by itself was quite informative to neuroscientists who would study the Gage case—it reinforced an increasing recognition of how different aspects of the brain specialize to some degree. Because key parts of Gage's brain had been untouched by the tamping iron, many aspects of neurological functioning were unaffected. But by all accounts, Gage was not himself after the accident. Although Gage had previously been lauded as efficient, polite, and capable, he was now marked by "animal propensities" and extreme outbursts in which he was erratic, impatient, restless, dishonest, and disrespectful toward others (Harlow, 1869, p. 14). Gage, in short, had greatly lost the ability to self-regulate his own thoughts, actions, and emotions. He was described as "a child in his intellectual capacity and manifestations," and he would abandon plans quickly and with little thought (Harlow, 1869, p. 14). In fact, his personality was so drastically different that his friends said he was "no longer Gage" (Harlow, 1869, p. 14).

Jump ahead almost 170 years to the present, when researchers are still studying Phineas Gage and his remarkable shift in personality. His skull is displayed in the Warren Anatomical Museum at Harvard Medical School, and while it is too fragile to be further examined, it earlier was subjected to careful medical imaging. Neuroscientists continue studying those scans to determine the exact nature and extent of Gage's injuries. The prominent conclusion is that while Gage's injuries were limited to a small portion of the brain, they hit the critical region of the prefrontal cortex that helps supervise and link the various brain regions that work together to make complicated decisions regarding moral decision-making and self-restraint (Van Horn et al., 2012). It is precisely for this reason that his transformation involved shifts in *behavior* in particular. To this day, Phineas Gage remains the textbook case for examining brain trauma, neuropsychological deficits, and changes in impulsive behavior.

In most instances, however, unexpected events and circumstances are not so spectacular and dramatic. They often involve shifts in normal aspects of everyday life that take on significance over time. These include shifts in social relationships with significant others (like parents, spouses, and friends) or in experiences with prominent social institutions (like schools, the labor market, and the criminal justice system). What specifically would make changes in these areas *unexpected*? In the examples we discuss below, there are two common patterns. The first involves a shift that is *new*—it is a departure from earlier circumstances. The second common pattern involves a development that is statistically unlikely for an individual, given his or her existing qualities. For example, as we have discussed earlier, a child with low self-control is not likely to thrive in the school environment— low self-control generally works against that goal. Thus, if he or she does thrive, this is unexpected, and it could be the basis for later improvements in self-control as the individual embraces the socialization he or she receives in school.

Regardless of which variation comes into play, there is a common theme behind it all: Unexpected events happen, and when they do, the reverberations can make their way to self-control. We consider this possibility for key areas of life in which unexpected events have been most linked to shifts in self-control or behavior.

Unexpected Changes With Parents

In thinking about adolescents, we should especially consider the importance of changes involving parents. Parent–child interactions significantly shape self-control from an early age, and there is notable stability in the quality of parenting from childhood to adolescence—children exposed to high-quality parenting in childhood often are treated to that same advantage in adolescence. And yet, stability coefficients on parenting quality are far from perfect—parents do sometimes change their approach (Kandel & Wu, 1995; Loeber et al., 2000). Importantly, these shifts appear to be consequential. In conducting a study of children who aged from 7 to 15 during the study period, Hay and Forrest (2006) found that shifts in the quality of parenting (as indicated by shifts in supervision and warmth) over time explained individual shifts in self-control—when the quality of parenting improved, so too did self-control; when it declined, self-control dropped also (see also Burt et al., 2006).

What explains shifts in the quality of parenting? Why do some parents alter their approach to such things as parental supervision and expression of warmth? Changes in the lives of the parents themselves are important—shifts in marital quality, economic hardship, occupational satisfaction, physical and mental health, and so forth all affect parents' well-being and, in the process, affect outcomes for their children. This squares well with an elaborate literature on the idea of *parenting stress* (Conger et al., 2002; Deater-Deckard, 2005; Warfield, 2005). This research reveals that parental stress over such things as economic hardship, problems in the workplace, and disruptions in child care can trigger harsh reactions to child transgressions and undermine parents' capacity to respond constructively to the challenges of parenting.

Unexpected Peer Associations

Increasing involvement with peers is a defining aspect of adolescence. Even adolescents who are diligently supervised by their parents will begin spending more time with friends. And, of course, their existing level of self-control likely will affect who they choose as friends. We would expect that those who are impulsive risk-seekers (i.e., those with low self-control) will be naturally drawn to friends who are similar in this regard. Conversely, those with high self-control should have friends who are similarly high in self-control. Although this type of self-selection certainly occurs on some level, several recent studies suggest that unexpected peer associations commonly emerge. Specifically, adolescents commonly experience changes in peer associations, and this sometimes has them shifting from prosocial to antisocial peers (or vice versa). Similarly, individuals sometimes have friends that are different than expected based on what we know of their self-control (Young, 2010). Indeed, much research on peer selection points to the importance of similarities on qualities *other than* self-control, including ascribed characteristics (like race and sex), grade level, interests, hobbies, and physical appearance. Residential proximity is a surprisingly critical factor—adolescents who live close to one another are more likely to become friends (Warr, 2002, pp. 26–28).

Thus, seemingly "unexpected" friendships can emerge, and when they do, there is good reason to expect them to influence self-control. Some adolescents will find themselves in unexpected friendships that encourage self-control—just as parents discipline impulsive or inconsiderate acts, so too do prosocial peers through their own brand of criticism or exclusion. On the other hand, some unexpected friendships may involve an antisocial influence in which peers actually encourage low self-control. Rebellon and Manasse (2004, p. 359) make this point in noting that in some groups, "peers may grant risk-takers a measure of status" and those willing to rebel against authority and "test boundaries" may be viewed as "more fun than the conformist" (see also Simons & Burt, 2011). Meldrum, Young, and Weerman (2012) considered these issues in their study of early adolescents who were followed for three years. They found that subjects experienced significant changes in the self-control and delinquency levels of friends, and when this happened, it translated into significant changes—those who shifted toward friends higher in self-control and lower in delinquency experienced improvements in self-control (and vice versa). Burt and colleagues (2006) reached a similar conclusion—increased time with deviant peers and decreased time with prosocial peers led to reductions in self-control over a two-year period (also see Meldrum & Hay, 2012).

Unexpected Developments at School

An example we referenced earlier involves a child with low self-control who enters the school setting. Success in school often requires diligence, thoughtfulness, persistence, and restraint—the very qualities those low in self-control often lack. Indeed, the common expectation is that children with low self-control will find the school environment boring at best and hostile at worst. This would follow from the school's natural emphasis on order and discipline (Gottfredson & Hirschi, 1990, pp. 162–163).

But is it always this straightforward? Hay, Meldrum, and Piquero (2013) considered this question for a sample of 800 adolescents who were studied at ages 10, 12, and 15. A key question was this: Does having low self-control necessarily lead to poor outcomes at school? They used an overall measure of school bonding that asked adolescents how much they agreed with statements like "I work hard in school," "I am happy to be at my school," and "I feel very close to at least one of my teachers." The analysis revealed a surprising conclusion: Although having low self-control was associated with lower school bonding, there were plenty of exceptions to that pattern. Indeed, among those in the lowest self-control group (the bottom 25% of the self-control distribution), nearly 20% were in the *top* 25% of the distribution when it came to thriving at school. Moreover, the adolescents who fit this pattern had a delinquency rate that was more than 50% lower than that of the low-self-control youths who were poorly bonded to school. Other studies confirm that attachment to school increases later self-control and reduces delinquency (e.g., Burt, Simons, & Simons, 2006). Simply stated, when this unexpected educational development occurs, positive outcomes often follow.

One question remains: *Why* were some children with low self-control able to thrive in school? Their low self-control presumably prevents that outcome. Two important factors likely come into play. First, many impulsive children will possess other qualities that compensate for self-control deficits. An amiable nature, an impressive talent, a charismatic personality, or an attractive appearance all could make school a hospitable and satisfying environment despite their self-control struggles. Also, some will be intelligent and intellectually curious; education may therefore capture their attention and set aside problems with self-regulation. In connection, there is a growing literature on the nontrivial number of gifted, talented, and high-IQ students who have been diagnosed with attention deficit disorder (Nicpon, Allmon, Sieck, & Stinson, 2011). It also is possible that their success at school follows not from their own alternative characteristics, but instead from the efforts of *others*. For example, passionate teachers, coaches, or school staff may see an impulsive girl not just in terms of the challenges she presents, but also in terms of her future potential, and they may invest in her accordingly. Laub and Sampson (1993, p. 311) speak of this dynamic in describing how those in influential positions might "take chances" on an individual with hopes "that their investment will pay off." Under such circumstances, a child may develop a strong commitment to school and to education in general despite having an individual quality that often works against that outcome.

IN FOCUS 6.2

The Mass Media and Self-Control: MTV's *16 and Pregnant*

Our discussion has focused on how key social environments and relationships—in the areas of family, peers, and school—can trigger self-control changes. Is it possible that certain influences in the mass media could also bring about such changes? Could something as simple as watching a television show change people's self-control? A recent study of the MTV network's reality show *16 and Pregnant* suggests that the answer could be yes. The show chronicles the lives of a small number of female teenagers facing the challenging task of a pregnancy. Far from glamorizing or trivializing this occurrence, the show is known for its "grim" and

(Continued)

(Continued)

"brutally honest" depiction of what these teenagers face in tackling important decisions and burdens when it comes to school, medical bills, dealing with the child's father, and adapting to the physical, social, and emotional turbulence from this extraordinary life occurrence (Bellafante, 2009; National Public Radio, 2014). Two behavioral economists, Melissa Kearney and Phillip Levine (2014), considered whether watching this show might encourage greater self-control among adolescent viewers. If so, it would suggest that a powerful media depiction of the consequences of impulsive behavior could inspire others to have greater interest in self-control. They used Nielsen ratings data to capture geographic variations in viewership of the show. They found that in areas in which the show was most popular, Google searches and tweets about birth control and abortion spiked exactly when the show was airing. Moreover, an analysis of fertility data suggested that viewership of the program contributed to an almost 6% reduction in the teen birth rate from June 2009 through the end of 2010.

Although one single study cannot definitively answer a complicated research question like this one, this is a promising result and a testament to how the mass media, social media, and the Internet can powerfully combine to affect behavioral tendencies, including those involving self-control. Sarah Brown, CEO of the National Campaign to Prevent Teen and Unplanned Pregnancy, describes it this way:

> The entertainment media can be, and often is, a force for good . . . One of the nation's great success stories of the past two decades has been the historic declines in teen pregnancy. MTV and other media outlets have undoubtedly increased attention to the risks and reality of teen pregnancy and parenthood and, as this research shows, have likely played a role in the nation's remarkable progress. (Wellesley College, 2014)

Changes Associated With Marriage

As people age from adolescence into early adulthood, different life course arenas and events become proximate drivers of behavioral change. Events with parents, peers, and school are replaced to some degree by such things as marriage, entry into the labor force, and parenthood.

Marriage especially has received extraordinary attention, much of it seemingly inspired by the possibility that troublemaking *men* in particular can be reformed by the love of a good woman. Such an idea has likely been around since the dawn of human existence. As early as human populations recognized that some men in their community were genuine troublemakers, there almost certainly were hopes that strong and patient women would step forward and lead them to mend their ways. And, of course, in theory, a troublemaking woman could also be reformed by the love of a good man.

As it turns out, either hypothesis is quite difficult to test. The problem is that troublemaking men *and* women are relatively unlikely to enter into high-quality marriages with prosocial spouses—their bad behavior (and the low self-control that underlies it) often prevents this. Thus, in any given dataset that behavioral scientists study, the solid marriages tend to be clustered among those individuals who are inclined to behave well in the first place. The very type of marriage needed to test this hypothesis—one in which a troublemaker marries "up," so to speak—is in short supply.

An ingenious study from Sampson, Laub, and Wimer (2006) tackled this analytical problem. With data in hand from 400 males followed from early childhood through adulthood, they asked this question: Did getting married lead to improvements in behavior? To answer it, they used a method known as *inverse probability of treatment weighting*. With this approach, their dataset more heavily weighted the cases in which a male got married and stayed married when he was *not* expected to do so. Marriages were deemed unexpected when the male had a background marked by crime, aggressiveness, and low self-control (among other things). These things hinder one's chances of getting and staying married, but their presence also raises the possibility that marriage can improve behavior, given that such individuals have clear room for improvement. Sampson and his colleagues found that when these cases are given heavier weighting—and thus not allowed to be dwarfed by other more common marital matches—an important conclusion emerged: Being married in a given year reduced one's rate of offending by approximately 35% in that year. Support for this pattern emerged across a wide range of analyses and data specifications, leading Sampson and his colleagues to suggest that marriage can trigger some men to make the miraculous shift from "a hell-raiser to a family man" (p. 498).

Similar findings have emerged in other recent studies (Bersani & Doherty, 2013; Bersani, Laub, & Nieuwbeerta, 2009; Doherty & Ensminger, 2013; King, Massoglia, & MacMillan, 2007), although there are lingering questions regarding whether females experience crime-reducing benefits of marriage to the same degree that males do. (One complication for females is that higher crime among males increases the chance that they will have a crime-involved spouse.) When individual reductions in crime *do* emerge from marriage, they are thought to be explained by the ways in which marriage increases commitment to conventional prosocial goals and reduces adherence to lifestyles and daily routines that encourage crime (Osgood & Lee, 1993; Sampson & Laub, 1993). Indeed, as part of this, marriage interrupts associations with the antisocial friends that reinforced prior involvement in crime (Warr, 1998).

But what about self-control—can marriage reduce crime by increasing self-control? This possibility has been neglected, but Forrest and Hay (2011) argued that marriage is likely to have this exact effect. They suggested that self-control is not a fixed trait, but instead is, at least in part, "a skill or resource that . . . can be learned or forgotten or employed or not employed" (p. 492). They argued that in three specific ways, marriage likely encourages the learning and use of self-control. First, marriage often introduces new standards of behavior. In all marriages, there will be expectations of consideration, compromise, attentiveness, and reliability, and these standards may be new for many prior offenders. Second, as an institution inherently oriented toward the long term, marriage likely increases self-control *interest*. Many prior offenders simply may not have cared much about self-control. Marriage may change that as the long-term interests of one's new family become a priority. And third, marriage may increase self-control by providing opportunities for self-control *practice*. We elaborate on this principle at a later point, but the simple idea is that self-control *strength* can be enhanced through the accomplishment of easy tasks that focus individuals on the successful use of self-control. As many married people will admit, the first months and years of marriage offer a crash-course in self-control practice, as opportunities abound for regulating thoughts, actions, and emotions to promote individual and marital well-being.

Forrest and Hay's (2011) analysis supports these possibilities. They studied approximately 2,000 individuals whose self-control was measured in late adolescence and then again in early adulthood. The average individual experienced an increase in self-control during this period, but this was substantially more true among those who also got married. Moreover, the greatest effects of marriage on self-control were experienced arguably by those who most needed this benefit—the positive effects of marriage on self-control were doubled in an analysis limited to those who used marijuana in adolescence. Forrest and Hay concluded that although more studies are needed on this issue, the initial evidence is that marriage can trigger significant self-control improvements.

Employment as a Turning Point

Employment in early adulthood may function in ways that are quite similar to marriage—for those coming out of adolescence with self-control deficits and problems with antisocial behavior, paid work can be a turning point toward a more conventional lifestyle (Uggen, 2000). Indeed, Forrest and Hay (2011) argued that employment can trigger self-control improvements for the same three reasons that marriage can. Specifically, employment introduces (a) new standards of behavior that are relevant to self-control (e.g., punctuality, reliability, conscientiousness), (b) new incentives for caring about self-control, and (c) new opportunities for self-control practice.

Although research on these possibilities is quite limited, there is promising evidence. For example, in criminology, many studies find that entry into employment is a significant predictor of criminal desistance (the cessation of criminal involvement). Sampson and Laub (1993) found this to be true in their study of delinquent males who grew up in disadvantaged Boston neighborhoods—job stability from ages 17 to 25 significantly decreased crime not just during those years, but also from ages 25 to 32. Indeed, job stability had effects that were quite broad—not only did it reduce arrests, but it was negatively associated with measures of excessive alcohol use and overall deviance. Support for an employment–desistance link also emerged in Uggen's (2000) evaluation of the National Supported Work Demonstration Project. This evaluation was able to use random assignment of formerly incarcerated offenders to control and experimental groups. Those in the experimental group were offered minimum-wage jobs, mainly in the construction and service industries. Uggen (2000) found that for offenders who were age 26 or under at the time of release, there were no differences between the experimental and control groups. For those over 26, however, the program appeared to successfully prevent crime—the experimental group had a rearrest rate roughly 20% lower than that of the control group for a three-year follow-up period.

There also has been attention to this issue in personality research that examines changes over the life course. Early work from Elder (1969), one of the early pioneers of the life course perspective, found that men who achieved greater occupational status than their fathers experienced greater shifts in personality than men who did not—by their 30s, they became more dependable, responsible, independent, and persistent in the face of struggles. More recently, in studying personality changes from age 18 to 26, Roberts, Caspi, and Moffitt (2003) found that work commitment/satisfaction and financial security led to within-individual improvements in emotional stability and constraint, two aspects of personality that are consistently linked to self-control.

Taken together, this research suggests that adulthood shifts in self-control may arise in part from changes and evolutions in employment. However, new research is needed, especially research focusing directly on the link between employment experiences and self-control in particular (rather than related behavioral or personality constructs).

Discovering (or Rediscovering) Religion

Those with an extensive history of problem behavior may at times break from that pattern because of transformative shifts in religious values. Behavioral scientists have in recent years devoted greater attention to the connection between religiosity and motivation to engage in self-control. As Reisig, Wolfe, and Pratt (2012; all quotes below from p. 1175) note, there are many reasons to expect that enhanced commitment to religious values could spur improvements in self-control. For example, the belief that key divergent outcomes hang in the balance upon death (e.g., eternal salvation versus eternal torment) can "serve as powerful inducements to improve self-control efforts." Moreover, religious activities like prayer and meditation provide explicit opportunities to self-monitor and reflect on the appropriateness of one's behavior; this, in turn, "may facilitate greater self-control efforts in the future." Finally, religion is a source of role models and prosocial influences that encourage self-control. In Reisig and colleagues' words, religion provides its believers with "moral guidelines to defer to and exemplars to emulate."

Several studies suggest that these mechanisms may in fact be operating—religious commitment, increases in religiosity, and circumstances that encourage religious thought are generally associated with higher self-control, even in studies that statistically account for background factors thought to promote both religiosity and self-control (McCullough & Willoughby, 2009; Rounding, Lee, Jacobson, & Ji, 2012). Pirutinsky (2014) offers compelling longitudinal evidence on this. His study of high-risk adolescent offenders found that individual increases in religiosity were associated with reductions in offending and that part of this association was explained by improvements in self-control resulting from enhanced religiosity.

Human Agency Revisited

The developments described above—regarding parents and peers during adolescence, marriage and employment in early adulthood, and religious change at any point in time—were described as unexpected events that can trigger changes in self-control and behavior. And importantly, the empirical studies cited above used analytical methods that did indeed try to isolate *unexpected* events—events that are unlikely given an individual's past. And yet, were they entirely unexpected? In raising that question, we return to the idea of human agency—"the purposeful execution of choice and individual will" (Laub, 2006, p. 244). We do so because researchers can never know *everything* about individual subjects. This leaves the distinct possibility that some unexpected events and changes occur because individuals *make them happen.* When this occurs, human agency would seem to be a big part of the story—individuals are taking an active role in redefining themselves and reshaping their future in ways that involve shifts in self-control.

This type of transformation has been especially studied in adult criminal offenders who have lived chaotic lives, often going in and out of prisons, jails, and drug treatment centers (Giordano, Cernkovich, & Rudolph, 2002; Laub & Sampson, 2004; Liem & Richardson, 2014; Maruna, 2001; Paternoster & Bushway, 2009). Their personal transformations occur when they reach that moment in which they have *had enough*—they are frustrated, weary of their lives, and ready for a change. At this moment, the person becomes open to "willfully changing his identity and both working toward something positive in the future and steering away from something feared" (a return to his old ways; Paternoster & Bushway, 2009, p. 1108). Most research in this area emphasizes that although there may be "epiphany" moments in which sudden realizations lead to rapid shifts, these transformations are often gradual and marked by intermittent ups and downs and advances and relapses (Bushway, Piquero, Broidy, Cauffman, & Mazerolle, 2001). Simply stated, the journey toward a new self is a meandering one, full of missed turns and flat tires.

Among those who complete the journey, there are common themes, the most notable of which involves the construction of a personal narrative that redefines oneself as different—as *better*—than prior lapses and transgressions would indicate. These narratives go by many names, including Maruna's (2001) "redemption scripts," Stevens's (2012) "prototypical reform story," Giordano and her colleagues' (2002) "cognitive transformations," and Liem and Richardson's (2014) "transformation narratives." Maruna's (2001) work has been especially influential in this area. His concept of redemption scripts involves a personal narrative in which ex-offenders affirm the basic goodness of their characters, renounce the corrupting influences of their past, and speak of their motivation to *make good,* a motivation often spurred on by some special person or outside force (including religion). The redemption script often is quite forgiving to oneself, and it need not be wholly accurate—instead, it simply must be a resonating and powerful narrative that envisions and inspires a better future.

Giordano and her colleagues (2002) have devoted special attention to the link between these personal narratives and some of the unexpected events we described above. They describe a process that gradually moves an individual toward creating pivotal events or, just as important, responding in favorable ways to opportunities that emerge—opportunities he or she likely would have squandered in the past. At the beginning of this process, the individual first becomes open to change and then becomes drawn to the positive developments (e.g., rehabilitative programming, job stability, prosocial romantic relationships) that can help him or her accomplish that change. The cognitive transformation then becomes complete as the person envisions a conventional, law-abiding "replacement self" that supplants the deviant self that is left behind. Over time, crime and a criminal lifestyle are no longer seen as "positive, viable, or even personally relevant" (p. 1002).

The point to emphasize, therefore, is that for all the major life developments that encourage shifts in self-control, there is some degree of human agency at work. Changes in one's circumstances at work, in the family, or in values and spiritual commitments are not simply *imposed* upon an individual—he or she often has experienced a personal cognitive transformation of some kind that encourages, embraces, and spurs on these changes.

SLEEPING, EATING, AND SUBSTANCE USE: SHORT-TERM FLUCTUATIONS IN SELF-CONTROL

We have focused on pivotal life transitions that trigger long-term shifts in self-control over the life course. Some shifts in self-control, however, will be short term in nature. This harks back to our earlier discussion of self-control *traits* and *states*—the trait component of self-control involves long-term tendencies and patterns, whereas the state component involves short-term fluctuations from one situation to another over short spans of time. Much research has considered the sources of short-term fluctuations, with special attention to how problems in the areas of sleeping, eating, and substance use lead to abrupt self-control lapses. This research fits nicely within Baumeister's self-control strength model that sees self-control as a personal resource that fluctuates over time within the individual—it can be depleted, restored, or strengthened, depending on immediate or recent experiences and challenges.

With regard to sleeping, there are two key conclusions: (1) Many people in the United States are sleep deprived (Centers for Disease

Control and Prevention, 2013; Colten & Altevogt, 2006; National Sleep Foundation, 2013),[2] and (2) sleep deprivation undermines self-control. Sleep offers the central nervous system an opportunity for recuperation and restoration and is therefore critical to cognitive functioning in general (Kopasz et al., 2010). If we get too little sleep, our cognitive functioning is undermined—at least to some degree—and the odds of impulsive behavior, including substance use and violence, go up. This has been found in community studies examining natural variations in sleep and self-control among individuals (Barber & Munz, 2011; Barnes & Meldrum, 2014; Meldrum, Barnes, & Hay, 2013; Peach & Gaultney, 2013), but also in experimental studies that randomly assigned individuals to various degrees of sleep deprivation (Kamphuis, Meerlo, Koolhaas, & Lancel, 2012).

Eating habits are a second commonly studied source of short-term self-control lapses. As we discussed earlier, self-control (as well as higher-order cognitive processes in general) appears to be metabolically expensive—the intense electric firing in your brain taxes your body's energy resources in the same way your cell phone relies on its battery to run energy-intensive apps. If the brain is deprived of its energy source—glucose in the bloodstream that comes from what we eat and drink—then self-control lapses are expected. Much research supports this perspective, finding that hunger and low blood glucose levels lead to short-term spikes in the likelihood of self-regulation failure (Bushman, DeWall, Pond, & Hanus, 2014; DeWall, Deckman, Gailliot, & Bushman, 2011; Gailliot, Schmeichel, & Maner, 2007). Of course, blood glucose levels that are too high (hyperglycemia) also present risks for health and behavior (WebMD, n.d.). Indeed, one recent study found that high consumption of sugary drinks was associated with heightened aggression among teenagers (Solnick & Hemenway, 2012).

One practical implication, therefore, is that the optimal diet maintains blood glucose levels within the recommended range of 70 to 100 mg/dl prior to eating.[3] While it may seem tedious, the best approach to diet (for those with no metabolic disorder) is straightforward and consistent with the recommendations for promoting overall health. The best diet is marked by steady and measured consumption of complex carbohydrates from whole grains, proteins, and unsaturated fats—such a diet helps maintain relatively consistent blood glucose levels over the course of the day. A common problematic diet, on the other hand, involves sporadic eating marked by a cycle of hunger, intense craving, and then consumption of foods with an excess of simple carbohydrates, including added sugar and highly refined grains. In the short run, these foods address the problem—they remove the feeling of hunger and the body converts sugar and other simple carbohydrates into usable energy quite quickly. However, it uses up this energy quite rapidly also, therefore quickening the rate at which another drop in blood glucose will be experienced. By extension, this quickens the rate at which a person will be vulnerable to another glucose-related lapse in self-control.[4]

And last, there is the issue of substance use, especially alcohol use. The evidence on alcohol is clear and compelling—alcohol consumption reduces inhibition, therefore producing short-term reductions in self-control (MacDonald, Zanna, & Fong, 1996; Sullivan, Harris, & Pfefferbaum, 2010; Weafer & Fillmore, 2012). This pattern has previously has been attributed to the "generalized toxic effects of alcohol on the brain" (Sullivan et al., 2010, p. 127), whereas the most recent research has sought to understand with greater specificity the exact neurological processes that alcohol and substance use undermine. Our basic theme, however, is the same regardless: Becoming intoxicated places one at risk for abrupt and severe drops in self-control. This probably occurs by reducing both self-control *interest* and self-control *ability* (Tittle et al., 2004). In terms of self-control interest, the euphoria of an intoxicated state primes a person's interest in rewards and sensations, perhaps producing a corresponding drop in concern about the costs and risks of action. With regard to ability, substance use impairs brain functioning in numerous ways. Of most relevance to self-control may be the way it undermines working memory (automatic processes regarding how to respond to specific stimuli) and set shifting (the ability to quickly change course when new stimuli are presented; Casbon, Curtin, Lang, & Patrick, 2003). Regardless of the exact process, the end result is that impulsive actions—getting in fights, yelling at one's friends and family members, wrecking a car, having unprotected sex with others, and spending all one's money—become immediately more likely when the individual is intoxicated.

POLICY IMPLICATIONS AND POSSIBILITIES

When it comes to policy implications, the key theme for this chapter is *reversal*. Changes in self-control absolutely can occur. Sometimes these changes are desirable and have individuals acquiring greater self-control than they previously had, but the opposite is possible also. The goal for policymakers is to use the research evidence on self-control reversals to advance the public good, pursuing an approach that leads self-control deficits to be reversed as much and as often as possible. The best opportunities begin in adolescence. Recall that unexpected self-control transformations during that period often follow from shifts in the quality of parenting, peer associations, and the school context. Policy-driven self-control reversals therefore often involve interventions that target these key arenas of social life. A number of effective such programs exist for adolescents. One is Multisystemic Therapy (MST), a home- and community-based program found to be successful with serious juvenile offenders (Henggeler, Schoenwald, Borduin, Rowland, & Cunningham, 1998). This program has three main goals: Improve family functioning (especially parents' capacity to monitor, discipline, and positively interact with the adolescent), remove offenders from deviant peer groups, and enhance youths' capacity to succeed in school. In this approach, a customized treatment plan is developed collaboratively between the family and a highly trained therapist with a low caseload. In the initial weeks of treatment, therapist visits are frequent and there is particular focus on improving family members' ability to get along with one another and peacefully solve problems. This improved family functioning then serves as the basis for gains in other areas of the adolescent's life, especially at school and with peers. For most families, the program lasts for three to five months. Many (but not all) evaluations of MST have found it to reduce later crime, often substantially. Given the program's focus on risk factors that have been empirically linked to self-control, there is good reason to expect that improvements in self-control are partially driving this program's success.

Functional Family Therapy (FFT) is a similar program that also has achieved strong evaluation results (Gordon, Graves, & Arbuthnot, 1995). It is designed to improve the quality of family interactions among juvenile delinquents at risk for being institutionalized. We mention it in part because of its established success, but also because one recent evaluation (Sexton & Turner, 2010) touched upon the critical issue of *program fidelity*, which involves how well a program is implemented. If a well-designed innovative program is to be successful, its implementation must closely adhere to the blueprints of the program. However, this is not always the case, and variations in implementation may be highly consequential. In studying more than 900 families that went through FFT in a western state, Sexton and Turner (2010) found that juveniles treated by therapists who closely adhered to FFT protocols were significantly less involved in crime over the following year than a control group that received usual services (mostly probation). The FFT group was especially lower (30% to 35% lower) on the most serious offenses, including felonies and violence. However, those treated by more careless therapists (who scored low on treatment adherence) actually did *worse* than the control group—they might have been better off without FFT. It is for this reason that successful programs devote such attention to ensuring proper implementation.

When it comes to adults in particular, we emphasized earlier that the most notable routes for self-control improvement involve prosocial shifts in the areas of marriage and employment. Admittedly, there is little that policymakers can do to directly encourage prosocial marriages and romantic relationships. On the employment front, however, there are promising possibilities. Recidivism research indicates that among prisoners in state and federal prisons, participation in vocational and prison work programs produce at least modest increases in employment and decreases in recidivism (Wilson, Gallagher, & MacKenzie, 2000). Uggen (2000) reached a similar conclusion in a randomized assessment of a national work placement program in which ex-offenders were trained and then offered minimum-wage jobs, mainly in the construction and service industries, although the program was effective only for individuals over the age of 26. As we noted earlier, at least part of the gains that come from employment may be operating through self-control. Employment introduces (a) new standards of behavior that are relevant to self-control (e.g., punctuality, reliability, conscientiousness), (b) new incentives for caring about self-control, and (c) new opportunities for self-control practice. Thus, policies that encourage stable employment also can promote self-control.

And last, we must emphasize perhaps the most promising policy approach for bringing about self-control reversals among adolescents or adults. This involves programs that act *directly* upon problems with self-control. Thus, rather than trying to affect the risk factors (e.g., family life, peer associations, employment in adulthood) that in turn affect self-control, these programs use individual or group therapy to explicitly improve self-control skills and behaviors.

These programs generally fit within a broad class of treatments known as *cognitive behavioral therapy* (CBT). CBT is based on a straightforward idea: If a person can consciously reflect on the thoughts, emotions, and habits that have created problems in high-risk situations in the past, they can alter those things to prevent self-control lapses in the future. CBT emerged in the 1960s, and in terms of its therapeutic lineage, its name is quite instructive—it blends a cognitive approach (emphasizing internal mental processes) with an emphasis on behaviorism (prioritizing behavior and action over mere good intentions or enhanced understanding of the self; Milkman & Wanberg, 2007). As Vaske, Galyean, and Cullen (2011) point out, this blended approach calls upon individuals to (a) identify high-risk situations and the cognitions that have led to impulsivity in the past; (b) replace impulsive cognitions with those that encourage prosocial behaviors and consideration of the long-term well-being of others; and (c) make general improvements in key cognitive areas. This includes "increasing self-control, increasing the ability to recognize short and long term consequences of behaviors, improving decision-making, and strengthening problem-solving skills" (Vaske et al., 2011, p. 91).[5]

Evaluation results for CBT are consistently impressive. Meta-analyses of experimental studies conclude that it reduces crime by as much as 30% (Landenberger & Lipsey, 2005; Lösel & Beelmann, 2003). Prominent examples of CBT include Aggression Replacement Training (Glick & Gibbs, 2011) and Thinking for a Change, both of which are used with juvenile and adult offenders. Thinking for a Change includes 20 lessons delivered in a structured group setting to offenders in the juvenile or criminal justice system. Consistent with the overall CBT approach, the lessons emphasize recognizing, confronting, and replacing thought patterns that have produced impulsive behaviors in the past. As one example of supporting research, Lowenkamp, Hubbard, Makarios, and Latessa

(2009) studied recidivism patterns among a sample of roughly 200 adult offenders (the average age was 32), about half of whom were referred to Thinking for a Change by a court or probation officer. In the follow-up period, 23% of the Thinking for a Change subjects were rearrested, a figure far lower than the 36% rate for the control group. Multivariate analyses revealed that these differences were maintained even after statistically controlling for ways in which the two groups differed prior to the intervention.

Ultimately, one promise of CBT involves the possibility that it may trigger the human agency transformations that jump an individual from a low-self-control trajectory onto a high one. As described earlier in this chapter, major life reversals among criminals and addicts typically involve a genuine shift in perspective in which the individual goes from embracing his or her criminal and deviant lifestyle to becoming weary of it, wanting to leave it in the past. Many factors must come together for this to happen, but exposure to CBT at a critical moment could be a part of that mix because of the way it encourages individuals to thoughtfully reflect on prior transgressions and envision different emotional and behavioral responses in the future. In this way, CBT could encourage the new personal narratives—Maruna's (2001) "redemption scripts," Stevens's (2012) "reform stories," Giordano and her colleagues' (2002) "cognitive transformations," and Liem and Richardson's (2014) "transformation narratives"—that inspire future changes among soon-to-be-rehabilitated offenders.

CONCLUSION

Winston Churchill once said, "There is nothing wrong in change, if it is in the right direction." So it is with changes in self-control. While most individuals remain stable in their levels of self-control after childhood, our discussion in the present chapter points out that other individuals *do* experience meaningful changes. For some, these changes are positive and "in the right direction"—such things as improved parenting, unexpected prosocial relationships, and guidance from dedicated teachers and mentors help some adolescents overcome earlier deficits in self-control. Comparable shifts are possible even in adulthood and can

follow from romantic relationships with prosocial partners or serendip-
itous opportunities for good employment. When these changes occur,
such individuals have jumped onto a different, more desirable (for
both themselves and society) self-control trajectory, one marked by a
thoughtful, reflective approach to decision-making and a willingness
to override impulses that conflict with higher-order standards and
long-term well-being.

But, of course, negative changes can occur also. A "storm-
and-stress" version of adolescence fraught with an intense maturity gap
(Moffitt, 1993) or intense dual-systems imbalances (Steinberg, 2010b)
will work against self-control even among those who were doing fine
when entering adolescence. Other unexpected and unfortunate events
may take place, including reductions in the quality of parenting,
increased proximity to delinquent peers, and changes in sleeping and
eating habits that undermine proper functioning of the PFC. And all
along the way, human agency—the individual's ability to exert his or
her own will to shape the future—comes into play.

Across all these developments, one thing is clear: *Change is possible.* This is, on balance, quite encouraging because of the possibilities
it opens up for using social policies and programs to encourage reversals of self-control deficits. Such things as Multisystemic Therapy,
Functional Family Therapy, and the many varieties of cognitive behavioral therapy have already achieved notable gains, often contributing to
major life transformations in adolescence, early adulthood, and beyond.

DISCUSSION QUESTIONS

1. Can you think of someone (someone you know or a fictionalized
   TV character) who, over time, ended up *breaking good*? What factors do you think underlie the transformation experienced by this
   person? How might changes in self-control have played a role in the
   transformation?

2. What relevance does the *maturity gap* discussed in the chapter have
   for understanding why adolescence is, for some, a dynamic period
   of change in self-control? What factors explain the emergence of
   the maturity gap in modern society?

3. In what ways could peers undermine the efforts of parents to instill self-control in their children? How might the salience of friendships during early adolescence explain why some individuals experience significant changes in their self-control?

4. What role does the brain play in contributing to changes in self-control during adolescence? What two *networks* discussed in this chapter are relevant to this discussion?

5. What young adult roles can account for changes in self-control? Do you think these role transitions have an impact on self-control *ability*? Self-control *interest*?

NOTES

1. Also, see the very recently published study from Burt, Sweeten, and Simons (2014). Notable shifts in self-control were found among subjects followed over a 15-year period from age 10 to 25.

2. Sleep deprivation is especially a problem for adolescents. Compared to preadolescence, adolescence is marked by later bed times, earlier school start times, and pubertal shifts thought to *increase* the number of needed hours of sleep (Colten & Altevogt, 2006). In connection, the National Sleep Foundation (2013) indicates that adolescents need roughly 8.5 to 9.25 hours of sleep per night, yet this is achieved by less than 15% of the adolescent population.

3. It must be emphasized that variations from these levels occur not just from dietary habits, but also from disorders that undermine the optimal metabolism of glucose. Such disorders appear to heighten the risk of violence and aggression (Raine, Phil, Stoddard, Bihrle, & Buchsbaum, 1998; Virkkunen & Huttennen, 1982). Most recently, DeWall and his colleagues (2011) found that individuals scoring high on a checklist of diabetic symptoms were significantly higher in aggression and significantly lower in self-control. Moreover, in looking at the 50 states of the United States, they found a significant correlation of .38 between state-level rates of violent crime and diabetes.

4. One caveat must be offered: Scientists continue to seek a better understanding of the link between glucose levels and self-control. It is possible that stable blood glucose promotes self-control through mechanisms that have little to do with how glucose fuels brain activity. Some have argued that the glucose demands of self-control and higher-order thinking are in fact not that high (Beedie & Lane, 2012). Additionally, some studies find that merely rinsing one's mouth with a high-glucose solution triggers greater self-control—actual consumption is not necessary (Hagger & Chatzisarantis, 2012). This raises the possibility that the benefits of optimal blood glucose levels are perceptual rather than metabolic in nature (Hagger, 2013). The comfort and contentment that come from steady blood glucose levels may free up one's mental and cognitive resources in ways that enhance self-control motivation. Alternatively, the

irritation and diversion of attention that comes from sagging blood glucose (and hunger) may do the opposite. Taking it all into account, there appear to be important connections between diet, glucose levels, and self-regulation, but the exact explanation for this is not clear.

5. One way to clarify the CBT approach is to contrast it with traditional psychotherapy. As Milkman and Wanberg (2007, pp. xii–xiii) point out, traditional psychotherapy is egocentric—"it helps people resolve their personal problems, feel better about themselves, and fulfill their inner goals and expectations." CBT, on the other hand, is a sociocentric approach that teaches specific cognitive skills and behaviors oriented around one's responsibilities to others and the community.

SEVEN

DO THE HARMFUL EFFECTS OF LOW SELF-CONTROL VARY ACROSS DIFFERENT CIRCUMSTANCES?

---◆---

The idea of *resilience* is one of the more exciting behavioral science stories of recent decades (Fergus & Zimmerman, 2005; Masten, 2001), and it illustrates a pattern central to this chapter. Resilience refers to a pattern in which highly disadvantaged children unexpectedly overcome their adversity to achieve competence and success over the life course. These are children born into intense poverty, perhaps to a single parent who did not finish high school, who often have been exposed to trauma and hardships involving such things as family violence, the death of a parent, or abuse and neglect. Prior research tells us of their expected struggles—with such things as crime, substance use, and school dropout—in adolescence and adulthood. And yet, somewhat miraculously, many disadvantaged children studied over long periods of time were not plagued by these problems. Indeed, some truly thrived (Luthar, 2003)—they did well in school, got along with peers, and then pursued conventional lines of success as adults in the areas of work and family.

Behavioral scientists naturally were drawn to these patterns and looked for explanations. Early scholarship focused on the remarkable and extraordinary nature of these resilient individuals. Masten (2001, p. 227) noted that they were seen as "invincible" and "invulnerable"— nothing could stand in their way. Beauvais and Oetting (2002) similarly observed the tendency to view resilient youth as "golden children" with magical abilities to overcome hardship. One book even dubbed them the "superkids of the ghetto" (Buggie, 1995).

As research continued, however, an interesting pattern emerged: Instances of resilience were more common than expected (Masten, 2001)—not common, just not quite as rare as one might think. This undermined the view that resilience followed purely from the super- hero qualities of these children. After all, superheroes are supposed to be really rare, right?

With that in mind, resilience research has over time come to emphasize a less sensational perspective—one that acknowledges the impressive determination of resilient youth but that also sees them as examples of a general behavioral science process in which the harmful effects of adversity vary across individuals and situations. They often materialize as expected, but sometimes they do not, and when the latter occurs, helpful other factors often have come into play to diminish the harmful effects of childhood adversity. Sometimes that helpful factor is an individual quality like high IQ or strong interpersonal coping skills—these enable smoother adaptations to hardship. Alternatively, some children benefit from social experiences with an adult mentor or participation in an effective intervention program (see Luthar, 2003, and Masten, 2001, for reviews). Regardless of what protective factor comes into play, the key theme of resilience research remains the same: The causes of behavior have effects that often depend on other factors. Simply stated, x leads to y in many instances, but not in other instances, and there may be interesting explanations for these varying effects.

This chapter considers a pattern like this for self-control research in particular. Theorists and researchers have long speculated that the harm- ful effects of low self-control systematically vary (Gottfredson & Hirschi, 1990; Grasmick, Tittle, Bursik, & Arneklev, 1993). Depending on other factors that come into play, these effects may be greater in some instances and lesser in others. Recent research supports this speculation, and in this chapter we identify those critical *other factors* that come into play—factors that work together with low self-control to affect the likelihood of crime and deviance. Considering the joint operation of these different causes offers more nuanced insight into how low self-control affects crime and deviance. It also generates practical insights that are relevant to public policy—a list of factors known to lessen the harmful effects of low self-control provides a checklist of protective factors that can be targeted in policies and programs. With that in mind, our discussion will turn ultimately to the policy implications of our arguments.

CONDITIONAL CAUSATION
AND LOW SELF-CONTROL: CONCEPTUAL ISSUES

Much of this book has described a pattern in which low self-control has a substantial effect on behavior. For example, those with low self-control may have a 40% greater chance of being involved in crime than those with high self-control (Burt, Simons, & Simons, 2006, Table 2; Hay, Meldrum, & Piquero, 2013, Table 2). And for simplicity's sake, we have often spoken of this large effect in a fairly singular sense—as if there were one effect that operates similarly across all individuals, contexts, and circumstances. But as the discussion of resilience just indicated, the situation likely is more complex than this—low self-control does not always translate into the same 40% increase. Under some circumstances, it may increase the odds of crime by as much as 50% or 60%, while under other circumstances, the effects of low self-control may be much lower than 40%, perhaps even approaching zero.

These possibilities involve a process that behavioral scientists refer to as *conditional*, *interactive*, or *moderated* causation. We offer each of those terms because they are the ones variously used in this literature; in practice, they all mean essentially the same thing, each describing a process in which the effect of a given cause depends on other factors. Such an effect is *conditional* in the sense that it depends upon the presence of other factors. Similarly, it is *interactive* in the sense that the effect depends on whether it "interacts with"—or "co-occurs with"—another variable. And such an effect is *moderated* in the sense that the presence of some other factor moderates—or changes—the original effect (the effect that exists when the moderating factor is not considered). Again, the meaning is the same with all—the effects of a given cause of behavior (like low self-control) systematically vary according to other factors.

Importantly, those other factors may at times *amplify* the effects of a given variable, while at other times they may *diminish* those effects. These patterns can be seen with a simple example unrelated to self-control. Everyone at times takes medication to battle a cold or allergies. When you do, you may notice the label that issues these warnings: "Do not consume alcohol while using this medication" and "Do not drive, use machinery, or do any activity that requires alertness." There is a good reason for these warnings: Many of these medicines include an antihistamine that reduces swelling in the nose and throat, but in the process of doing so also makes people feel drowsy. And, of course, alcohol also increases drowsiness. When these things are consumed in conjunction with one another, the two interact such that the increase in drowsiness is even greater than what would be expected—there is a "multiplicative" effect of using these two substances together. Thus, through this interaction, the effect of taking cold or allergy medicine on drowsiness is conditional upon alcohol consumption; specifically, its effects on drowsiness are significantly *amplified.*

However, for other drug interactions, a *diminishing* pattern may be in effect. This sometimes is true for antibiotics that are taken to eliminate an infection. Many antibiotics will not have this desired effect if they are taken in conjunction with dairy consumption. The calcium in milk or yogurt decreases the digestive system's absorption of the antibiotic, therefore preventing the antibiotic from accomplishing its intended task. Thus, through this interaction, the effects of the antibiotic are diminished when dairy consumption is present.

We can take this same logic and apply it back to the topic of low self-control. There are some conditioning factors that play an amplifying role—when these factors are present, the effects of self-control on crime (and other outcomes) become even greater. This means that the differences in crime between those with low and high self-control are greater than they normally would be. Thus, under such circumstances, self-control takes on added importance. Other factors, however, may *diminish* the effects of self-control. When this occurs, the differences in crime between those with low and high self-control are lessened. They may even approach zero. When this occurs, it points to a process in which the other factor is able to essentially push low self-control to the side, rendering it largely inconsequential. Normally it would cause problems, but under these circumstances it does not.

IN FOCUS 7.1

Amplified and Diminished Effects

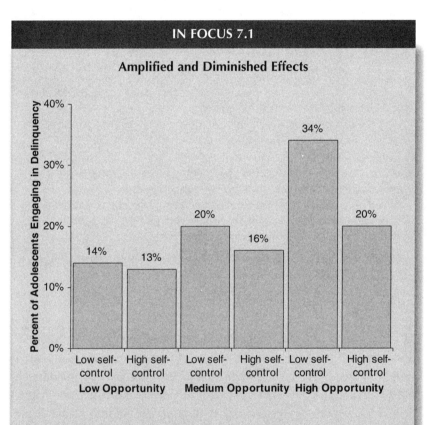

This figure presents hypothetical data that nicely illustrate the manner in which the frequency of criminal or delinquent opportunities moderates the effects of self-control on delinquency. The *y*-axis (the vertical axis) shows the prevalence of delinquency—the percentage of adolescents who committed a delinquent act during a given time period—while the *x*-axis identifies the groups of interest: low- and high-self-control groups that vary across low, medium, and high levels of delinquent opportunity. Notice that in the medium opportunity condition, there is a detectable but somewhat modest

(Continued)

(Continued)

effect of self-control. Specifically, there is a 4-percentage-point difference in the prevalence of delinquency between those with low and high self-control—16% of those with high self-control have committed a delinquent act, but this goes up to 20% for those with low self-control. Importantly, this difference between the low- and high-self-control groups changes when we examine the other two values of opportunity. When opportunity levels are high, the difference jumps to 14 percentage points (with a prevalence of 34% for the low-self-control group and 20% for the high-self-control group). This indicates an amplifying effect of criminal opportunity—increased opportunity amplifies the behavioral differences between those with low and high self-control. On the other hand, when the frequency of opportunities is low, there is no meaningful difference in the prevalence of delinquency between the low-self-control group (14% prevalence) and the high-self-control group (13% prevalence). This therefore indicates a diminishing effect of low delinquent opportunity. Importantly, although the numbers we present here are hypothetical, this is the basic pattern found in research considering interactive effects between self-control and criminal/delinquent opportunities (see Grasmick et al., 1993; Hay & Forrest, 2008; Kuhn & Laird, 2013; LaGrange & Silverman, 1999; Longshore, 1998).

CRIMINAL OPPORTUNITY

In criminology, criminal opportunity has received the most attention as a potential moderator of the effects of low self-control. This attention followed from an argument made by Gottfredson and Hirschi (1990): Although low self-control puts one *at risk* for giving in to criminal temptations, for this risk to be transformed into actual crime, a criminal opportunity—a situation in which crime is possible and easily accomplished—must exist as well.[1] Smoking pot, for example, requires access to marijuana, an opportunity that might be especially afforded to those whose friends smoke pot. This idea suggests that the presence of criminal opportunities amplifies the effects of low self-control—when criminal opportunities are abundant, low self-control is more easily translated into actual crime, thus leading the differences in crime between those with low and high self-control to become greater.

To consider how this may often play out, imagine two 15-year-old males who both have low self-control compared to the typical 15-year-old male. These two males should be more involved in delinquency than their high-self-control counterparts in the neighborhood. However, imagine that one of these males is quite unique when it comes to opportunities for delinquency because his parents do little to monitor his behavior and whereabouts. For example, after school, he returns to a home in which no parent is present. He largely is free to do as he pleases, and this involves plenty of time hanging out with friends away from the supervision of adults. Indeed, his parents may not know where he is or who he is with—they do not keep track of who his friends are, and therefore do not know if they are bad influences. Our second male, however, is different—although he has similarly low self-control, in these areas of supervision and monitoring, his parents are at least doing an average job.

In comparing these two males, we would expect the unsupervised one to be at least moderately more delinquent because of how often his low self-control will get coupled with easy opportunities for delinquency. Moreover, when we compare him to the other males in the neighborhood—the ones with higher self-control—we would expect him to be *substantially* more delinquent. That difference follows in part from his lower self-control, but the difference is amplified by the absence of parental supervision that offers him such a steady supply of situations in which he can translate his delinquent temptations into actual delinquency. For him, such things as stealing small items from stores, committing acts of vandalism, and experimenting with alcohol are all like "shooting fish in a barrel"—success is almost guaranteed.

A number of studies support the existence of a pattern like this (Grasmick et al., 1993; Hay & Forrest, 2008; Kuhn & Laird, 2013; LaGrange & Silverman,1999; Longshore, 1998). Much of this research has focused on adolescents in particular, and across these studies, criminal opportunity has been measured in varying ways. Some studies have used indicators of parental supervision in line with the example cited above. In other instances, opportunity has been measured with indicators of time spent with friends. This approach builds on the consistent finding that much delinquency is committed in the presence of peers and that peers are a major source of delinquent opportunities. In connection, some have argued that delinquency is comparable to a "pickup" game of basketball—if someone is there with friends, he or she has the opportunity to play in a game that spontaneously emerges, but if not, then he or she has missed out on the opportunity (Osgood et al., 1996). Last, some studies have taken a more direct approach to measuring criminal opportunities—they simply have asked individuals to indicate how frequently they find themselves in situations in which they could easily commit a criminal act without fear of getting caught.

Taken together, these studies suggest a number of conclusions. Most notably, they find substantial variation in criminal opportunity— some individuals have or perceive an extraordinary number of criminal opportunities, while for others, this is much less the case. For example, in Longshore's (1998) study of 500 convicted offenders, subjects perceived an average of 13 opportunities to commit a property crime over a six-month period; however, while some individuals perceived nearly zero opportunities, others perceived up to 200. Also, these variations in opportunity are consequential. Opportunity generally has significant independent effects on crime—more opportunities are associated with greater involvement in crime and delinquency, even after statistically controlling for varying levels of self-control.

And in reference to our specific focus in this chapter—conditional effects of self-control—this research typically indicates that the presence of criminal opportunities significantly amplifies the effects of low self-control (Grasmick et al., 1993; Hay & Forrest, 2008; Kuhn & Laird, 2013; LaGrange & Silverman,1999; Longshore, 1998). For example, in one of the first tests of this thesis, Grasmick and his colleagues (1993) found that the effects of low self-control on crimes of force and fraud were at least two to three times greater when perceived criminal opportunity was high. Similarly, Hay and Forrest (2008) found that differences in crime between those with low and high self-control were twice as large when adolescents returned from school each day to a home in which no adult was present. Time spent with peers and unsupervised time away from home played similar roles—the more there were of these things, the greater the gap in crime between those with low and high self-control.

ASSOCIATION WITH DELINQUENT PEERS

Some researchers have considered not just whether adolescents spend a great deal of time with peers, but also whether those peers are highly delinquent. If they are, peer associations could amplify the effects of low self-control on delinquency. This would follow in part from the pattern we just described in which peer associations increase opportunities for delinquency. However, delinquent peers offer more than just opportunity—they also may *actively encourage* delinquency. In the language of social learning theorists, this involves the *reinforcement* of delinquency (Akers, 1998), something captured also in the concept of peer pressure. Such peer pressure may intensify the harmful effects of low self-control—a given level of low self-control will be translated into even greater delinquency when coupled with strong encouragement from delinquent peers.

A number of studies support this possibility. Desmond, Bruce, and Stacer (2012) found, for example, that adolescents were more likely to report using alcohol, tobacco, and other drugs if they were lower in self-control, and this effect was stronger among those who also reported having more peers who used the same substances. Similar conclusions emerged in studies from Longshore and Turner (1998) and Kuhn and Laird (2013).

However, not all studies reach this conclusion (Ousey & Wilcox, 2007), and some reach an opposite conclusion. Meldrum and his colleagues (2009), for example, found that self-control had strong effects among those with few delinquent peers but quite diminished effects among those with many delinquent peers. Why would such a result emerge? Why would differences in crime between those with low and high self-control be more pronounced among those with *fewer* delinquent peers? In asking that question, one standard caveat applies: Studies with different samples, measures, and analytical approaches can generate different findings in ways that sometimes can appear quite random. This is why important research questions are never conclusively answered with just one study. With the Meldrum, Young, and Weerman (2009) study, however, there is an interesting possibility that goes beyond that standard caveat. Specifically, in some instances, a highly delinquent peer group may represent what Mischel (1977) referred to as a "strong" environment—one in which the pervading norms, values, and behavioral expectations are so powerful that they diminish the effects of individual qualities like self-control. Simply stated, in strong environments, group norms and influences dominate over individual tendencies. With delinquent peer groups in particular, the "push" toward crime may at times be strong to the point that crime will be common among those who are low *or* high in self-control. This is consistent with what Meldrum and his colleagues (2009) found—those in the most delinquent peer groups were relatively high in delinquency regardless of their level of self-control.

Taking it all into account, what should we conclude? Based on the existing research, the most common pattern is one in which delinquent peers amplify the harmful effects of low self-control, thereby producing greater differences in crime between those who are low and high in self-control. Nevertheless, this will not always be the case. Moreover, in some instances, the criminogenic push of the delinquent peer group may be strong enough to crowd out the effects of an individual quality like low self-control. Under such circumstances, crime and delinquency may be quite common across the entire self-control continuum.

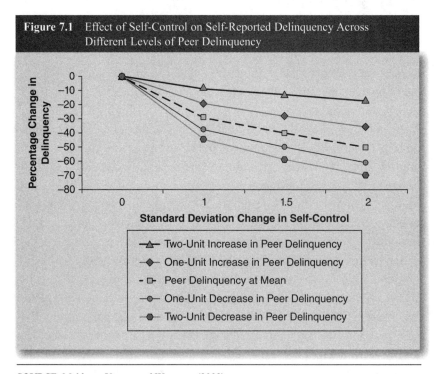

Figure 7.1 Effect of Self-Control on Self-Reported Delinquency Across Different Levels of Peer Delinquency

SOURCE: Meldrum, Young, and Weerman (2009).

SOCIAL BONDS

Social bonds to conventional people, goals, and institutions represent another potentially important moderating factor. These conventional influences often may allow those with low self-control to bypass some of its harmful effects on behavior—their low self-control may be pushing them toward an impulsive and antisocial pattern of behavior, but these conventional influences can divert them back in a more prosocial direction. Wright, Caspi, Moffitt, and Silva (2001) presented this argument in their model of life course interdependence, reasoning that the effects of stable individual traits like low self-control should be diminished by conventional social bonds that arise from such things as employment, family attachment, and commitment to educational goals.

Many but not all studies have supported this pattern. In contrast to it, Doherty (2006) found that while self-control and strong social bonds in adulthood (e.g., employment, stable marriage, service in the military) each uniquely explained whether or not an offender ended his or her criminal career in adulthood, no significant interaction between the two was found. Other studies have often pointed to a diminishing effect of strong social bonding. This was the case in Wright and his colleagues' (2001) analysis—the criminogenic effect of low self-control was attenuated among young adults who had the most stable employment, greatest education achievement, and strongest family ties.

Also, in a national study of high school students, Li (2004) found that having stronger beliefs in conventional behavior and greater involvement in conventional activities (e.g., working on homework) diminished the effect of low self-control on delinquency. Similarly, Gerich (2014) found a weakened effect of low self-control on alcohol use among Australian college students living in social environments that promoted social conformity.

NEIGHBORHOOD DISADVANTAGE

There has been a tendency in criminology to study individual behavior in ways that ignore the broader community and neighborhood context. There is good reason to expect, however, that individual characteristics like low self-control manifest themselves differently across communi-ties that vary on such things as the level of poverty, the presence of criminal subcultures, and the extent of disorder and social disorganiza-tion. If so, rather than studying individual qualities *or* community environments, researchers should study both of these causal forces and how they interact to explain crime and antisocial behavior (Tonry, Ohlin, & Farrington, 1991).

One distinct possibility is that the effects of low self-control on crime are amplified in an economically disadvantaged community. The poorest communities often are plagued by a wide array of social disad-vantages that encourage the emergence of criminal and aggressive subcultures (Anderson, 1999). In such a context, low self-control may take on added importance—if an individual lacks self-control, this will be coupled with a community context that encourages crime, and the result will be a stronger connection between low self-control and crime. A number of studies have considered this possibility, with most revealing an amplification effect of this kind. Lynam and his colleagues (2000), for example, studied roughly 400 adolescents who were spread across roughly 90 neighborhoods in Pittsburgh. They were interested in effects of impulsivity and measured it in ways that are consistent with our conception of low self-control. They found that among adolescents who lived in the most economically disadvantaged neighborhoods, impulsivity had a strong effect on crime. In contrast, it had almost no effect in affluent neighborhoods—in those neighborhoods, impulsive teens were no more likely to engage in delinquency than their less impulsive peers. Similar conclusions were reached in studies from Meier, Slutske, Arndt, and Cadoret (2008) and Jones and Lynam (2009)—the differences in crime and delinquency between those with low and high self-control were amplified by residence in a socially and economically disadvantaged neighborhood.

Once again, however, not all studies have reached this conclusion. Vazsonyi, Cleveland, and Wiebe (2006) found that the effects of self-control on delinquency were largely invariant across communities that differed in socioeconomic status. Moreover, in studying Chicago neighborhoods, Zimmerman (2010) found that there was no effect of low self-control on crime for adolescents in poor communities but a strong effect for those who lived in wealthier communities. This pattern may also be explained by Mischel's notion of strong environments that we previously discussed—the pervading norms, values, and behavioral expectations in a highly disadvantaged community may be powerful enough to diminish the effects of individual qualities. On the other hand, in wealthier neighborhoods—those that lack a strong push toward crime—an individual quality like low self-control may sometimes have greater freedom to exert its effects. It bears emphasizing, however, that the most common empirical pattern is one in which social and economic disadvantages in the community amplify the harmful effects of low self-control, thereby producing greater differences in crime between those who are low and high in self-control.

WEAK MORAL VALUES

Per-Olof Wikström has in recent years suggested that under some circumstances, whether or not a person has self-control is largely *inconsequential* for crime. In making this argument, he suggests that the key question that self-control provokes—"Should I or should I not give in to a criminal temptation?"—does not come into play for many individuals, even when they encounter an opportunity for crime.

A hypothetical scenario—one that has you doing some horrible things—helps illustrate this possibility. Imagine you are driving along an isolated stretch of road and you pass an elderly woman whose shiny new Cadillac has suffered a flat tire. The woman looks fatigued and disoriented—she may have been stranded for some time. It's a hot humid day, and she looks dehydrated. In her weakened state, she has wandered away from the car to seek the shade of a nearby tree. However, she left her expensive-looking purse sitting on the hood of her car. By the looks of this woman and her car, two things seem obvious to you: (1) Her purse likely contains something valuable and (2) this listless old woman is in no condition to stop you from taking it. Moreover, as you scan the area, you once again notice how isolated this stretch of road is—you have not seen another car for some time.

Under these circumstances, grabbing the purse would be easy. It would be like taking candy from a baby, only easier. With this in mind, you decide to take the purse and leave the old woman to fend for herself. You do so with this convenient rationalization: Life is rough and we all face hardships, including flat tires and lost purses. In taking her purse, you will give her a chance to discover how resilient she can be in the face of adversity. What doesn't kill her will only make her stronger—she'll be just like those superkids of the ghetto!

But would you really do this? *No, of course you wouldn't!* We genuinely believe that, and you might refrain from this crime for reasons that have little to do with self-control. If it *did* have to do with self-control, here is how the process would play out: You would see the woman's unguarded purse as an opportunity to advance your self-interest, and this would be tempting, but your high self-control would lead you to override this temptation. Wikström (2004), however, argued that this is *not* how it would play out. From his perspective, when a situation like this is encountered, most individuals do not see stealing the purse as a genuine behavioral option—it runs too far afoul of their moral values, so much so that they are not consciously aware of a temptation. And if there is no temptation, there is no need for self-control.

Wikström (2004) presents this as part of his *situational action theory*, which sees the propensity to commit crimes as governed mainly by moral values and habits. Moral values are rules about what is right or wrong behavior in a given situation, while moral habits involve automated prosocial responses to familiar circumstances. Wikström argues that these values and habits dictate whether we see criminal behaviors as action alternatives. If our values and habits are such that crimes do not enter our minds as viable alternatives, then self-control is not needed. And in the terminology of this chapter's discussion, this would be an interactive process that *diminishes* the effects of low self-control—strong moral values and habits render self-control less consequential, such that there should be few differences in crime between those with low and high self-control. Either type of person—those low and high in self-control—would avoid crime because their values and habits stopped them from even considering it.

There is a corollary of this: When moral values and habits are *not* so prosocial, then self-control *should* matter. And this could come into play in many ways. Most notably, there are many criminal and antisocial acts that are morally murky, so to speak—the difference between right and wrong is not so clear or important. Moreover, there are some individuals who have a weaker commitment to basic moral values and habits. Among these individuals, self-control should matter greatly because they encounter many situations in which antisocial behavior is seen as a morally acceptable alternative.

Few studies have examined this issue, but they often support the argument that the effects of low self-control depend on moral values. For example, Schoepfer and Piquero (2006) collected data from nearly 400 college students on their self-control, their moral beliefs, and their willingness to assault and steal. Regarding the latter, participants were asked to read scenarios and place themselves in the position of its actors who at times assaulted others or committed thefts. On a scale from 0 to 10, they rated the likelihood they would act as the person in the scenario did if they were to face the same circumstances. Consistent with the arguments above, Schoepfer and Piquero (2006) found that the most pronounced effects of self-control on willingness to assault or steal were among those with weaker moral beliefs. Wikström and Svensson (2010) reached the same conclusion in their study of 14- to 15-year-olds in the United Kingdom. They found that when there were strong moral objections to crime, self-control was of little conse-quence—crime was low among those both low and high in self-control. However, when moral beliefs were weak, there was a strong effect of self-control that came from a big spike in criminal involvement among those with low self-control. Simply stated, when low self-control was coupled with the absence of any moral constraints, crime was substan-tially more likely (see also the supporting research from Zimmerman, Botchkovar, Antonaccio, and Hughes, 2012).

The conclusions therefore are fairly consistent, but we should emphasize that few studies have examined this issue and there is con-trary research that finds effects of self-control that do not depend on moral values (Antonaccio & Tittle, 2008). Moreover, we also wonder whether the line between self-control and moral beliefs is as stark as Wikström has argued. In connection, an important question is this: Where do moral values come from? Moral values and habits may evolve over the life course and follow in part from prior levels of self-control—perhaps a person's prior willingness to override antisocial impulses and defer immediate gratification sets the stage for defining certain actions as immoral and developing habits in which such actions are avoided. In support of this possibility, the correlation between self-control and moral beliefs may be as high as .60 (Antonaccio & Tittle, 2008; Wikström & Svensson, 2010)—when someone has higher self-control, they often will have stronger moral beliefs.

Taking this all into account, we draw two main conclusions. First, at any given point in time, there is good reason to believe that effects of self-control on behavior depend on the strength of moral values and habits. Strong moral condemnation of an act often diminishes the consequences of low self-control; correspondingly, when moral beliefs are weaker, low self-control likely takes on added importance. Second, we suspect that much can be learned in future research that considers how early self-control tendencies affect the development of moral beliefs and habits over the life course.

IN FOCUS 7.2

The Evolutionary Origins of Moral Values

The research in this chapter suggests that those with especially strong moral values often need not rely on self-control because temptations that are morally problematic may, for them, not even be tempting at all. And yet, there is good reason to expect that the link between self-control and moral values is more complicated than this. The two may be intertwined in fascinating ways, with each developing partly in reliance on the other. Most notably, a person's self-control may lead him or her to have stronger moral values (if self-control is the temperamental quality that encourages diligent reflection on morality). It also is possible, however, that morality helps a person have high self-control (because those with strong morality have powerful higher-order standards to draw upon in overriding behavior).

We suspect that future research will yield more insights on the interconnections between self-control and morality, and in considering that possibility, we are drawn to the fascinating research done at Yale University's Infant Cognition Center. It has considered the evolutionary origins of moral values, discovering that a capacity for morality likely is "hardwired" into our brains to some degree. They have reached this conclusion by asking a novel question: Do babies know something about morality, and if so, how soon do they know it? If humans can demonstrate moral behavior prior to even talking or walking, there is good reason to suspect that an inherent biological capacity for morality is at work. In short, a capacity for morality may be a key facet of human nature that we each acquire and develop from conception.

Research at Yale's "baby lab" (as some have called it) has supported this view in laboratory studies that are almost as entertaining as Walter Mischel's marshmallow studies with 4- and 5-year-olds nearly five decades earlier. The task for these baby morality studies was straightforward: Infants must be placed in a setting in which a moral decision could be made, and a clever way of allowing them to communicate their moral preferences had to be devised. An opening passage in Paul Bloom's (2013, p. 7) book *Just Babies: The Origins of Good and Evil* perfectly captures the experiments they designed and the observations Bloom and others have made over the years:

> The one-year-old decided to take justice into his own hands. He had just watched a puppet show with three characters. The puppet in the middle rolled a ball to the puppet on the right, who passed it right back to him. It then rolled the ball to the puppet on the left, who ran away with it. At the end of the show, the "nice" puppet and the "naughty" puppet were brought down from the stage and set before the boy. A treat was placed in front of each of them, and the boy was invited to take one of the treats away. As predicted, and like most toddlers in the experiment, he took it from the "naughty" one—the one who had run away with the ball. But this wasn't enough. The boy then leaned over and smacked this puppet on the head.

Study after study reinforces this observation, indicating that babies show a natural understanding of the difference between right and wrong, often as early as the sixth month of life. And just like the boy above, they sometimes even get *mad* at the immoral and unfair actions of others. Bloom offers a provocative conclusion on this: "Certain moral foundations are not acquired through learning. They do not come from a mother's knee, or from school or church; they are instead the products of biological evolution" (p. 8).

Of course, Bloom goes on to emphasize that social environments and experiences influence whether this *foundation for morality* is one day translated into *actual moral behavior*. This is an issue that merits greater attention in future research. As our comments in this chapter suggest, we see the intersection between morality and self-control over the life course as a promising issue to consider in this area of research.

CONSIDERING SELF-CONTROL AS A MODERATOR VARIABLE

In each of the discussions above, we have considered a causal arrangement in which self-control is the causal variable and some other factor (e.g., opportunity) plays a moderating role. In such an arrangement, the question is whether the effects of self-control are changed (in either an amplifying or diminishing way) when the moderating factor (e.g., high criminal opportunity) comes into play. Some studies, however, have considered a reversed arrangement in which the "other" factor is the causal variable and low self-control is the moderator. In this arrangement, the question is whether the presence of low self-control alters the effects of other variables. This type of arrangement is also instructive to consider because, regardless of whether low self-control is the causal or moderating variable, such research gives insight on the basic question of how low self-control works with other variables to affect involvement in criminal and antisocial behavior.

One commonly studied research question in this regard involves legal deterrence variables. A long line of criminological theory—dating back to the 18th- and 19th-century writings of philosophers like Cesar Beccaria and Jeremy Bentham—argues that criminal involvement is strongly influenced by people's perceptions of whether their criminal acts would provoke legal punishments. If punishments are fairly certain to occur and are relatively severe, then crime is avoided. The research testing this argument has a long and complicated history, one that often suggests that legal punishments do not affect behavior as directly as we would like. That said, on balance, there is evidence that a person's perceptions of the certainty and severity of legal punishments have at least a modest deterrent effect on crime.

Some scholars have considered this issue in conjunction with self-control. One possibility is that low self-control diminishes the effects of legal punishments. Those with low self-control may be least influenced (or deterred) by the threat of punishment because they fail to consider consequences—legal or otherwise—of their behavior. Those with low self-control simply *act*—contemplation about the certainty and severity of legal consequences will not much matter. In an early study assessing this possibility, Nagin and Paternoster (1994) found evidence that tended to support this stance. In particular, they found that the negative influence of perceived informal sanctions on intentions to steal and engage in assaultive behavior was *diminished* among study participants who had the lowest levels of self-control.

While similar conclusions have been reached in other studies (e.g., Piquero & Pogarsky, 2002; Pogarsky, 2002), Wright, Caspi, Moffitt, and Paternoster (2004) point out that these studies have largely been based on college samples and examined intentions to commit crime (rather than real criminal acts). In their analyses of long-term data from a birth cohort in New Zealand, Wright and his colleagues (2004) examined the interactive effect between sanction risk and low self-control when predicting actual reports of criminal behavior. Contrary to prior work, they found that the deterrent effect of perceived legal punishments was *amplified* among those with the lowest self-control—when self-control was high, legal punishments did not matter. This finding points to the possibility that those with the highest self-control often build strong conventional ties in the areas of education, family, and work. These factors introduce strong inhibitions, therefore making the deterrent effect of legal sanctions irrelevant. Those with low self-control, on the other hand, are quite open to crime, and they therefore may be more responsive to perceptions of legal punishments. Pogarsky (2007) reached a similar conclusion, and together these studies indicate that those with low self-control do in fact think about the future risks of crime. Their perceptions may not always be accurate, and they have a tendency to discount the value of future (rather than present) risks and rewards (Piquero, Paternoster, Pogarsky, & Loughran, 2011). Nevertheless, they do form perceptions about the likelihood of legal punishments, and because they perceive fewer other obstacles to crime, these perceptions may be quite consequential. Thus, low self-control may amplify the effects of legal punishments on crime, although there still is much to learn on that possibility.

Robert Agnew's (1992, 2001) influential general strain theory provides another line of research that considers low self-control as a moderating factor. This theory argues that crime and aggression often are a response to the strainful aversive experiences that people face. Such things as harsh parental discipline, criminal victimization, discrimination, and hassles at work or school lead to negative emotions like anger and frustration that prime the individual for some sort of corrective action. Sometimes this involves retaliation against those responsible for their strain; in other instances, aggression is directed toward others as the individual's anger creates a general openness to aggressive, combative, and rebellious behavior. Either way, strainful events and relationships should increase crime and aggression, and this prediction has been supported in much research (Botchkovar & Broidy, 2013).

Agnew has emphasized, however, that not all strained individuals will resort to crime and aggression—other factors come into play to moderate the relationship between strainful experiences and involvement in crime. Low self-control is expected to be one such factor. Specifically, Agnew contends that low self-control should amplify the association between strain and delinquency—those with low self-control will be more likely to respond to strain in impulsive, short-sighted, and emotional ways that involve greater antisocial and aggressive behavior. Those with high self-control, on the other hand, are more likely to deliberate on their situation and pursue a prosocial, constructive response to strain. Some studies suggest that self-control plays exactly this moderating role. Agnew, Brezina, Wright, and Cullen (2002), for example, studied strainful circumstances among a sample of early adolescents, finding that strain in family, school, and neighborhood contexts increased crime. Importantly, these effects were especially high among those with low self-control and essentially zero among those with very high self-control. Hay and Meldrum (2010) reached a similar conclusion in examining the effects of being a bullying victim on thinking about suicide and engaging in self-harming behavior (cutting or burning oneself). Bullying victimization and its harmful effects have received significant attention in recent years. There is good reason to expect, however, that the harmful effects of bullying are conditional upon other factors, and self-control could easily be one such factor. Hay and Meldrum's analyses of data from a sample of middle and high school students supported that possibility, revealing that when self-control was high, the effects of being bullied on self-harm and suicidal ideation were lessened, often by as much as 35% to 40%. This was the case for those exposed to traditional, face-to-face bullying, but also for those exposed to newer forms of cyberbullying in which the Internet or cell phones are used to ostracize others. This is consistent with the idea that self-control helps promote thoughtful, long-term adaptations to strainful circumstances.

CAN SELF-CONTROL MODERATE
THE EFFECTS OF SELF-CONTROL?

Most approaches to self-control treat it as a durable long-term trait, but recall from earlier discussions that it can also be seen as a temporary state that fluctuates from one situation to the next or across short spans of time. These different views of self-control have sometimes been seen as contradictory and opposing, but the two may both capture interesting aspects of the self-control puzzle. At any given time, a person can be thought of as having two dimensions of self-control: a trait level that involves a long-term, somewhat stable trajectory, and a state level that follows from the immediate circumstances in a given situation or short span of time. Of course, trait and state levels of self-control should often be the same—those with high trait self-control often will find themselves in high-self-control states, and vice versa. However, as the preceding chapter indicates, self-control states can diverge from trait levels of self-control in response to different experiences. And this raises an interesting possibility: Perhaps there is a statistical interaction between trait and state levels of self-control, such that the effects on behavior of one dimension depend on those of the other.

A number of studies have considered that possibility (e.g., DeWall, Baumeister, Stillman, & Gailliot, 2007; Dvorak & Simons, 2009; Gailliot, Schmeichel, & Baumeister, 2006; Muraven, Collins, Shiffman, & Paty, 2005). They often measure trait self-control with the standard measures, such as the Brief Self-Control Scale (Tangney, Baumeister, & Boone, 2004) discussed in Chapter 3. Shifts in self-control states, on the other hand, are measured in terms of exposure to circumstances expected to use up one's short-term self-control resources (thus producing a low-self-control state). Muraven and his colleagues (2005) considered this in studying young adults who were followed for three weeks. On a daily basis, using Palm Pilots provided to them, they reported how much they felt stressed or overwhelmed by that day's events and experiences. These feelings were conceptualized as depleting one's state self-control, given that stressful circumstances require one to use up self-control resources. As expected, the researchers found that on days in which subjects felt greater stress, they were more likely to drink to excess. Importantly, however, the magnitude of this effect depended on trait self-control—this effect of stress on alcohol consumption was roughly twice as large for those with low trait self-control, leading Muraven and his colleagues (2005, p. 145) to conclude that "individuals high in trait self-control may have a larger pool of resources at their disposal and therefore are less affected by self-control demands than individuals lower in trait self-control."

DeWall and his colleagues (2007) also considered this issue in a clever laboratory experiment with a sample of undergraduate students. At the start of the study, all participants were asked to read through a page from a psychology textbook and cross out all instances of the letter *e*. This simple task required little effort or self-control, but as the study progressed, half the participants were randomly assigned to a more difficult task. They were asked to cross out the *e* in all instances except when it was immediately followed by a vowel or was in a word that had a vowel appearing two letters before the *e*. Not surprisingly, this task was perceived as more tedious and burdening, and in line with that, it was conceptualized as depleting self-control states (relative to the task of crossing out every *e*).

The researchers then had all participants read a scenario in which they were asked to envision themselves in a bar with a romantic partner whom they were "absolutely in love with." As the scenario continues, another person enters the situation and starts "eyeing up" and flirting with the romantic partner (who seems to be enjoying the attention). The aggrieved subject confronts the unwanted visitor, and the situation escalates to the point of potential violence, at which point the subject spots a beer bottle on the bar counter and considers smashing it over the other's head. DeWall and his colleagues found that, on average, those subjects who faced the more difficult *e*-crossing task were significantly more willing to smash the beer bottle over the unwanted visitor's head. This supports the basic view that circumstances that deplete our self-control resources (and therefore produce low-self-control states) increase the likelihood of aggression in a given situation. Interestingly, however, the researchers found that this average effect obscured differences across the sample. Specifically, among those with high trait self-control, the difficult *e*-crossing task had no effect on their willingness to smash the beer bottle over the interloper's head. However, for those low in trait self-control, there was a quite pronounced effect—those with the more difficult *e*-crossing task were substantially more willing to resort to violence in this situation.

Taken together, these studies suggest an interesting interaction between trait self-control and one's exposure to experiences that trigger low-self-control states. Specifically, high trait self-control seems to act as a buffer against the complications that often arise in response to the daily demands, stressors, and hassles that life throws at us. Those individuals with high self-control certainly may be aware of these demands, stressors, and hassles, but they are better able to cope with them to limit their harm. Conversely, those with low trait self-control are more likely to respond with antisocial or destructive behavior that includes drinking to excess or acting aggressively. This affirms a basic theme of this chapter: Self-control is quite important, but this importance often follows not just from its powerful independent effects on behavior, but also from how it interacts with other critical circumstances, experiences, and qualities.

POLICY IMPLICATIONS AND POSSIBILITIES

This chapter has pointed to protective factors that diminish the effects of low self-control on crime, deviance, and harmful behavior. This raises an interesting policy possibility: the harmful consequences of low self-control can be reduced without actually affecting an individual's level of self-control. Instead, we must simply design policies that promote the protective factors that diminish its effects.

Of course, in reality, this would never be our first policy option—the most efficient and effective policy approach will involve preventing self-control deficits from ever occurring in the first place; and short of that, we would like to reverse such deficits once they do emerge. Those two mechanisms—prevention and reversal—have been prioritized in our earlier discussions of policy implications, but they will not always be possible. The justice and social service systems will always find themselves dealing with disadvantaged children whose lives have gotten off to a genuinely rough start. For many children, by the time these systems get involved, the window for accomplishing true prevention has already passed, and reversal may be difficult also—as we have noted, once a low-self-control trajectory is under way, it often persists.

Thus, although reversal efforts should be continued whenever possible (because unexpected changes can occur), these circumstances call for an alternative policy approach, one that invokes the mechanism of *suppression*. The goal with suppression efforts is to introduce protective factors that reduce the harmful consequences of low self-control. Even if these protective factors cannot eliminate the self-control deficit, they may strip it of its potency—the self-control deficit persists, but it no longer translates into actual acts of crime and deviance. Thus, policy efforts might focus on improvements in the key moderating factors we earlier identified: criminal opportunities, association with delinquent peers, social bonds, the neighborhood context, and moral commitments.

Of these, the most likely target for suppression efforts involves the prospect of limiting criminal opportunities. We earlier described the compelling research showing that low self-control leads to less crime and deviance under circumstances of low opportunity. Additionally, efforts to address the other moderating factors—including peer associations, social bonds to conventional others, and moral values—are not likely to be inspired by efforts to merely suppress the harmful consequences of low self-control. Instead, such efforts are more rehabilitative in nature, and therefore likely are focused on trying to reverse any self-control deficits that exist. Opportunity, on the other hand, is notably compatible with the idea of suppression—an emphasis on limiting criminal opportunities necessarily highlights the idea that the internal motivations and inclinations of offenders often cannot be manipulated, but their bad behavior can be reduced if we restrict their access to situations in which the inclinations are easily acted upon.

So, if we were to restrict criminal opportunities, how might this be done? With adolescents, this might be accomplished with adolescence-specific parent-training programs like Functional Family Therapy (FFT; Gordon, Graves, & Arbuthnot, 1995) that are touted for improving levels of parental supervision and monitoring. When adolescents are out of school, it is critical for parents to know where they are, who they are with, and what they are doing. However, this requires a certain amount of parenting skill, given that parental supervision and monitoring rely a great deal on adolescents' willingness to provide information to their parents (Kerr, Stattin, & Burk, 2010). Proven programs like FFT impart the needed skills. In the process, perhaps they will reverse self-control deficits by improving family functioning; however, even if major improvements in self-control do not occur, benefits may still accrue from greater parental supervision and the resulting reduction in opportunities.

Another proven program is Big Brothers Big Sisters of America. This program has a rich history in the United States—it has been pairing at-risk youths with volunteer mentors from the community for more than 100 years. It started in New York in 1904 when Earnest Coulter, the clerk for the New York Children's Court, solicited promises from 39 volunteers to befriend at least one at-risk youth.[2] Jumping ahead to the present, the program now is active in all 50 states. Mentors are matched with children and adolescents on the basis of shared goals and interests, and the pair spends roughly three to five hours per week together for at least 12 months, but often longer. Rigorous randomized controlled studies have yielded impressive results on such things as drug and alcohol use and violence (Grossman & Tierney, 1998). At least some of this effect may be occurring as a result of suppression— the greater time spent with mentors may help suppress the harmful effects of key risk factors, including low self-control.[3]

Formal criminal justice efforts that physically prevent opportunities for crime represent another potential source of suppression. This approach will be more common for adults and older adolescents who are an immediate threat to the community. Even with these cases, however, there should be a key cost–benefit balancing act in play. Any formal sanction involving institutionalization is quite expensive, and the rate of recidivism for such sanctions is quite high, with some evidence suggesting that the harsh conditions of institutionalization leave some offenders worse off than they were before. Nevertheless, for serious violent offenders, incarceration may often be needed to physically prevent opportunities for crime. Incarceration clearly does not eliminate the self-control deficit (it might make it worse), but it physically prevents the individual from committing acts of crime against the general population. For less serious offenders, however, other criminal and juvenile justice options are preferred. Evaluations indicate that electronic monitoring programs that use GPS technology to supervise offenders' whereabouts without having to incarcerate them can reduce criminal opportunities (Killias, Gilliéron, Kissling, & Villettaz, 2010; Padgett, Bales, & Blomberg, 2006). Importantly, however, policymakers must be mindful of avoiding net-widening dynamics (Blomberg, 1980) that extend criminal justice sanctions to offenders who might be better dealt with outside the justice system. Another promising approach is case management, which involves assigning a social or mental health worker to an at-risk individual to coordinate continued services and supervision (Enos & Southern, 1996; Healey, 1999). Programs of this kind are especially effective (and cost efficient) when dealing with mentally ill or developmentally disabled adults who enter the criminal justice system (Healey, 1999).

One final approach merits emphasis. In each of the policy possibilities described above, suppression efforts have focused specifically on individuals with low self-control and considered how their specific circumstances might be altered. An alternative approach involves focusing on the broader community in which the individual lives. This follows from the research indicating that the most serious problems with crime, deviance, and harmful behaviors tend to be geographically clustered in a small number of communities. If such communities can be changed for the better, there will be, among other things, fewer situations in which low-self-control individuals in the community can easily translate their low self-control into actual criminal and deviant acts. One successful community-wide intervention is the Communities That Care (CTC) program developed by the Social Development Research Group at the University of Washington (Hawkins, Catalano, & Arthur, 2002; Monahan, Hawkins, & Abbott, 2013). CTC provides a structure for bringing together community stakeholders to envision the community they want to build and put in place the programs needed to turn that vision into reality. This occurs in CTC training events delivered over the course of 6 to 12 months by certified CTC trainers. The communities decide on the priorities, and the CTC trainers provide the implementation expertise to target the risk and protective factors that a community prioritizes and the research expertise to evaluate progress. Randomized controlled studies find that CTC communities have a lower incidence of crime, substance use, and key risk factors; moreover, as a result of their long-term experiences with the CTC program, these communities are much more likely than non-CTC communities to take an evidence-based scientific approach to solving problems in their neighborhood.

CONCLUSION

Low self-control increases behavior problems, but the extent of that increase almost certainly varies. This is a critical complicating issue to consider. It suggests that we cannot speak of low self-control purely in terms of its average effect. Instead, we must recognize that effects vary in systematic ways, with self-control operating in conjunction with other important factors to affect the probability of crime, deviance, and harmful behavior. The research highlighted in this chapter suggests that the differences in problem behavior between low- and high-self-control individuals are especially likely to be amplified when there is a high supply of criminal opportunities, frequent association with delinquent peers, weak social bonding with conventional others, residence in a disadvantaged neighborhood, and weak moral commitment. Alternatively, the consequences of low self-control are diminished when it is coupled with the converse of these factors (i.e., low opportunity, association with prosocial peers, strong conventional bonding, an advantaged neighborhood context, and strong moral values).

We caution readers, however, to keep in mind the "strong environments" dynamic that at times comes into play. Specifically, if the amplifying circumstances just noted ever produce pervading norms and values that are sufficiently powerful, they may diminish rather than amplify the effects of individual qualities like self-control. This occurs if group norms and influences—such as those from highly delinquent peer groups—are powerful to the point that they trample individual tendencies. In such instances, the "push" toward crime is strong enough to make it common among those who are low *or* high in self-control. The point to emphasize is that this possibility of moderating effects truly is a complicating factor—it greatly limits our ability to make simple generalizations about the average effects of low self-control.

This chapter also highlighted a novel possibility in which state and trait components of self-control statistically interact to affect the likelihood of crime and deviance. Specifically, high trait self-control (one's long-term enduring pattern of self-control) seems to act as a buffer against the daily demands, stressors, and hassles that may lower state self-control (the level of self-control in a specific instance or situation). The specific pattern is one in which stressful circumstances or hassles are more likely to lead to criminal, deviant, and harmful behaviors among those with low trait self-control. Those with high trait self-control, on the other hand, are better able to cope with stress in ways that limit its harm.

And last, this chapter emphasized key policy implications of these findings. Most notably, efforts to reduce crime, deviance, and harmful behaviors sometimes may rely on the mechanism of suppression— when self-control deficits can neither be prevented nor reversed, the final policy alternative involves suppressing their harmful effects. Suppression efforts introduce protective factors that diminish the harmful consequences of low self-control. Our discussion focused especially on efforts to reduce the harmful effects of low self-control by decreasing criminal opportunities, something that can be done with a wide variety of social service and criminal justice programs and policies. The most notable include mentoring programs with juveniles (like the Big Brothers Big Sisters program) and formal criminal justice interventions with adults (like electronic monitoring and case management).

DISCUSSION QUESTIONS

1. What is the difference between an *amplifying* and a *diminishing* effect? Can you think of examples not discussed in the chapter in which the influence of one variable on another is amplified or diminished by some other factor?

2. Write out a list of all the instances where you conceivably *could have* engaged in criminal behavior over the past week. Based on what was discussed in the chapter, in what ways might these

    opportunities be more or less attractive to individuals who have more or less self-control?

3. Why might living in an economically disadvantaged community amplify the effect of low self-control on delinquent behavior? In other words, what physical, social, and/or cultural factors in neighborhoods could make it easier for low self-control to lead to delinquency?

4. Do you think people who are low in self-control are more likely or less likely to be deterred by the threat of formal (arrest and incarceration) and informal (loss of prestige, ending of relationships) sanctions for criminal behavior?

5. Think of an experiment on your own in which you deliberately try to deplete the *state* self-control of study participants to see if they will subsequently engage in antisocial behavior. What is the task that you will randomly assign to your participants, and what will be your measure of antisocial behavior? How might the impact of depleting the state self-control of your study participants on their engagement in antisocial behavior be moderated by their *trait* self-control?

NOTES

1. For those readers especially interested in the theoretical nuances, we must elaborate on Gottfredson and Hirschi's positions. In later writings (Gottfredson & Hirschi, 2003; Hirschi & Gottfredson, 1993), they downplayed the importance of criminal opportunity as a moderator of self-control's effects. In doing so, they still maintained that criminal opportunities are necessary for low self-control to produce a criminal act, but they insisted that opportunities are abundant to the point that they have little causal significance. The simplest daily events—walking into a store, passing by a house, visiting a bar—provide ample opportunities for crime. The ubiquity of opportunity means that it does not matter much because those with low self-control can easily create their own opportunities or spot those that develop. Thus, what really matters is self-control, and this is Gottfredson and Hirschi's steady position—self-control is always *the* factor that drives the process. Everything else—including the presence or detection of opportunities—follows from the person's level of self-control. It bears emphasizing, however, that these arguments have not been supported. Individual differences in the frequency of criminal opportunities (measured subjectively or objectively) have been observed in various studies, and these differences have effects on behavior that are independent of the effects of self-control (Grasmick et al., 1993; Hay & Forrest, 2008; Longshore, 1998).

2. This history is described well on the program's website (www.bbbs.org).

3. After-school programs that occupy early adolescents in the hours after school also can be helpful in limiting criminal opportunities. However, such programs have not been found to consistently reduce crime. It is useful to consider the ways in which after-school programs may differ from mentoring. A chief benefit of mentoring may be the interpersonal bonds that it offers. Thus, it enhances supervision in a context that also encourages prosocial attachments and commitments. Gottfredson, Gottfredson, and Weisman (2001) suggest that after-school programs that encourage prosocial attachments and commitments may be the most effective type of after-school program.

⊰ EIGHT ⊱

SELF-CONTROL AND CRIME OVER THE LIFE COURSE: BRINGING IT ALL TOGETHER

T he preceding chapters have presented a vast array of ideas, arguments, and empirical conclusions. It is time now to bring them all together. Our ultimate goal for this chapter is to provide a theoretical framework—or, more clearly, a series of frameworks—for understanding how differences in self-control emerge early in life and evolve over the life course, and how these differences affect behavior all along the way. In providing this framework, we draw from the key themes already developed in the preceding chapters, and we make no attempt to reproduce the specificity of our earlier discussions. Instead, we paint the basic contours of our arguments in fairly broad strokes, encouraging readers to refer to earlier chapters and their cited research whenever greater precision is wanted.

In summarizing our arguments, we have found that a useful approach is to metaphorically "walk" an individual through the various stages of the life course, highlighting the key factors that affect the causes, consequences, and development of self-control over time. We begin with truly the earliest stages of life, focusing on the genetic qualities inherited at conception and the risks for neuropsychological

209

deficits faced prenatally and in the earliest years of life. Very early in life, social interaction—especially with parents—also takes on extraordinary significance. The habits and interactions that occur then will in turn influence the earliest manifestations of self-control. This sets the stage for the social experiences that will come later in childhood, adolescence, and even adulthood—experiences that will themselves have implications for self-control. Across it all, we will see the many ways in which stability in self-control is encouraged over the life course. We also, however, will explore the ways in which such things as human agency, chance occurrence, and outside influences can produce unexpected self-control changes.

In presenting these ideas, we rely heavily on diagrams—"pictures" that are replete with boxes representing different variables and arrows that connect them. Such diagrams nicely clarify the causal sequences we are predicting. We should emphasize, however, that these diagrams necessarily are simplifications. Their greatest merit—the way they clarify central arguments—also is in some sense a weakness, given that no diagram can include every relevant variable or every feasible connection between variables. That said, such diagrams are, on balance, quite useful for forcing scholars to be clear about what they are proposing. Indeed, we believe that any behavioral science argument worth making ought to be reducible to a diagram that leaves little question about the central processes being advanced.

There is one last point to emphasize before getting under way: The models and arguments we present are rooted in the results from prior research—research we have described in the preceding chapters. Thus, in developing these models, we have pieced together the facts and patterns that can be reliably gleaned from the impressive research to date. True enough, in many instances, we must make inferences because certain interesting possibilities have been considered only indirectly or in a limited manner. But even then, there is strong empirical justification for the arguments that follow. Thus, in presenting these arguments, we are indebted to the scores of behavioral scientists—from all over the world and from a wide array of academic disciplines—who have painstakingly and rigorously contributed new insights on the links between self-control and behavior.

THE CAUSES OF INITIAL SELF-CONTROL
DIFFERENCES IN THE FIRST DECADE OF LIFE

The Prenatal Period and Infancy

The causes of self-control differences emerge truly in the earliest stages of life. These most notably include the genetic code that a child has inherited from his or her parents upon conception. A fetus's inherited DNA provides a set of instructions for how biological development should proceed, and the best research indicates that this is highly relevant to self-control—in the first decade of life, children will develop a level of self-control that often is quite similar to that of their parents, and this intergenerational transmission follows in part from the genetic similarities between parents and children.

Importantly, however, genetics are not the only important prenatal factor—there also is the environment. For a developing fetus, that environment is the mother's womb. The prenatal experience unquestionably goes better for some children than it does for others. The habits, circumstances, and challenges that a mother faces loom large, and it should be emphasized that some of this is beyond the control of the mother and her family—such things as economic disadvantage, medical complications, and tragic misfortune all can come into play. Anything that affects the physical environment of the womb can have implications for the child's development. If the mother uses alcohol, drugs, or tobacco, the developing fetus is exposed to the portions of these substances that pass through the placenta. Each has been linked to later neuropsychological deficits that reflect impaired functioning of the brain's prefrontal cortex, and this has implications for later self-control. Additionally, the mother's nutritional intake during the prenatal period is also critical, given that malnutrition undermines biological development (Franzek, Sprangers, Janssens, Van Duijn, & Van De Wetering, 2008; Morgane et al., 1993). Other complications during gestation or the birth itself also come into play—such things as anoxia (oxygen deprivation), eclampsia (seizures), cesarean delivery, respiration problems, meconium (presence of stool in the lungs), and prematurity/low birth weight can have dramatic implications for early brain development and later self-control.

IN FOCUS 8.1

The Effects of Prenatal Famine on Addiction

Researchers face challenges when trying to determine if one thing truly causes another, and this certainly applies to the study of nutrition and its developmental impacts on self-control and antisocial behavior. The ideal approach—from a methodological standpoint—would involve randomly assigning mothers in the first trimester of their pregnancy to various nutritional regimens, with some being assigned to a nutrient-rich diet and others being assigned to a nutrient-deficient one. Yet, purposely subjecting developing fetuses to nutrient-deficient diets to study the effects on antisocial behavior would, of course, be a horrible thing to do, and no committee on research ethics would approve such a study.

There are, however, alternative study designs that inform our understanding of the importance of nutrition early in life. One involves the "natural experiments" that sometimes arise during the course of history and enable researchers to study the consequences of naturally occurring events. One example of this occurred in the Netherlands during World War II when a failed attempt by the Allied forces to push back German movements into the Netherlands led the German authority to restrict food transports into the country. As a result, food rations fell dramatically, and a significant portion of the Dutch population, including pregnant women, experienced a short-term famine with average daily caloric intake often failing to exceed 1,000 calories. This became the "Dutch hunger winter" of 1944–1945, and researchers have carefully studied its long-term effects. One such study sought to determine whether individuals who were prenatally exposed to the Dutch hunger winter were more likely to suffer addiction as adults (Franzek et al., 2008). To answer this question, researchers analyzed data on a large group of Dutch adults, some of whom were registered as having an addiction problem while others had no recorded history of addiction. All participants, however, were born between 1944 and 1947 (the period inclusive of the hunger winter). Using records available to them, the researchers identified when each study participant was conceived, and whether any of the three trimesters when their mothers were carrying them overlapped with the 1944–1945 hunger winter.

The researchers found that men who were prenatally exposed to the hunger winter during the first trimester of their mother's pregnancy were more likely to have an addiction problem as adults than were men who were not prenatally exposed to the 1944–1945 hunger winter. And indeed, this is consistent with other Dutch hunger winter studies finding effects on such things as schizophrenia, neurological development, and behavior (e.g., Neugebauer, Hoek, & Susser, 1999). Studies that specifically focus on self-control have not been done, but given (a) the strong link between self-control and early brain development and (b) the detrimental effect of prenatal malnutrition on brain development (Prado & Dewey, 2014), there is good reason to expect strong linkages.

When the child is born, some of these factors continue to exert an effect. For example, if the child is breastfeeding, then the mother's alcohol, tobacco, or drug use continues to affect development. Moreover, whether the child is breastfeeding or not, malnutrition (either from too few calories or from deficiencies in specific vitamins and minerals) may be a problem in disadvantaged families. Additionally, once out of the womb, environmental toxins can come into play. Lead is a special concern because of its link to long-term neurological problems. Children living in old, dilapidated housing and in industrial areas of large urban centers are at greatest risk for lead exposure (Narag, Pizarro, & Gibbs, 2009).

The child's exit from the womb also introduces the social element of life, and this is especially marked by interactions with parents. In the initial hours, days, and weeks of life, strong bonds of attachment ideally develop between parents and the child in ways that encourage healthy development, including maturation of the prefrontal cortex (Feldman, Rosenthal, & Eidelman, 2014). Long before the child is capable of initiating complex social interaction, various forms of parent-directed social interaction—skin-to-skin contact, soothing in the wake of distress, playing with and reading to the child—assist the child's biological and cognitive development. And, of course, the absence of these things will hinder brain development.

Also, some children do not just lack attachment and security—they find themselves on the opposite side of the family continuum by being exposed to abuse and neglect. This takes a genuine toll on their development, to such a degree that abuse and neglect has been conceptualized as amounting to *toxic stress* (Shonkoff et al., 2012). When children have ongoing exposure to traumatic circumstances, stress hormones like cortisol surge and undermine the body's regulation of inflammation, therefore producing a chronic "wear and tear" on its organs, including the brain (with particular implications for PFC functioning). This process can occur in utero as well—the surges in cortisol experienced by an abused or traumatized pregnant mother make their way to the child. Whether in utero or during the postnatal period, children exposed to long-term or intense stress during critical periods of brain development will be at a neurological disadvantage—the architecture of their brains lowers the likelihood that they will be able to optimally self-regulate in the years that come.

The Toddler Years and Early Childhood

As children advance into the toddler years, the first notable inklings of self-control are possible—they can maintain focus on a given stimulus, comply with requests, and engage in basic forms of emotional regulation (Graziano, Calkins, & Keane, 2011; Rueda, Posner, & Rothbart, 2005). During this period, social interaction with parents is critical. The path toward high self-control is advanced by an authoritative parenting style (demandingness plus responsiveness; Gray & Steinberg, 1999; Larzelere, Morris, & Harrist, 2013). In the toddler years, this especially involves strong parent–child attachment, praise of good behavior, diligent (but supportive) supervision, and the avoidance of hostile, punitive, or overcontrolling parenting. Beyond toddlerhood, and up through roughly age 10 to 12 (prior to adolescence), these same dimensions of authoritative parenting will be relevant. Naturally, the exact way they are applied to a 10-year-old will differ from that for a 2-year-old, and as the child gets closer to adolescence, authoritative parents will devote greater attention to encouraging such things as individuality and psychological autonomy. Nevertheless, the common theme over the first decade of life is that authoritative parents will be warm, supportive, and attentive, but they also will have high expectations for the child's behavior and will supervise and instruct accordingly.

Importantly, these parent–child interactions will not simply involve the parent influencing the child—the child is a critical player as well. Under the best circumstances, the supportive and diligent approach from parents is welcomed and reciprocated by the child. This is captured well by Kochanska's (2002, p. 192) description of a *mutually responsive orientation* in which the parent and child "are responsive and attuned to each other, are mutually supportive, and enjoy being together." Moreover, they mutually understand their relationship as a "cooperative enterprise" in which each is invested in the well-being of the other and the family. When a mutually responsive orientation emerges between the parent and child, a family more easily accomplishes its socialization goals, including the development of self-control among children.

As you might expect, these ideal interactions between parents and children are most likely to emerge in families that are free of the risks for neuropsychological deficits emphasized above, including prenatal and postnatal exposure to toxins, poor nutrition, and toxic stress from abuse and neglect. Two mechanisms most explain this. First, key background characteristics of parents, including their levels of education, economic stability, intelligence, and self-control, similarly affect the likelihood both of preventing neuropsychological deficits in their children and of parenting authoritatively in ways marked by a mutually responsive orientation. Second, to the extent that the child enters the toddler and childhood years free of complicating neuropsychological deficits, the task of parenting is easier. This involves the *child effects* process described in Chapter 4. Toddlers and children who can sustain attention and practice age-appropriate forms of self-regulation often provoke positive, prosocial, and constructive forms of parenting. In turn, this type of parenting assists the child's neuropsychological development and spurs greater gains in self-control in the coming years. On the other hand, a difficult child—one who does not sustain attention for long, throws frequent and extreme tantrums, and responds poorly to socialization attempts—is more likely to provoke negative and harsh forms of parenting that further reinforce existing relative deficits in self-control. Thus, from the earliest point in life, there will be a correlation between a child's neuropsychological risks and the quality of parenting he or she receives. That said, the correlation will be far from perfect—there will be negative cases that do not fit the expected pattern, including children with high neuropsychological risks who are exposed to strong parenting (and vice versa).

Diagramming These Arguments

Figure 8.1 summarizes our predictions about the process by which self-control differences emerge in the first decade of life. The exogenous qualities of parents get the ball rolling, so to speak. By exogenous, we simply mean that these qualities are temporally prior to any of the other variables in the causal process—these are the preexisting qualities that parents bring into their experience as parents. Most notably, these include their genetic qualities, but they also include a number of specific individual characteristics that are readily observable and have been easily measured in much research (and that often may be connected to genetic qualities). Examples of these characteristics are prior education level, economic stability and well-being, and values about

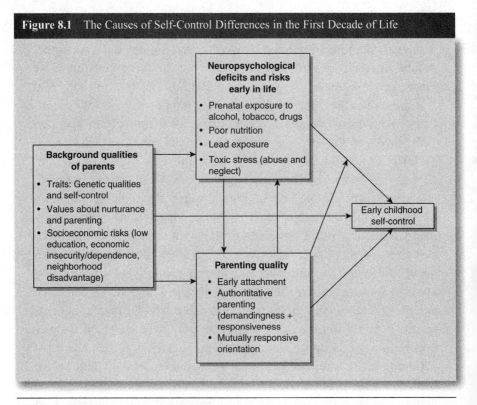

Figure 8.1 The Causes of Self-Control Differences in the First Decade of Life

NOTE: For all of the diagrams in this chapter, the bullet points provided in each box provide examples of the types of variables we expect to be important.

parenting (e.g., harsh vs. nurturant). And, as we have emphasized, parents' level of self-control is itself quite significant.[1]

As Figure 8.1 shows, we expect these background qualities to have two direct effects. First, they will affect the family's ability to avoid neuropsychological risks for their children. For example, parents with high education levels and high self-control will ensure during the prenatal period that the developing fetus receives strong nutrition and is not exposed to alcohol, tobacco, or drugs. Moreover, economic stability during the prenatal and postnatal periods provides access to quality health care that prevents or mitigates harmful health complications. A second direct effect of parents' background qualities is on the approach they take in socialization efforts. For example, parents with high education and with values that emphasize nurturance are more likely to initiate critical attachment processes in the initial days, weeks, and months of life. Also, as the child advances into toddlerhood and childhood, authoritative parenting and a mutually responsive orientation will be especially common.

In turn, neuropsychological risk and parenting quality will be the most direct causes of variation in self-control among children in the first decade of life, and this will be for the reasons elaborated upon previously, especially in Chapter 4. Neuropsychological risks or observed neuropsychological deficits are linked to suboptimal performance of the prefrontal cortex, and therefore should predict lower self-control. High-quality parenting, on the other hand, predicts high self-control because the activities and involvements implied by such things as parental demandingness, responsiveness, and a mutually responsive orientation encourage children to embrace and internalize their parents' norms and values and to behave in ways that are more thoughtful and reflective. All these things increase the chances that they will override impulses to ensure that their behavior adheres to higher-order standards.

A few additional aspects of Figure 8.1 merit emphasis. Notice that it includes arrows running in both directions between neuropsychological risk and parenting quality. As we earlier emphasized, neuropsychological deficits will partially determine whether this is an "easy" or "difficult" child, and this will, on average, affect the type of parenting he or she receives. However, parenting quality will also affect neuropsychological risk—parents who are warm, attentive, and responsive help advance their child's neuropsychological development. Thus, these two potent variables will affect one another, but each in turn has independent direct effects on the child's self-control.

Also, Figure 8.1 specifies that in addition to these independent effects, neuropsychological risk and parenting quality will have an interactive effect on self-control. Specifically, we argue that parenting quality will moderate the effects of neuropsychological deficits and risks. This is illustrated with the arrow from parenting quality that is drawn *into* the arrow between neuropsychological risk and self-control. With the variables labeled in the way they are in Figure 8.1, the specific nature of the interaction should involve a *diminishing* pattern in which the effects of neuropsychological risk on self-control—the differences in self-control between those with low and high neuropsychological risk—are *reduced* by high-quality parenting. Simply stated, exposure to high-quality parenting can help overcome the harmful effects of neuropsychological deficits.

And last, we must emphasize the direct arrow that is drawn between the exogenous qualities of parents and the child's self-control. Although effects of exogenous parental qualities on self-control often will be indirect—operating through neuropsychological risk and parenting quality—direct effects are expected also. This most notably will be true for the genetic qualities of parents. Its effects will not always be entirely or even mostly explained by parenting quality or exposure to the neuropsychological deficits and risks that can be measured in a given study.

THE CHILD GROWS INTO AN ADOLESCENT

The Link Between Childhood and Adolescent Self-Control

By the time children enter early adolescence, they have at least a decade of development and influences under their belt. Indeed, they likely have developed something of a "latent trait"—an established set of tendencies, habits, and propensities—in the area of self-control. And this is critical for understanding the development of self-control over the course of adolescence. Regardless of how powerful and sensational the experience of adolescence may be, the adolescent version of an individual does not emerge out of nowhere—a history has been established.

A key implication is that the most consistent predictor of an adolescent's self-control is the level of self-control he or she possesses when emerging from childhood. This is where our explanation for self-control development in adolescence begins. This explanation is provided in Figure 8.2. We should focus first on its top portion above the dashed line. This part describes processes that promote self-control stability in adolescence. Briefly, childhood self-control predicts adolescent self-control, which in turn predicts adolescent involvement in crime and deviance.

More specifically, though, and as the figure indicates, childhood self-control should predict adolescent self-control through both direct and indirect routes. The direct route is indicated by the top arrow that directly connects those variables (without eliciting a role from any other variable). This direct path reflects a straightforward continuity in self-control that follows from the *latent trait* idea emphasized especially in Chapter 5. This is the idea that once individuals reach early adolescence, their self-control is to some degree a stable and enduring reflection of *who they are.* The complicated mix of genetics, neuropsychological risk, and social environmental experiences (especially with parents) has produced an enduring self-control propensity that sticks as they advance through adolescence. There is, in short, "an initial propensity or proneness . . . that has reverberations over time" (Nagin & Paternoster, 2000, p. 119), and this stable propensity follows from all the first-decade-of-life processes specified earlier in Figure 8.1.

But there also is the *indirect* route. Through state-dependence processes described in Chapter 5, childhood self-control translates into relationships and experiences in adolescence that are themselves consequential for self-control. Through processes of social sorting and selection, high-self-control children will be exposed to prosocial influences that make them more attentive to the higher-order standards that encourage the overriding of impulsive behavior. They will be more committed to school and have encouraging experiences there. They also will be more likely to associate with prosocial peers. In the family

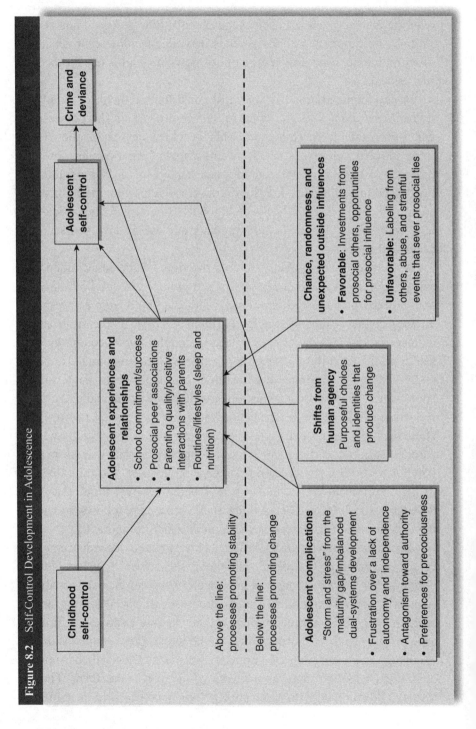

Figure 8.2 Self-Control Development in Adolescence

Childhood self-control

Adolescent self-control

Crime and deviance

Adolescent experiences and relationships
- School commitment/success
- Prosocial peer associations
- Parenting quality/positive interactions with parents
- Routines/lifestyles (sleep and nutrition)

Above the line: processes promoting stability

Below the line: processes promoting change

Shifts from human agency
Purposeful choices and identities that produce change

Chance, randomness, and unexpected outside influences
- **Favorable:** Investments from prosocial others, opportunities for prosocial influence
- **Unfavorable:** Labeling from others, abuse, and strainful events that sever prosocial ties

Adolescent complications
"Storm and stress" from the maturity gap/imbalanced dual-systems development
- Frustration over a lack of autonomy and independence
- Antagonism toward authority
- Preferences for precociousness

environment, they will encounter more prosocial, positive forms of parenting (because their successful navigation of adolescence makes them an easy child to parent in positive, prosocial ways). And last, their higher self-control will give rise to healthier routines and lifestyles, including better sleep, nutrition, and physical health and lower proximity to opportunities for intoxication. As a result, they will be less vulnerable to physiologically or metabolically rooted drops in self-control. In this sense, the strength of their self-control "muscle" will not be depleted so badly and will be more consistently replenished.

For children with low self-control, on the other hand, a very different pattern is likely. Their transition into adolescence will be more turbulent, especially when it comes to people and settings that prioritize diligence, thoughtfulness, and sustained focus—the very qualities most missing in those with low self-control. For these individuals, adolescence is more likely to include problems at school and weak commitment to education, association with antisocial peers, and hostile and negative interactions with parents. Moreover, they are more likely to develop lifestyles and routine activities—inadequate sleep and nutrition and greater opportunities for intoxication—that make them more vulnerable to temporary reductions in self-control and incomplete replenishment of self-control reserves. All these things are likely to lead to greater deficits in their relative level of self-control as they advance into adolescence.

The end result, therefore, is that childhood self-control should be strongly related to adolescent self-control in part because of continuity associated with a latent trait dimension of self-control and in part through a mediated process in which childhood self-control affects adolescent experiences and relationships in the areas of school, peers, interaction with parents, and lifestyles and routine activities. Adolescent self-control, in turn, is the primary proximate cause of adolescent crime and deviance (although we expect that prosocial experiences and relationships will also affect crime and deviance).[2]

The Process for Self-Control Change

The process we just described highlights the powerful tendency toward stability in self-control, with childhood self-control leading to adolescent experiences and relationships that often reinforce preexisting levels of self-control. That said, stability will be far from absolute—there *will be* exceptions in which the level of childhood self-control does not translate into the expected level of adolescent self-control. Some high-self-control children will turn into low-self-control adolescents, and vice versa. These unexpected changes must be explained. *Something else* is coming into play to alter the typical pattern.

Our view of that *something else* prioritizes the two critical dynamics of adolescence emphasized in Chapter 6. These two dynamics are genuine wild cards; each presents the possibility of major deviations from the patterns established to that point. First, there is the maturity gap in which adolescents are "chronological hostages of a time warp between biological age and social age" (Moffitt, 1993, p. 687). This likely is most intense in the stretch between roughly 13 and 17 years of age when puberty and sexual maturation has teenagers quickly advancing to biological adulthood. Despite those advances, adolescents are denied adult social status in key ways, constantly subject to the authority and decision-making of their parents and other adults and having little power over the things about which they most care. This understandably can lead to frustration and a greater inclination to rebel against the adult authority seen as so burdensome.

The second major dynamic is the imbalanced dual-systems development emphasized by Steinberg (2010b). Two major neurological systems in flux during adolescence are the socioemotional network (responsible for reward-seeking behavior) and the cognitive control network (responsible for controlling impulses in favor of long-term goals). Near the beginning of adolescence, the socioemotional network zooms forward in response to surges in dopamine linked to puberty. This greatly enhances the positive sensations associated with reward-seeking behaviors (Casey, Getz, & Galvan, 2008). The cognitive control network, on the other hand, advances much more gradually. This network is governed in large part by changes in the prefrontal cortex (PFC) that increase the speed and efficiency with which it connects with and coordinates other parts of the brain. Ultimately, these changes produce a cognitive control network that can match and contain adolescent surges in reward-seeking from an advancing socioemotional network. But again, this happens gradually, so during a good portion of adolescence, the cognitive control network is playing catch-up to the surging socioemotional network and its enhanced priority on reward seeking.

What does all this mean for self-control? All else being equal, the maturity gap and imbalanced dual-systems development exert downward pressure on self-control—on average, the merits of self-control simply will be less valued during the teenage years than they would have been otherwise. However, as we have emphasized, biological and psychological development does not occur in a uniform fashion—different individuals will experience adolescence in different ways. Some adolescents will have few complications as they coast through adolescence in relatively seamless, easy ways. Others, however, will intensely experience the maturity gap and imbalanced dual-systems development. These are the cases marked by a genuine "storm-and-stress" version of adolescence.

One critical question involves measurement: How can we spot an adolescent of this kind? Needless to say, directly observing a maturity gap or imbalanced dual-systems development would not be easy. Indeed, direct observation of the latter likely requires brain imaging, which is unavailable in most behavioral science research. Fortunately, however, there likely are easily assessed indirect indicators, including attitudes and preferences that follow from these two difficult-to-observe dynamics. Most notable may be adolescents' reports of such things as frustration over a lack of autonomy/independence, antagonism toward adult authority, and preferences for precociousness (e.g., an adolescent's desire to "rush into adulthood"). Adolescents who experience the most intense feelings of these kinds are likely the ones in whom the storm-and-stress complications are most manifest.

And the difference between these teenagers and those with a less turbulent adolescence is critical—this variation gets the process of self-control change going, sending some individuals in one direction, others in a different direction, and "reshuffling" the self-control deck, so to speak. This is captured in the bottom portion of Figure 8.2 that falls below the dashed line. All the processes below that dashed line promote changes in self-control. A central part of this involves the ways in which adolescent complications lead to decreases in self-control through—you guessed it—both direct and indirect routes. The direct route reflects how these complications affect decision-making in ways that do not require other variables to come into play. All else being equal, adolescents in the throes of an intense maturity gap or dual-systems imbalance will be less likely to override immediate impulses when exposed to a given temptation. Through the indirect route, on the other hand, adolescent complications affect self-control by reducing prosocial experiences and relationships in the areas of school, peers, family life, and lifestyle. Intense adolescent complications will, on average, lead to increases in school-related problems, involvement with antisocial rather than prosocial peers, strained relationships with parents, and weaker adherence to healthy lifestyles and routine activities.

As the bottom portion of Figure 8.2 indicates, however, adolescent complications are not the only factor driving changes in adolescent relationships and experiences. Such things as human agency, chance and randomness, and the consequential investments of others also should matter. In this regard, we are borrowing from life course criminology's focus on how unexpected shifts in behavior and experiences follow from varied sources. The important point to emphasize regarding human agency is that adolescents are not automatically funneled into different experiences and relationships—there is an element of choice involved. Indeed, as youths enter adolescence, they develop the cognitive sophistication needed to purposely and consciously embrace certain identities and tendencies. They become more fully capable of thinking about their *future selves* (Silver & Ulmer, 2012) and their *interest* in self-control (Tittle, Ward, & Grasmick, 2004) and then adjusting their lifestyle accordingly. This can involve shifts in a prosocial/high-self-control direction, but the opposite also is possible and, during adolescence, may indeed be quite common. In either case, quickly developing adolescents are exercising choice in ways that influence the experiences and relationships they encounter.

In addition to human agency, such things as chance, randomness, and unexpected outside influences may come into play (Laub & Sampson, 1993, p. 317). Through the sheer luck of the human experience, adolescents sometimes end up in good friendships and prosocial roles that put them on a trajectory toward greater self-control. Moreover, parents, teachers, coaches, and other adult mentors may invest in an adolescent in ways that produce unexpected shifts in his or her experiences and relationships

(Laub & Sampson, 1993, p. 311). But, of course, things can cut the other way as well. Through a mix of misfortune or the influences of others, adolescents may unexpectedly experience abuse and ostracism, a harmful victimization, or entanglement with the criminal justice system, all of which may sever prosocial ties. Similarly, rather than investing in an adolescent, influential adults may label, stigmatize, or discount him or her in ways that further encourage antisocial experiences and relationships that facilitate greater than expected decreases in self-control.

In summary, the process depicted in the bottom portion of Figure 8.2 is one in which the storm and stress associated with adolescence is experienced to differing degrees by adolescents. An intense experience of this directly lowers one's interest in self-control but also indirectly reduces self-control by affecting exposure to the types of adolescent experiences and relationships that themselves affect self-control. Exposure to those experiences and relationships is in flux during adolescence already—such things as human agency, the randomness and chance of life, and the unexpected influences of others affect these things as well.

In the end, such a process can translate into significant shifts in self-control during adolescence. This may involve greater absolute levels of self-control if the complications of adolescence are minimal and if prosocial environments and relationships take root. For some, however, there may be absolute reductions in self-control—they may show less self-control during adolescence than they did at the end of childhood. In such cases, the storm and stress of adolescence conspired with antisocial experiences and relationships to send the adolescent in a backward direction. And with these absolute changes, relative changes—changes in people's position in the self-control distribution—will occur as well. In this sense, the self-control rank ordering among individuals is "reshuffled" to some degree—those starting adolescence at a medium or high position sometimes are passed by others, and the opposite pattern can occur also.

THE ADOLESCENT GROWS INTO AN ADULT

In extending this model into adulthood, many of the critical themes just established continue to be important. This can be seen in Figure 8.3,

226

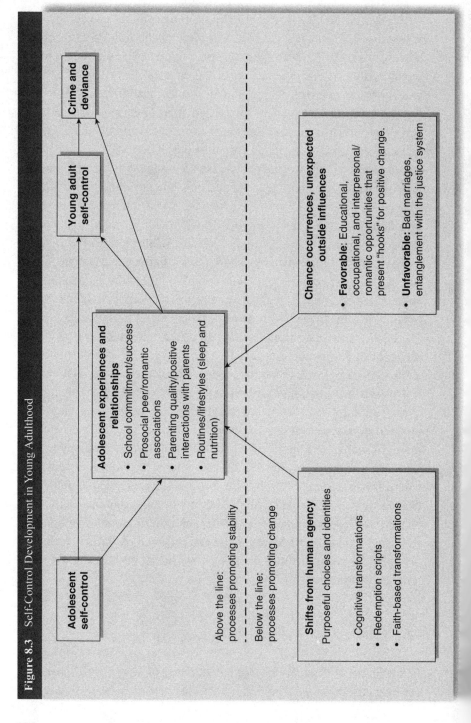

Figure 8.3 Self-Control Development in Young Adulthood

Crime and deviance

Young adult self-control

Adolescent self-control

Adolescent experiences and relationships
- School commitment/success
- Prosocial peer/romantic associations
- Parenting quality/positive interactions with parents
- Routines/lifestyles (sleep and nutrition)

Above the line: processes promoting stability

Below the line: processes promoting change

Chance occurrences, unexpected outside influences
- **Favorable:** Educational, occupational, and interpersonal/romantic opportunities that present "hooks" for positive change.
- **Unfavorable:** Bad marriages, entanglement with the justice system

Shifts from human agency
Purposeful choices and identities
- Cognitive transformations
- Redemption scripts
- Faith-based transformations

which diagrams the causes of self-control development in young adult-hood. This figure is also divided between top and bottom portions that promote stability and change, respectively. As the top panel of Figure 8.3 shows, self-control levels at earlier stages of life (especially the most recent period of adolescence) significantly predict adulthood self-control. This occurs for the two reasons that were operative earlier as well. First, there is a direct path that reflects a *latent trait* dimension of self-control in which individual qualities and prior experiences produce a self-control tendency that persists over time. Second, there is an indi-rect route that reflects a state dependence process in which adolescent levels of self-control affect relationships and experiences in young adult-hood that are themselves consequential for self-control. Then, the final part of the causal sequence involves crime and deviance—young adult self-control is presented as a primary proximate cause of young adult crime and deviance, although we have no doubt that prosocial experi-ences and relationships will exert their own effects also.

In considering this indirect route, the most salient experiences and relationships in adulthood are analogous to but slightly different from those in adolescence. For example, being committed to school in ado-lescence often gets replaced in adulthood by such things as completing a higher education degree or having stable employment. Similarly, in the area of family, interactions with parents are most salient during adolescence, whereas entry into a stable marriage and parenthood may be the most salient family factors in adulthood.[3] Without question, those who leave adolescence with greater self-control are more likely to experience these prosocial life course events, and this helps explain high self-control and low involvement in crime and deviance.

Once again, though, there is the possibility of change, and this is reflected in the portion of the figure below the dashed line. Prior self-control will not be the only determinant of prosocial experi-ences and relationships in young adulthood. Human agency, chance, and unexpected outside influences all play a role here as well. By adulthood, many of the notable shifts that individuals experience will be in the prosocial direction and will involve improvements in self-control. The destabilizing complications of adolescence often have passed by now, and prosocial adult roles and responsibilities (like those just noted) increasingly take root, even among many individuals who were previously low in self-control and high in offending during adolescence. Thus, when life course researchers have examined early adulthood and considered such things as human agency, chance, and unexpected outside influences, attention has been directed especially to things that trigger a pattern of "breaking good" rather than "breaking bad."

As part of this, much research has examined social psychological shifts in which individuals who have lived chaotic lives marked by crime, substance use, and life complications grow weary of their old ways and seek a new beginning. This often involves the emergence of a personal narrative that emphasizes a brighter, better future. This is captured well in research on the "redemption scripts" (Maruna, 2001) and "cognitive transformations" (Giordano, Cernkovich, & Rudolph, 2002) common among those who have turned their lives around. This involves the development of a new self-identity, one in which a "replacement self" supplants the deviant self that is left behind. Research in this area has at times also emphasized faith-based turnarounds that reinforce the human agency transformations under way (Maruna, 2001; Schroeder & Frana, 2009).

These identity shifts can play a critical role in priming the individual to take advantage of unexpected prosocial opportunities that emerge—opportunities they perhaps would have squandered in the past. This is where human agency can work together with chance and unexpected outside influences. If individuals are well into a prosocial cognitive transformation—if their replacement self truly is starting to supplant their previous deviant self—then they are likely to seize upon fortunate new opportunities that offer good prospects for the future. This might involve an appealing employment possibility or a second chance at completing their education. It also might involve interpersonal opportunities, including chance encounters that set the stage for romantic relationships with prosocial partners willing to overlook their troubled past. All these opportunities—in the areas of education, work, and interpersonal relationships—represent what Giordano and her colleagues (2002) have referred to as "hooks for change." These things provide the *possibility* for change, and human agency shifts like those described above can turn that possibility into reality. Ultimately, this complicated mix of human agency, random good fortune, and the investments of others can produce unexpected increases in prosocial experiences and relationships—increases that are independent of the effects of earlier levels of self-control. These prosocial influences in turn increase self-control in young adulthood.

It bears emphasizing once again, however, that human agency, chance, and outside influences can conspire to produce self-control deterioration rather than improvement. Such things as bad marriages, shifts in the economy that lead to unemployment, experiences with discrimination, entanglement in the criminal justice system, and human agency shifts of an antisocial variety all are possible. Each of these negative developments can in turn affect self-control adversely by decreasing prosocial experiences and relationships and increasing anti-social experiences and relationships. Across all these possibilities, the common theme is this: A person's self-control is never set in stone. Change is indeed possible.

Extending the Model Later Into Adulthood

And if we were to extend our model into middle and then later adulthood, what would this look like? In reality, we know very little about that because of the near absence of self-control research that has followed individuals beyond early adulthood. We strongly suspect, however, that the most defensible prediction model would be very sim-ilar to the one we just described. Self-control at earlier stages of life would predict middle and later adulthood self-control, in part because of the stability associated with a latent trait and in part because of how earlier self-control encourages prosocial experiences and relationships that reinforce future self-control. Importantly, however, change is still possible, and this is where human agency, chance events, and the unex-pected influences of others come into play. There is every reason to believe that self-control continues to be potentially malleable deep into life. On this issue, we refer you again to a small number of personality studies that followed individuals over unusually long stretches of time—sometimes as much as 40 or 50 years (Roberts, Wood, & Caspi, 2008). Those studies found *some* stability in personality traits over time, but the amount of stability was far from overwhelming, therefore prompting Roberts and his colleagues (2008, p. 379) to note that "we might not recognize the 70-year-old from what we knew when he or she was 20." Thus, as individuals advance deeper into their lives, they continue to be molded by the experiences and relationships they encounter.

MODERATED EFFECTS ACROSS THE ENTIRE LIFE COURSE

This brings us now to the final major piece of our perspective—one that emphasizes the conditional effects of self-control. Notice that in Figures 8.2 and 8.3, our causal sequence ended with a simple specification: Self-control → crime and deviance. Recall, however, an argument we made in Chapter 7: The effects of self-control are often more complex than this. Although there typically is an effect of self-control on crime, such as that captured by the simple arrow above, other factors come into play to influence its magnitude. Under some circumstances, the effect of self-control (the difference in crime between those low and high in self-control) is amplified (it becomes stronger), whereas in other instances, it is diminished (it becomes weaker).

Prior research and theory suggest that conditional effects of this kind often follow a specific pattern. Specifically, when conditional effects are observed, the most likely pattern is one in which circumstances that themselves encourage crime and deviance will amplify the effects of self-control. Thus, when low self-control occurs in conjunction with other criminogenic factors, its harmful effects will become greater. In this regard, low self-control takes on added importance.

The bar chart in Figure 8.4 summarizes our expectations in this area. The chart's y-axis captures the expected difference in crime between those with low and high self-control, whereas the x-axis captures how this expected difference varies across different moderating and conditioning circumstances. The first bar, on the very left side of the x-axis, pertains to the normal difference in crime— the one that would be observed if we took no steps to consider the role of moderating or conditioning factors. This difference is moderate in size. It is increased, however, by a number of amplifying circumstances specified in Chapter 7. Most notably, the effect of self-control becomes greater when it occurs in conjunction with a high supply of criminal opportunities, association with delinquent peers, weak moral beliefs, weak bonds to conventional society, and residence in a disadvantaged neighborhood. In varying ways, each of these factors liberates the low-self-control individual, allowing low self-control to more easily translate into a greater number of actual criminal acts (thus increasing the difference between their frequency of offending and the frequencies of high-self-control individuals). Figure 8.4 also shows the corresponding diminishing role played by the converse of these criminogenic circumstances. Thus, in the same way that the criminogenic and antisocial factors just noted amplify the differences in crime between those low and high in self-control, the presence of prosocial factors is expected to *diminish* those differences. Thus, differences in crime between those low and high in self-control will be diminished by such things as an absence of criminal opportunities, association with prosocial peers, strong moral condemnation of crime, strong bonds to conventional society, and residence in a middle-class or affluent neighborhood.

Moderated Effects and "Strong" Environments

The patterns just emphasized may sometimes be reversed in substantively meaningful ways. In short, criminogenic circumstances will not always amplify the differences in crime between those with low and high self-control—they may sometimes diminish them. In considering this possibility in Chapter 7, we described the "strong environment" phenomenon (an idea borrowed from Mischel, 1977). This occurs when a particular social context or environment is powerful to the point that it greatly diminishes the effects of individual qualities like self-control. If such an environment is powerfully antisocial and criminogenic, the "push" toward crime may be strong enough to ensure that crime is common among those who are low *or* high in self-control. This may be especially likely to occur in neighborhoods with extremely concentrated disadvantage or in antisocial peer groups or gangs marked by especially strong reinforcements for crime and delinquency. Such environments do not merely liberate those with *low* self-control—they encourage criminal and deviant behavior across the entire self-control continuum.

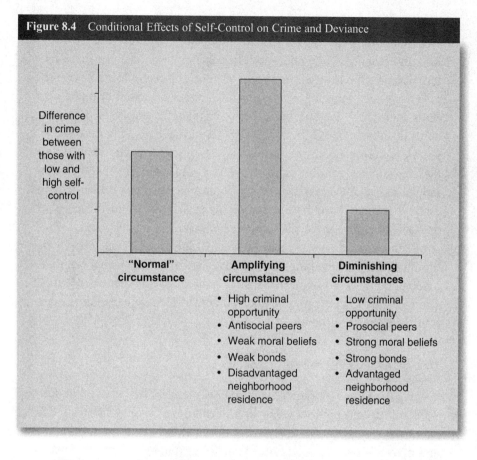

Figure 8.4   Conditional Effects of Self-Control on Crime and Deviance

We must emphasize that a conditional relationship in which criminogenic circumstances diminish (rather than amplify) the effects of self-control does not necessarily mean that the strong-environment phenomenon is operating. Other evidence and considerations are needed. Most notably, if the strong-environment phenomenon is operating, key aspects of sampling and measurement should be consistent with this possibility—there should be a compelling case that a strong environment really is being captured. For example, in a study of the moderating effects of community disadvantage, the sample must include severely disadvantaged communities and the measures used must be able to identify them as such. Moreover, if the moderating variable truly is capturing a strong-environment phenomenon, the findings should support this possibility. Specifically, the moderating variable probably will have a strong independent effect on crime. Also, diminished differences in crime and deviance between those with low and high self-control should be occurring in large part because the strong environment elevates crime and deviance to surprisingly high levels among those with reasonably high self-control.

Interactive Relationships Between State and Trait Self-Control

Self-control can be seen as a fairly durable long-term trait, but temporary fluctuations around some long-term average are also likely. This gets at the idea that an individual's self-control comprises both trait and state components. In Chapter 7, we described research suggesting that these trait and state components statistically interact to affect crime and deviance. Specifically, stressful or burdensome circumstances expected to undermine the temporary state component of self-control increase the probability of an immediate act of crime or deviance. However, the magnitude of this effect will be influenced by trait self-control. For those with low trait self-control, the jump in criminal and deviant probabilities will be especially high, whereas for those with high trait self-control, any increase in the probability of crime or deviance may be quite small.

This is illustrated in the causal sequence shown in Figure 8.5. The arrow with a positive relationship between stressful and burdensome experiences and low state self-control reflects how such things as getting fired from a job, getting ostracized by peers, or dealing with the hassles of a tumultuous marriage can use up one's self-control resources and increase the probability of an immediate lapse in self-control and an aggressive, criminal, or deviant act. Figure 8.5 includes other arrows, however, that specify a moderating role played by trait self-control. Specifically, low trait self-control will *amplify* those effects, such that the relationships will be especially strong among those with low trait self-control. This is indicated by the arrows (with positive signs) drawn from low trait self-control into the associations among stressful and burdensome experiences, low state self-control, and the probability of crime and deviance.

Much of the empirical evidence indicating this pattern comes from laboratory studies in which subjects are randomly assigned to an

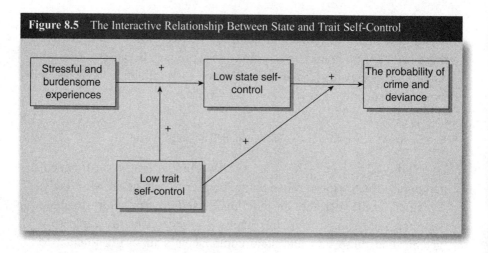

Figure 8.5 The Interactive Relationship Between State and Trait Self-Control

experimental group that receives a stressful or burdensome task or a control group that does not. There are key methodological benefits of such studies, but the notable drawback is that the stressful tasks imposed in the laboratory do not capture the true stress that individuals experience in their real lives. Also, criminal acts in the laboratory generally are of minor significance or hypothetical in nature. However, criminological research on Agnew's general strain theory addresses these voids. That research has examined the effects of real-life stressful circumstances, especially among adolescents and including such things as combative interactions with parents, getting picked on by other kids, and having negative experiences at school. Consistent with the causal sequence in Figure 8.5, this research has at times found that the effects of these things on real-life crime and deviance are amplified among those with low trait self-control. We see this interactive relationship as a critical piece of the self-control puzzle—when individuals with low self-control meet with stressful and burdensome experiences, the chances of a criminal or deviant response are especially high.

CONCLUSION

There is ample evidence that self-control has implications for an individual's health, social relationships, personal achievement, and behavior across the different stages of life. The outcomes for a person with severe deficits in self-control will tilt heavily in a negative direction—there will be early childhood struggles with behavior, difficulty in school, rocky interpersonal relationships, and struggles in the labor market. And once adolescence and adulthood commence, there may be substantial problems with crime and violence, entanglement in the criminal justice system, and addiction. Our focus in this chapter was to put all of this together to create a model of how self-control operates with these other critical aspects of life to affect behavior over the life course.

True to the themes that we emphasized in the early pages and chapters of this book, our approach was guided by a few defining principles. First, we would take a life course perspective that sees self-control not as a fixed, set-in-stone quality that someone *has or does not have*, but instead, as something that is subject to development across the different stages of life, including the prenatal period, infancy and childhood, adolescence, and then adulthood. Second, we would take a multidisciplinary approach in which we brought together varied perspectives on self-control, including the insights not just from our home discipline of criminology, but also from the important work done in other fields, especially psychology and the broad behavioral scientific study of the biosocial underpinnings of behavior.

And last, we would develop a model that reflected the complicated empirical patterns that had consistently emerged in recent self-control research. Our view was this: The time in which the links between self-control and behavior could be described in a bare-bones, simple, parsimonious manner is long gone. Innovative new research put a stake through the heart of that approach. We now know too much, thanks to the efforts of an army of behavioral scientists turning out an incredible volume of new self-control research every year.

New theoretical models were needed to catch up to this research, and these models necessarily needed to be, relatively speaking, complicated—there would need to be different types of variables capturing genetic, biological, and environmental forces; there would need to be varied causal processes reflecting both direct and indirect sequences by which self-control affects behavior over the life course; there would need to be attention to moderating variables that specified the circumstances by which self-control effects are amplified or diminished; there would need to be a sensitivity to alternative possibilities for stability and change; there would need to be some allowance for the role of human agency and chance occurrence, two factors often neglected in prior theorizing; and there would need to be a recognition that self-control is itself a nuanced concept, one that within any individual can be seen not just as an enduring long-term trait, but also as a short-term state subject to temporary fluctuations.

The models presented in these chapters and illustrated in our various diagrams capture these features. They reveal a process by which key self-control differences emerge quite early in life in response to genetics, exposure to neuropsychological deficits and risks, and experiences in the family environment, especially with parents. The differences developed then often route individuals into later relationships and experiences that reinforce initial levels of self-control and help connect early differences in self-control to later differences in behavior. And yet, the prospects for self-control change of both the good and bad variety are ever present, driven by such things as biological development (especially involving adolescence), unexpected developments and chance occurrence (including the investments of others), and human agency. And to complicate matters further, the effects of self-control on behavior are far from uniform—they often will vary according to the characteristics of individuals or the social environments in which they operate.

The models we have presented are far from perfect. There will be things we have neglected or missed altogether. There will be ideas and concepts we have failed to explain as clearly as we could have. There may even be things that turn out to be just wrong. All of this follows in part from our imperfections as scientists, but importantly, also from the very nature of science itself—in the world of science, our state of knowledge is always incomplete and subject to new insights and discoveries. Thus, we present these models as nothing more or less than this: our best approximation of what behavioral scientists currently know about the causes, consequences, and development of self-control over the life course. In future years, this approximation necessarily will be revised to account for new insights and understanding. For now, however, it organizes much of what we presently know.

DISCUSSION QUESTIONS

1. The model presented and discussed places heavy emphasis on the importance of parenting for the development of self-control early in life. Using what you have learned, develop an explanation as to why attachment between parents and children in the first few days, weeks, or months of life may make it easier for parents to instill self-control in their child during later periods of development (e.g., adolescence).

2. Self-control development during adolescence is described as a result of both a *direct* and *indirect* effect of childhood self-control. Discuss the difference between these two types of effects, drawing on examples from your own life and people you know who may fit the direct and indirect patterns described.

3. The model presented in this chapter is probabilistic—it anticipates that individuals who are lower in self-control will be *more likely* to engage in crime and other analogous behavior across the life course. However, there will inevitably be deviations from the expected pattern. Some individuals who are low in self-control will end up refraining from crime, while some individuals who are high in self-control will nonetheless commit criminal acts. What do you think explains the existence of these *negative* cases that do not fit the normal pattern?

4. Chance and randomness were discussed as two things that may influence the development of self-control and behavior across the life course, particularly during young adulthood. Can you think of any circumstances that you or someone else has experienced that, had things played out in a slightly different manner, could have had potential long-term implications for behavior, social relationships, or self-control trajectories?

5. Very little research has considered the consequences of self-control in later life. If *you* were to extend the model presented in this chapter to cover *later* adulthood, what would you include? Would there be direct and indirect effects? Moderating effects? Do you think other process besides self-control might become stronger predictors of behavior?

NOTES

1. We see this not as an exhaustive list of relevant background qualities, but as just an illustration of the idea that parents possess a variety of background qualities that shape the family environment they create for children.

2. Also, while not included as part of Figure 8.2, we expect that the critical factors emphasized in Figure 8.1—including background qualities of parents, neuropsychological deficits and risks, and parenting quality to affect adolescent experiences and relationships in ways that are not fully explained by the effects of those variables on childhood self-control. In short, childhood self-control is not the only mechanism through which earlier social and biological circumstances affect adolescent experiences and relationships.

3. We expect, however, that relationships with parents continue to be important in adulthood, especially early adulthood (Johnson, Giordano, Manning, & Longmore, 2011; Siennick, 2011).

NINE

SELF-CONTROL AND CRIME: INFLUENCING POLICY AND LOOKING TO THE FUTURE

————•◦◆◦•————

In the preceding chapter, we offered our overview of a theoretical process—one in which individual self-control tendencies emerge early in life, develop over the course of adolescence and adulthood, and explain variations in crime, deviance, and harmful behavior all along the way. In this final chapter of the book, we shift to a related priority: We summarize how this theoretical process informs policies and programs for reducing the human suffering from self-control deficits and related problem behaviors. We addressed these policy implications and possibilities in previous chapters, but in this chapter, we bring those arguments together into a cohesive whole. We take an approach similar to Chapter 8, walking an individual through the various stages of the life course, ranging from the prenatal period all the way through adulthood. Only this time, instead of emphasizing the naturally occurring causes and consequences of self-control, we focus on the specific points for social service, juvenile justice, and criminal justice intervention.

Our goal is to put self-control theory and research to work to suggest ways in which the human condition can be advanced. The criminologist Mark Warr (2002, p. 124) aptly described the need for such efforts:

> In a society beset by the hard realities of crime, a theory of crime causation ought to be something more than an intellectual exercise or mere armchair speculation. It should be pressed to offer some means to prevent or control crime in the real world.

We could not agree more. Behavioral science research should be about more than understanding human behavior—it ultimately should make human societies better places to live. This is a lofty goal, but as we discuss, it is attainable—increasingly sophisticated policy evaluation research offers insight on the effectiveness and cost-efficiency of various interventions. Efforts in this area can shape the well-being of entire societies, benefitting both those individuals whose self-control is enhanced and the broader population around them. This can result in lower crime rates, less addiction, fewer high school dropouts and unwanted pregnancies, and a society that is generally more productive, efficient, and happier.

Does this sound too optimistic? We understand there may be skepticism—while we have described the extraordinary effects of self-control on the lives of individuals, can we make a jump from these individual dynamics to larger dynamics involving the broader welfare of a society? We think we can, and in making that assertion, we are inspired by the acclaimed Harvard psychologist Steven Pinker. Before describing our specific points of public policy intervention over the life course, we share his recent arguments about the historical significance of self-control.

SELF-CONTROL AS A DRIVER OF SOCIETAL ADVANCE

Steven Pinker writes books that are *big* in the literal and figurative senses—they are long, dense, and detailed, and they tackle issues of great enormity in the behavioral sciences. His most recent work—*The Better Angels of Our Nature: Why Violence Has Declined*—is no exception. Pinker seeks to understand trends in violence over the course of human history, starting with the earliest forms of human society and moving up through the modern day. He makes the seemingly counter-intuitive argument that we presently live in the *least violent* stretch of human history. You might be asking yourself, is it really possible that human societies are *less* violent now than they previously were? A typical day in our news media suggests otherwise. It is replete with stories of violence, including not just traditional violent street crimes, but also violence from war, genocide, hate crimes, and terrorism. And yet, Pinker sees this as an *improvement* over earlier times. His simple point is this: As bad as it may be now, it was worse earlier.

He painstakingly provides the historic evidence leading to this conclusion. He reviews archaeological research on prehistoric grave-yards and their skeletons—research that reveals a shockingly high incidence of bashed-in skulls, cut marks from spears and arrowheads, and self-defense injuries, especially fractured ulnar bones. He also reviews evidence on the remarkable regularity of rape, torture, murder, arbitrary execution, and slavery in medieval agrarian societies in which "the rule of law" simply meant that powerful tyrants and landowners did what they wished. And then moving up closer to the present—a time in which the incidence of violence and crime are historically recorded by governments—he shows evidence that rates of crime and deaths from violence have largely moved downward during the past century.

Pinker then offers an elaborate explanation for the historic trends that gave rise to this long-term reduction in violence. Self-control plays a star-ring role in that explanation. Pinker points specifically to a centuries-long civilizing process, emerging especially in Europe in the 17th and 18th centuries, in which books, articles, and other artifacts shed light on an unmistakable cultural shift encouraging key principles of self-regulation: "Control your appetites; Delay gratification; Consider the sensibilities of others; Don't act like a peasant; Distance yourself from your animal nature" (Pinker, 2011, p. 71). Pinker suggests that the greater emphasis on self-control came from the emergence of modern commerce (which increased interdependency between individuals) and stronger central gov-ernments (which provided predictability and order, thus encouraging a longer-term orientation). Regardless of its source, however, Pinker illus-trates that the emerging cultural emphasis on self-control touched all aspects of life, ranging from the nonviolent (how people spoke, how they conducted themselves at meals) to the violent (whether they raped a vulnerable woman, assaulted someone who had wronged them, or launched themselves quickly into war with a neighboring community). In his words, "a culture of honor, in which men were respected for lashing out against insults, became a culture of dignity, in which men were respected for controlling their impulses" (p. 592).

And without question, these changes did not simply improve behavior—they laid the groundwork for the extraordinary advances of human civilization in the centuries that would follow. As Pinker rightfully points out,

> no aspect of life is untouched by the retreat from violence. Daily existence is very different if you always have to worry about being abducted, raped, or killed, and it's hard to develop sophisticated arts, learning, or commerce if the institutions that support them are looted and burned as quickly as they are built. (p. xxi)

Simply stated, a safer, more secure society marked by greater respect for the value of regulating impulses is one that can flourish, and this is precisely what happened in many societies, especially in England and mainland Europe, for an important stretch beginning about 400 years ago. So with this historic example in mind, our perspective is girded by two key convictions: (1) Wide-scale improvements in self-control are indeed possible, and (2) such improvements can fundamentally shape the well-being of a society.

USING POLICY TO PROMOTE SELF-CONTROL OVER THE LIFE COURSE

The life course perspective tells us that different stages of life are marked by different developmental needs and capabilities. This has major implications for policies and programs to promote self-control. Specifically, efforts in this area must be tailored to the unique aspects of different life stages, including the prenatal period, the toddler and childhood years, adolescence, and adulthood.

The Prenatal Period

In using public policy to promote self-control over the life course, it is never too early in a child's life to start. Home visitation programs like the Nurse–Family Partnership (Olds et al., 2007) are a good example of this. These programs emphasize nurse visits to the homes of high-risk, first-time mothers both during pregnancy and in the first years of the child's life. These visits have three main goals that evolve over the course of this period: (1) improving the mother's health and nutrition during the prenatal period, (2) improving the quality of parenting once the child is born (and preventing abuse and neglect), and (3) providing guidance and referrals that keep the parents' lives on track. Such programs can prevent the emergence of neuropsychological deficits and encourage positive social interactions between parents and children. In connection, they can create a sense of family stability and harmony that gets the child off to a solid start and prevents the toxic stress that Shonkoff and his colleagues (2012, pp. e235–e237) have described—a syndrome in which sustained stressors like child abuse, neglect, parental substance use or depression, and maternal stress during the prenatal period undermine the child's brain development and prefrontal cortex functioning in particular. As children grow older, a healthy and well-functioning brain will be critical to their efforts to assess risks and rewards, regulate impulses, and learn from social experiences.

IN FOCUS 9.1

The Power of Words Early in Life

In describing the critical role that parents play in children's lives, we often have emphasized such things as attachment, monitoring, and discipline. However, an emerging line of research suggests an additional route through which parents may assist in the development of self-control among young children—simply *talking* to them. In an ambitious study on child development, Hart and Risley (1995) recorded and observed more than 1,300 hours of parent–child interactions over more than two years to investigate whether parents of different socioeconomic backgrounds talk to their toddlers differently. It took them more than five years to transcribe, code, and tabulate all

(Continued)

(Continued)

the data, but their findings have shed great light on child development and the effects of poverty. Most notably, they found that high-education parents with professional occupations (e.g., lawyers, scientists, teachers) speak to their young children *way* more than middle-class or lower-class parents. The average child in a poor household hears about 600 words per hour; in a professional household, it is about 2,100. Extrapolating their data, Hart and Risley estimated that by age 4, a child raised in a professional family will have heard almost 45 million words, while a child from a lower-class household will have heard around 13 million words.

These differences in language exposure early in life have major implications and are thought to contribute greatly to achievement gaps in education between those from advantaged and disadvantaged families. There are complex neurological processes at play, but the logic is straightforward: Fewer words means less cognitive stimulation, and this translates into deficits in cognitive and neural development down the road. This has implications that go way beyond educational performance—this lower level of cognitive development also predicts low self-control and problems with behavior. In this sense, self-control, academic achievement, and behavior are influenced by some of the same early experiences (Davis, Sanger, & Morris-Friehe, 1991; Gallagher, 1999; Stattin & Klackenberg-Larsson, 1993). In connection, Beaver, DeLisi, Vaughn, Wright, and Boutwell (2008) found that lower language skill scores in kindergarten are contemporaneously and longitudinally related to lower levels of self-control, a finding which held even when taking into account potential genetic influences. A common theme underlying this research is that such varied things as educational performance, language skills, self-control, and behavior all are "drawing from the same well," so to speak—all significantly rely on sophisticated brain development in the early years of life. One of the simplest and best things parents can do to facilitate this is to speak early and often with children—the more words, the better.

These ideas have also inspired policy interventions with high-risk families. One prominent example is the Bellevue Project for Early Language, Literacy, and Educational Success (Mendelsohn et al., 2011). With this program, mothers of newborns were randomly assigned to receive a curriculum promoting verbal interactions with their children. This occurred in conjunction with their visits to a primary care physician. Initial evaluations reveal that mothers in the experimental group were significantly more likely to read to children and speak with them while engaging in play activities. The above research suggests that such interactions are likely to improve the cognitive and language skills of these children; in the process, self-control will likely be improved also.

The Toddler and Childhood Years

Parenting is a difficult task, with each stage of the child's life presenting unique challenges (along with the obvious joys and fulfillment). In the toddler and childhood years, the most obvious challenge is that children are developing a refined sense of what they desire, but their skills for obtaining these things are primitive. This creates the potential for an incredible number of parent–child conflicts over such things as child compliance, issues of fact, and the parents' unwillingness to give in to child demands. These conflicts can be valuable learning experiences for the child, or alternatively, they can solidify a coercive, combative dynamic between the parent and child. From a policy standpoint, this is where effective parent training programs like Triple P (Sanders, Dittman, Farruggia, & Keown, 2014) and Incredible Years (Menting, Orobio de Castro, & Matthys, 2013) come into play. These programs focus on such things as how to effectively use rewards and punishments and how to discipline, supervise, and communicate in positive and effective ways. Through such training, parents can develop a simultaneous emphasis on responsiveness (warmth) and demandingness (supervision and structure). Moreover, parent–child interactions can come to resemble Kochanska's (2002 p. 193) notion of *mutually responsive orientations* in which parent and child alike understand the relationship as a "mutually cooperative enterprise"—parental responsiveness to the child enhances trust, and the child responds in kind with responsiveness to the parents' needs and acceptance of their values. Quite early in life, children who are part of such a dynamic show developing signs of self-control—they can resist tempting but prohibited objects, they persist longer in tasks, they experience guilt after a transgression, and they show empathy and concern for someone who is distressed.

Policy efforts during these years can also go outside the family to include school enrichment programs like the Abecedarian Project (Masse & Barnett, 2002) and the PATHS (Promoting Alternative Thinking Strategies) curriculum (Weissberg & Greenberg, 1998). The latter focuses explicitly on encouraging self-control among elementary school children. It uses role-playing and teacher-led lessons to promote better decision-making in the face of temptations and risks. Children are coached on such things as understanding the difference between feelings and behaviors, delaying gratification, controlling impulses, and understanding the perspectives of others. This program encourages children to approach risky or uncertain situations in terms of a traffic signal—they are taught to "Stop, calm down" (red light), "Slow down, think" (yellow light), and then "Act, try my plan" (green light). This program's success likely reflects in part its ability to simply promote thoughtful, reflective habits among children, but there is good reason to believe that its benefits go deeper than this—it appears to encourage higher-order control of the prefrontal cortex and strengthen communication between different hemispheres of the brain (Riggs, Greenberg, Kusché, & Pentz, 2006). Importantly, a program of this kind can be delivered specifically to children who are at special risk for self-control deficits and can benefit from reversal efforts. In practice, however, it is often delivered on a more universal basis that is geared toward wide-scale prevention of self-control deficits. In this sense, it can help promote self-control skills among entire classrooms and schools of children.

Adolescence

The self-control policy challenge during adolescence is twofold. First, when some adolescents exit childhood, they already are far along on a low-self-control trajectory relative to others their age. Such adolescents have a history of impulsive behavior and are being sorted and selected into antisocial relationships and experiences (with parents and peers and at school) that reinforce that pattern. In these instances, reversal efforts are paramount—self-control deficits that already exist must be reversed. The second challenge involves adolescents who appear to be doing fine; even among them, complications are potentially looming. As we discussed in Chapter 6, the biological, psychological, and social changes of the teenage years carry the possibility of a storm-and-stress version of adolescence for some. Two dynamics that we especially emphasized are an adolescent maturity gap (Moffitt, 1993) and imbalanced dual-systems development (Steinberg, 2010b), both of which encourage rebellious, risky, and precocious tendencies, therefore producing lower levels of observed self-control. Also, unexpected shifts in relationships and experiences with parents, peers, and school can lead to problems where there previously were none. All of this suggests the need for continued prevention, especially in early to middle adolescence.

When it comes to reversal efforts, policymakers have many model programs at their disposal. One notable intervention is Multisystemic Therapy (MST), a home- and community-based program that has been successful with serious juvenile offenders (Henggeler, Schoenwald, Borduin, Rowland, & Cunningham, 1998). This program has three main goals: (1) improve family functioning (especially parents' capacity to monitor, discipline, and positively interact with their adolescents), (2) remove offenders from deviant peer groups, and (3) enhance the youths' capacity to succeed in school. In this sense, the program is not directly focused on self-control, but instead is focused on the key life arenas—the home, the peer group, and the school—that are the best social environmental predictors of self-control. If these areas of life can be improved, self-control deficits can be reversed. Functional Family Therapy (Gordon, Graves, & Arbuthnot, 1995) takes a similar approach with its focus on improving the quality of family interactions among juvenile delinquents at risk for being institutionalized. Another promising approach involves mentoring programs like Big Brothers Big Sisters of America (Grossman & Tierney, 1998), which matches mentors from the community with at-risk youth. These programs could produce self-control improvements, although as noted in Chapter 7, their success may also come from suppressing opportunities for impulsive and risky behavior in the hours after school.

There also are reversal programs that specifically target self-control, and most of these take a cognitive behavioral therapy (CBT) approach. These programs use individual and group therapy to encourage youths to consciously reflect on the thoughts, emotions, and habits that have created problems. CBT essentially retrains individuals on how to perceive and respond to life's inevitable frustrations and adversities. The training is designed to enhance their ability to identify high-risk situations and the impulsive cognitions they have previously provoked, and then, in turn, replace impulsive cognitions with those that encourage specific prosocial behaviors and responses (Vaske, Galyean, & Cullen, 2011). Varieties of CBT abound, but Aggression Replacement Training (Glick & Gibbs, 2011) and Thinking for a

Change (Lowenkamp, Hubbard, Makarios, & Latessa, 2009) are especially visible CBT programs backed by strong evaluation results for
struggling adolescents.

As noted above, because the disruptions of adolescence can potentially derail even those who are doing well, there also should be continued prevention efforts that target the broader adolescent population. CBT
programs reign supreme here as well. Model programs include Life
Skills Training (Botvin, Griffin, & Nichols, 2006) and the Positive
Action program (Lewis et al., 2013), both of which use a classroom-based
model for promoting self-regulation skills among middle and high
school students. Such programs encourage such things as setting personal goals, self-monitoring progress, assessing problem situations,
considering the consequences of different actions, and making decisions
with a future orientation in mind. There is a key premise underlying
universal prevention programs of this kind: If we want adolescents to
exercise self-control, training on *how this is done* must continue beyond
childhood, and doing this in the schools provides a fruitful opportunity
to reach a broad adolescent population.

Adulthood

When social service and criminal justice systems deal with adults,
the challenges are often quite daunting. By this point in the life course,
the individual may have built up long-term patterns of dysfunction,
often including intermittent stays in prison, jail, and drug treatment
centers. Moreover, the long-term persistence of problems suggests a
background and history marked by a dense mix of risk factors, including neuropsychological deficits, combative family relationships, and
poor outcomes in the areas of school and work. Under such circumstances, nothing short of a wholesale transformation is needed. The
good news is that the research literature is replete with stories of such
transformations actually occurring. The bad news, however, is that
these transformations are difficult to predict and the route to personal
transformation is far from steady.

Efforts to bring about such reversals unquestionably rely on CBT,
including many of the programs just noted (see Milkman & Wanberg,
2007, for a discussion of common CBT approaches in the correctional

system). CBT offers the best hope for fundamentally transforming people's perspectives on their lives and behavior. Without question, any benefits of CBT for hardened adult offenders will require a heavy dose of human agency. Mere exposure to an often effective intervention may not be enough; indeed, adults plagued by major self-control deficits and long-term antisocial behavior likely have already squandered prior experiences with programs that are often successful with other individuals. Thus, the best chance for policy success will involve the intersection between an effective CBT program and an individual who is ready for change. As we previously noted, qualitative evidence on successful personal transformations often involves narratives in which people reach a point in which they have simply had enough—they are frustrated by their frequent screw-ups and the accompanying hassles, and they are primed and ready to take a new direction (Giordano, Cernkovich, & Rudolph, 2002; Maruna, 2001). In connection, some CBT programs include training sessions and components to explicitly assess one's openness to change (Milkman & Wanberg, 2007). For those ready for change, CBT can trigger the emergence of a "replacement self" (Giordano et al., 2002) that supplants the deviant and impulsive self left behind.

Importantly, these CBT approaches can work in conjunction with other services that encourage prosocial relationships and experiences. These include vocational, job training, and job placement programs that produce at least modest increases in employment and decreases in recidivism (Uggen, 2000; Wilson, Gallagher, & MacKenzie, 2000). Also, for those individuals exiting the corrections system, programs specifically designed to encourage smooth reentry in the areas of employment, housing, and family life may be beneficial (Lawrence, Mears, Dubin, & Travis, 2002).

Despite all these efforts, there still may be adults whose self-control deficits, crime, and deviance persist. In such instances, reversal may seem unlikely to succeed. That said, criminological research indicates that just about all individuals will ultimately desist from crime and pursue a less troublemaking existence (Laub & Sampson, 2003); it simply is difficult to predict when this will occur, and for some individuals the turnaround may occur well into adulthood. This suggests a strategy in which CBT and other reversal efforts continue to be provided on a strategic basis, but suppression efforts that limit the harmful consequences of self-control deficits will also be needed. The most notable suppression effort involves incarceration. This severe and costly sanction obviously should be reserved for the most serious offenders. For other offenders, suppression efforts can include community-based sanctions like electronic monitoring, intensive supervision probation, and case management. Such efforts may not eliminate self-control deficits, but they may reduce the frequency of opportunities in which low self-control can easily translate into actual acts of crime and deviance.

COMMUNITY-BASED PROGRAMS
RELEVANT TO ALL STAGES OF THE LIFE COURSE

Some effective efforts will focus not just on low-self-control individuals (or those at risk of becoming such), but instead on entire communities. This follows from a key conclusion from research in the social and behavioral sciences: Key social problems—including crime and its various causes—often are quite geographically clustered in the most economically disadvantaged areas. If genuine gains are going to be made, the conditions of life in those communities must be improved. Community-wide policy efforts therefore can be initiated, and these efforts can lead to improvements across different stages of the life course and can work through the key mechanisms of prevention, reversal, and suppression. Many such programs exist (see Hope, 1995; Sherman, Farrington, Welsh, & MacKenzie, 2002). One model example is the Communities That Care (CTC) program (Hawkins, Catalano, & Arthur, 2002; Monahan, Hawkins, & Abbott, 2013). This program is the opposite of a *top-down* program in which policymakers or program staff dictate to a community about its needs. Instead, CTC provides a structure for empowering communities to chart their own futures. Through a long-term collaboration, community stakeholders work with CTC staff to identify their priorities and the programs they want in place. CTC staff then provide the program implementation expertise to put the community's plan in action in an evidence-based manner. CTC also provides expertise on how to monitor implementation and evaluate progress. Ultimately, programs of this kind offer the opportunity for interested communities to invest heavily in their own futures in an evidence-based, best-practices approach that combats root causes of community social problems.

EVIDENCE OF PROGRAM SUCCESS

As we described in Chapter 3 (see In Focus 3.3), the specific programs we have highlighted are backed by strong research evidence—rigorous evaluations (often randomized controlled studies) reveal significant improvements among participants that are sustained over time. As a result, most of these programs have been designated as model or promising programs by organizations (including the Institute of Behavioral Science at the University of Colorado and the National Institute of Justice) that track what works in the prevention and rehabilitation programming.

In some instances, we have also provided evidence on the cost effectiveness of these programs. Such evidence comes from cost–benefit analyses that add up the total cost of administering a program and then compare it to societal benefits that come in the form of reduced government spending and lower costs to victims that follow from less crime and better life course outcomes among participants. We noted, for example, that Nurse–Family Partnership programs have been found to save $3 to $4 for every $1 spent on the program. This is just one example of a cost-effective program that targets those at risk for self-control deficits and related behavior problems. Table 9.1 provides benefit and cost data for four types of programs that are commonly used in the correctional system and that are highlighted in this chapter: Functional Family Therapy, Multisystemic Therapy, Aggression Replacement Training for juveniles, and cognitive behavioral therapies in adult prisons. For each program, Table 9.1 provides four pieces of information:

- The expected reduction in crime among program participants
- The financial cost (per participant) of providing the program
- The estimated benefits (per participant) of the program, which include victimization benefits (lower crime means lower costs

of victimization) and taxpayer benefits (from lower government costs)
- The dollar value of benefits for every $1 spent on the program

The key theme of Table 9.1 is that investments in these effective programs more than pay for themselves. Most of the programs are in fact quite affordable—the cost per participant ranges from a high of $7,076 for Multisystemic Therapy to a low of $517 for CBT programs with adults. Because CBT is often administered in group therapy sessions, its cost per participant is low. This can be seen also with the relatively low cost ($1,449) of Aggression Replacement Training (a form of CBT) administered to juveniles. Importantly, for all programs, the costs are far outweighed by their benefits, with total benefits per participant ranging from roughly $11,000 for CBT programs to more than $32,000 for Functional Family Therapy. These benefits are a straightforward result of lower crime—fewer crimes means lower costs to victims and to taxpayers who would have paid the bill for the courts and corrections that would have occurred.

Putting it all together, the most cost-efficient type of program— the one yielding the greatest benefits for each $1 spent on it—is CBT with adults (with $21 in benefits). This efficiency comes mostly from its lower cost, because its effects on reoffending are in fact somewhat slight (it reduces later offending by an average of 7%). This impressive "bang-for-your-buck" makes it an important tool for dealing with adults, but its modest effect on reoffending along with its late-in-life relevance obviously means that this would not be a good stand-alone approach to self-control improvement and crime reduction. Instead, earlier intervention that can affect crime and self-control over the life course is needed, and as Table 9.1 reveals, these interventions are cost efficient as well, generating between $3 and $10 of savings for every $1 spent. A key benefit of these programs is that they target younger offenders; thus, their successes can prevent criminal justice systems from needing as many CBT programs for adult offenders in later years.

And this connects to a key theme we have emphasized: The earlier we successfully intervene, the more efficient we are in promoting self-control and reducing crime. Central to this idea are the

Table 9.1 Cost Effectiveness of Major Interventions				
Program	*Expected reduction in crime (per participant)*	*Cost in dollars (per participant)*	*Benefits in dollars* (per participant)*	*Benefits for every $1 spent*
Functional Family Therapy	18%	$3,134	$32,248	$10.29
Multisystemic Therapy	13%	$7,076	$23,112	$3.27
Aggression Replacement Training (juveniles)	9%	$1,449	$15,325	$10.58
Cognitive behavioral therapy (adult prisons)	7%	$517	$11,204	$21.69

SOURCE: U.S. Department of Justice.

NOTE: *These figures were provided in the 2013 U.S. Department of Justice report "Changing Lives: Prevention and Intervention to Reduce Serious Offending" (Welsh et al., 2013). Also, the figures for estimated benefits include victimization benefits (lower costs of victimization) and taxpayer benefits (lower government costs).

especially early-in-life policy tools at our disposal, including nurse home visitation, preschool enrichment, and parent training. These programs offer the possibility of shaping an entire lifetime of outcomes among those born into disadvantaged circumstances. Importantly, this theme of *intervene early with disadvantaged children* has gained traction not just among criminologists and psychologists who study crime and aggression, but also among prominent economists concerned with improving the efficiency and productivity of our entire society (Heckman, 2006; Heckman & Masterov, 2007). Their point is a simple one: For any given at-risk child, it is more efficient to pay for programs that prevent cognitive and self-control deficits from emerging in the first place than it is to pay much higher costs down the road from such things as crime, addiction, negligent accidents, greater dependence on social welfare programs, and lost economic productivity. As Heckman and Masterov (2007, p. 488) succinctly note, "redirecting funds toward the early years is a sound investment in the productivity and safety of American society."

CONCLUDING THOUGHTS

In our Preface, we vowed to use this book to build a comprehensive perspective on the link between self-control and crime and to accomplish three goals in doing so. First, we would bring to light the insights that have accumulated in recent decades in an ever-expanding body of behavioral science research on self-control. Second, we would capture the multidisciplinary nature of modern-day self-control research by incorporating the valuable insights from criminology, psychology and neuropsychology, sociology, economics, genetics, pediatrics, and a whole host of other disciplines that have examined self-control. And last, we would put public policy issues at the forefront—we wanted to consider not just how self-control might affect behavior, but also what this says about how to use public policy to advance human well-being.

In looking at the pages and chapters between that Preface and these concluding thoughts, we feel satisfied by all that the book has covered, but also impressed by how our goals can never be fully accomplished. The arguments and models we constructed were built from the findings of empirical research, and as best we can tell, the army of behavioral scientists who conduct this research never actually rest. Exciting findings are added to the self-control puzzle every day, and they come from all parts of the academic universe. Our knowledge therefore is always tentative—whatever we know today will be augmented by new insights that emerge tomorrow.

And yet, at some point, a book must end—its authors cannot keep waiting for tomorrow's findings. And to end at this point works well, because while we know that knowledge is tentative, there clearly are key pieces of the self-control puzzle that are entrenched. These are pieces we can rely on, and the arguments of this book have been built around them. Most notably, we know that self-control is a quality of unusual and wide-ranging significance, affecting not just involvement in crime but a whole host of other life events and outcomes. We know that early in life, the explanation for why a person develops or fails to develop self-control is complicated rather than simple—there is no *one important thing*; instead, many factors come into play, some occurring even before a child is born, many occurring in the few years after that. We know that the first decade of life is critical—the self-control tendencies and habits developed then often persist into adolescence and adulthood as individuals are sorted and selected into social relationships and experiences that reinforce existing levels of self-control. In this sense, self-control operates as a trait—a characteristic way of thinking, feeling, and acting that tends to persist over time. We know, however, that self-control shifts are not only possible, but surprisingly common. Some shifts are short term in nature, pointing to temporary fluctuations in self-control states that arise from changing circumstances, habits, and preferences. But we know that long-term changes in self-control also occur as individuals navigate complicated transitions in adolescence and adulthood—shifts in the areas of family, peers, education, and work can all matter. In this sense, self-control is never set in stone; it is, instead, a malleable trait that can fluctuate as new or unexpected circumstances emerge. And last, we know that human agency is critical. From a relatively early point in the life course, people are not merely passive entities governed by powerful forces beyond their control. Instead, there is a degree of *choice* whereby we actively define ourselves, shape our environments, and chart our futures.

This complicated process has extraordinary implications for the lives of individuals. Those with high self-control often capably advance their health, happiness, and security as they advance into childhood, adolescence, and adulthood, whereas those with lower self-control often fare quite poorly. A key theme of our perspective, however, is that these varied developments affect more than just the specific individuals involved—when individual tendencies are aggregated across entire populations, the consequences of low self-control pile up quickly and deeply. Thus, there are significant public policy implications at stake—governments, justice systems, and our society in general have a great deal riding on this.

This presents a difficult challenge, but our interest is squarely on the extraordinary opportunity it affords. Evidence-based approaches to promoting self-control can greatly enhance our society's well-being by reducing the hassles and complications that follow from self-control deficits. Imagine a world with fewer crimes and negligent accidents, less addiction, and lower levels of school failure, unwanted pregnancy, and social dependence. This would not just be a safer and more harmonious society; it would be a more productive and efficient one—one in which individuals come closer to achieving their human potential, and in which fewer of our resources must be set aside to combat social ills. All of this is attainable, at least to some degree. As the policy research in this chapter has described, strategic interventions at key stages of the life course are investments in the future that more than pay for themselves. The best such investments start early in life to promote the health and well-being of disadvantaged children and their families. These are the children most at risk for struggles with self-control; they therefore offer the greatest opportunity for large-scale gains.

Our discussion of effective programs and treatments points to how systematic policy efforts can make a difference. But what if we look beyond governments and their policies—what if we look to ourselves, and specifically, to the cultural values that shape our society? Can widespread cultural shifts that promote self-control also be part of the solution? Culture is an elusive concept—it deals with abstract norms and values for how we define behavior as right versus wrong or wise versus foolish. The issue of culture has been greatly neglected in this area, perhaps because self-control seems like such an individualistic concept. However, as we have noted in many instances, we strongly suspect that individual self-control tendencies are in fact shaped by broad, macro-level cultural forces.

In connection, Charles Tittle and Patricia McCall (Tittle, 2011; Tittle & McCall, 2006) have considered that self-control is not just a quality of individuals, but also a feature of broader social units like neighborhoods, cities, regions, and societies. They view a "self-control culture" as one in which "most people value self-control, admire efforts to develop it and exercise it, and attempt to help other people develop it" (Tittle, 2011, p. 105). When such a culture emerges in an area, it takes on a life of its own, above and beyond the individuals who may have contributed to its formation. The neighborhood, community, or society that shares this culture therefore is more than just the sum of its individual members—it is the sum of its individual members *plus* the emerging cultural values that shape behavior and persist over time as they are passed from one person or generation to the next. This points to an exciting possibility: Shifts in our cultural emphasis on self-control could produce widespread improvements in our society's ability to avoid the costly and harmful behaviors that follow from self-control deficits.

We see signs that shifts of this kind have in fact been under way for some time. We see this, for example, in Pinker's compelling argument, reviewed at the outset of this chapter, that in the 17th and 18th centuries, an emerging cultural priority on self-control laid the groundwork for the economic, technological, and democratic advances that would follow in the industrialized world. These advances produced the societies we know today—societies that, when compared to their medieval predecessors, are more willing to think about future costs and benefits and exercise some self-control.

Indeed, in thinking about recent decades, we see a long list of behaviors and actions that were common not long ago but are now frowned upon or outlawed. This includes such things as smoking in public buildings, driving while intoxicated, smoking or drinking alcohol while pregnant, riding in a car without using a seat belt, allowing parents to commit acts of violence against their children, and allowing companies to add lead to gasoline and paint or dump toxic waste into public waterways. In each instance, these actions offer someone an immediate benefit, gratification, or convenience, but our culture (and often the legal system) now deems them inappropriate threats to the well-being and future of our citizens. This is no insignificant thing. On the contrary, this is roughly what a culture of self-control looks like. Over time, our society has become, in relative terms, more likely to *look before it leaps* and less likely to *throw caution to the wind*.

We obviously still have far to go. As the pages of this book have revealed, stories of crime, addiction, negligence, and impulsivity are still too common among our citizens, governments, and social institutions. And yet, the changes that *have* occurred provoke thought—could further shifts toward a culture of self-control loom in our future? We see the connection between the self-control tendencies of individuals and the broad cultural forces around them as perhaps yet another piece that will be added to the self-control puzzle—a puzzle that seeks to organize our understanding of the causes, consequences, and development of self-control over the life course. Rest assured, there is an army of behavioral scientists ready at a moment's notice to consider this possibility and related others.

DISCUSSION QUESTIONS

1. Stephen Pinker's discussion of how books published in the 17th and 18th centuries encouraged people to delay gratification is illustrative of early efforts at promoting social messages to large numbers of people. Can you think of any specific public media campaigns today found on billboards, radio or TV, or in magazines that encourage people to exercise self-control? Conversely, can you think of any examples of media messages that may actually *discourage* self-control? Do you think any of these messages (either positive or negative) influence people's behavior?

2. If you had $10,000 that you could spend on an individual at any stage of his or her life course to help promote this person's self-control, at what point in the life course do you think use of the money would be most effective? Why? In what ways would you spend the money?

3. *Prevention*, *reversal*, and *suppression* are three key terms that have been discussed throughout the book with regard to addressing deficits in self-control. Discuss the differences between each of these strategies, citing examples of programs that would be illustrative of each of the terms.

4. Do you think that programming targeted at adult offenders (e.g., cognitive behavioral therapy) really impacts their *ability* to exercise self-control, or rather promotes and encourages their *interest* in exercising self-control?

5. If you were asked to design a program to address the self-control deficits of high-risk adolescents, what would the components of your program be? In describing your model program, explain how its components would target the aspects of self-control discussed throughout the book.

REFERENCES

Abe, T., Hagihara, A., & Nobutomo, K. (2010). Sleep patterns and impulse control among Japanese junior high school students. *Journal of Adolescence, 33,* 633–641.

Aos, S., Lieb, R., Mayfield, J., Miller, M., & Pennucci, A. (2004). *Benefits and costs of prevention and early intervention programs for youth* (No. 04–07, p. 3901). Olympia, WA: Washington State Institute for Public Policy.

Agnew, R. (1992). Foundation for a general strain theory of crime and delinquency. *Criminology, 30*(1), 47–88.

Agnew, R. (2001). Building on the foundation of general strain theory: Specifying the types of strain most likely to lead to crime and delinquency. *Journal of Research in Crime and Delinquency, 38*(4), 319–361.

Agnew, R., Brezina, T., Wright, J. P., & Cullen, F. T. (2002). Strain, personality traits, and delinquency: Extending general strain theory. *Criminology, 40*(1), 43–72.

Akers, R. L. (1998). *Social structure and social learning.* Los Angeles, CA: Roxbury.

Albert, D., Chein, J., & Steinberg, L. (2013). The teenage brain: Peer influences on adolescent decision making. *Current Directions in Psychological Science, 22*(2), 114–120.

Alexander, R. D. 1989. Evolution of the human psyche. In P. Mellars & C. Stringer (Eds.), *The human revolution: Behavioural and biological perspectives on the origins of modern humans* (pp. 455–513). Princeton, NJ: Princeton University Press.

Anderson, E. (1999). *Code of the street: Decency, violence, and the moral life of the inner city.* New York, NY: Norton.

Anderson, P. J., De Luca, C. R., Hutchinson, E., Spencer-Smith, M. M., Roberts, G., Doyle, L. W., & Victorian Infant Collaborative Study Group. (2011). Attention problems in a representative sample of extremely preterm/extremely low birth weight children. *Developmental Neuropsychology, 36*(1), 57–73.

Antonaccio, O., & Tittle, C. R. (2008). Morality, self-control, and crime. *Criminology, 46*(2), 479–510.

Ayduk, O., Mendoza-Denton, R., Mischel, W., Downey, G., Peake, P. K., & Rodriguez, M. (2000). Regulating the interpersonal self: Strategic self-regulation for coping with rejection sensitivity. *Journal of Personality and Social Psychology, 79*(5), 776–792.

Bakermans-Kranenburg, M., & van Ijzendoorn, M. H. (2011). Differential susceptibility to rearing environment depending on dopamine-related genes: New evidence and a meta-analysis. *Development and Psychopathology, 23*(1), 39–52.

Barber, L. K., & Munz, D. C. (2011). Consistent-sufficient sleep predicts improvements in self-regulatory performance and psychological strain. *Stress and Health, 27,* 314–324.

Barkley, R. A. (1997). *ADHD and the nature of self-control.* New York, NY: Guilford Press.

Barnes, J. C., & Meldrum, R. C. (2014). The impact of sleep duration on adolescent development: A genetically informed analysis of identical twin pairs. *Journal of Youth and Adolescence.* doi: 10.1007/s10964-014-0137-4

Baron, S. W. (2003). Self-control, social consequences, and criminal behavior: Street youth and the general theory of crime. *Journal of Research in Crime and Delinquency, 40*(4), 403–425.

Baumeister, R. F., Gailliot, M., DeWall, C. N., & Oaten, M. (2006). Self-regulation and personality: How interventions increase regulatory success, and how depletion moderates the effects of traits on behavior. *Journal of Personality, 74*(6), 1773–1802.

Baumeister, R. F., Heatherton, T. F., & Tice, D. M. (1994). *Losing control.* San Diego, CA: Academic Press.

Baumeister, R. F., & Tierney, J. (2011) *Willpower: Rediscovering the greatest strength.* New York, NY: Penguin Books.

Baumeister, R. F., Vohs, K. D., & Tice, D. M. (2007). The strength model of self-control. *Current Directions in Psychological Science, 16*(6), 351–355.

Baumrind, D. (1991). The influence of parenting style on adolescent competence and substance use. *Journal of Early Adolescence, 11*(1), 56–95.

Baumrind, D. (1996). The discipline controversy revisited. *Family Relations,* 405–414.

Bearman, P. S., Jones, J., & Udry, J. R. (1997). *The National Longitudinal Study of Adolescent Health: Research design.* Retrieved from www.cpc.unc.edu/addhealth

Beauvais, F., & Oetting, E. R. (2002). Drug use, resilience, and the myth of the golden child. In *Resilience and development* (pp. 101–107). New York, NY: Springer.

Beaver, K. M., & Belsky, J. (2012). Gene–environment interaction and the intergenerational transmission of parenting: Testing the differential-susceptibility hypothesis. *Psychiatric Quarterly, 83,* 29–40.

Beaver, K. M., DeLisi, M., Vaughn, M. G., Wright, J. P., & Boutwell, B. B. (2008). The relationship between self-control and language: Evidence of a shared etiological pathway. *Criminology, 46*(4), 939–970.

Beaver, K. M., Gibson, C. L., DeLisi, M., Vaughn, M. G., & Wright, J. P. (2012) The interaction between neighborhood disadvantage and genetic factors in the prediction of antisocial outcomes. *Youth Violence and Juvenile Justice, 10*(1), 25–40.

Beaver, K. M., Shutt, J. E., Boutwell, B. B., Ratchford, M., Roberts, K., & Barnes, J. C. (2009). Genetic and environmental influences on levels of self-control and delinquent peer affiliation results from a longitudinal sample of adolescent twins. *Criminal Justice and Behavior, 36*(1), 41–60.

Beaver, K. M., & Wright, J. P. (2005). Evaluating the effects of birth complications on low self-control in a sample of twins. *International Journal of Offender Therapy and Comparative Criminology, 49*(4), 450–471.

Beaver, K. M., Wright, J. P., & DeLisi, M. (2007). Self-control as an executive function: Reformulating Gottfredson and Hirschi's parental socialization thesis. *Criminal Justice and Behavior, 34*(10), 1345–1361.

Beedie, C. J., & Lane, A. M. (2012). The role of glucose in self-control: Another look at the evidence and an alternative conceptualization. *Personality and Social Psychology Review, 16*(2), 143–153.

Bellafante, G. (June 10, 2009). Real life is like "Juno," except maybe the dialogue. *New York Times.* Retrieved April 1, 2014, from http://article.wn.com/view/2009/06/11/Real_Life_Is_Like_Juno_Except_Maybe_the_Dialogue/

Bellinger, D. C. (2008). Neurological and behavioral consequences of childhood lead exposure. *PLoS Medicine, 5*(5).

Belsky, J., & Beaver, K. M. (2011). Cumulative-genetic plasticity, parenting and adolescent self-regulation. *Journal of Child Psychology and Psychiatry, 52*(5), 619–626.

Benda, B. B. (2005). The robustness of self-control in relation to form of delinquency. *Youth and Society, 36*(4), 418–444.

Benoit, E., Randolph, D., Dunlap, E., & Johnson, B. (2003). Code switching and inverse imitation among marijuana-using crack sellers. *British Journal of Criminology, 43*(3), 506.

Bersani, B. E., & Doherty, E. E. (2013). When the ties that bind unwind: Examining the enduring and situational processes of change behind the marriage effect. *Criminology, 51*(2), 399–433.

Bersani, B. E., Laub, J. H., & Nieuwbeerta, P. (2009). Marriage and desistance from crime in the Netherlands: Do gender and socio-historical context matter? *Journal of Quantitative Criminology, 25*(1), 3–24.

Blomberg, T. G. (1980). Widening the net: An anomaly in the evaluation of diversion programs. In M. W. Klein (Ed.), *Handbook of criminal justice evaluation* (pp. 571–592). Beverly Hills, CA: SAGE.

Bloom, P. (2013). *Just babies: The origins of good and evil.* New York, NY: Crown.

Boals, A., vanDellen, M. R., & Banks, J. B. (2011). The relationship between self-control and health: The mediating effect of avoidant coping. *Psychology and Health, 26*(8), 1049–1062.

Botchkovar, E., & Broidy, L. (2013). Accumulated strain, negative emotions, and crime: A test of general strain theory in Russia. *Crime and Delinquency, 59*(6), 837–860.

Botvin, G. J., Griffin, K. W., & Nichols, T. D. (2006). Preventing youth violence and delinquency through a universal school-based prevention approach. *Prevention Science, 7*(4), 403–408.

Boutwell, B. B., & Beaver, K. M. (2010). The intergenerational transmission of low self-control. *Journal of Research in Crime and Delinquency, 47*(2), 174–209.

Bowlby, J. (1988). *A secure base: Parent–child attachment and healthy human development.* New York, NY: Basic Books.

Bretherton, I. (1992). The origins of attachment theory: John Bowlby and Mary Ainsworth. *Developmental Psychology, 28*(5), 759.

Buggie, S. E. (1995, December). Superkids of the ghetto. *PsycCRITIQUES, 40*(12), 1164–1165.

Burke, J. D., Pardini, D. A., & Loeber, R. (2008). Reciprocal relationships between parenting behavior and disruptive psychopathology from childhood through adolescence. *Journal of Abnormal Child Psychology, 36*(5), 679–692.

Burnett, S., Sebastian, C., Cohen Kadosh, K., & Blakemore, S. J. (2011). The social brain in adolescence: Evidence from functional magnetic resonance imaging and behavioural studies. *Neuroscience and Biobehavioral Reviews, 35*(8), 1654–1664.

Burt, C. H., Simons, R. L., & Simons, L. G. (2006). A longitudinal test of the effect of parenting and the stability of self-control: Negative evidence for the general theory of crime. *Criminology, 44*(2), 353–396.

Burt, C. H., Sweeten, G., & Simons, R. L. (2014). Self-control through emerging adulthood: Instability, multidimensionality, and criminological significance. *Criminology, 52*(3), 450–487.

Burton, V. S., Cullen, F. T., Evans, T. D., Alarid, L. F., & Dunaway, R. G. (1998). Gender, self-control, and crime. *Journal of Research in Crime and Delinquency, 35*(2), 123–147.

Bushman, B. J., DeWall, C. N., Pond, R. S., & Hanus, M. D. (2014). Low glucose relates to greater aggression in married couples. *Proceedings of the National Academy of Sciences, 111*(17), 6254–6257.

Bushway, S., Brame, R., & Paternoster, R. (1999). Assessing stability and change in criminal offending: A comparison of random effects, semiparametric, and fixed effects modeling strategies. *Journal of Quantitative Criminology, 15*(1), 23.

Bushway, S. D., Piquero, A. R., Broidy, L. M., Cauffman, E., & Mazerolle, P. (2001). An empirical framework for studying desistance as a process. *Criminology, 39*(2), 491–516.

"Buy this dad a brain." (2008, October 7). *Smoking Gun*. Retrieved from http://www.thesmoking gun.com/documents/crime/buy-dad-brain

Cance, J. D., Ennet, S. T., Morgan-Lopez, A. A., Foshee, V. A., & Talley, A. E. (2013). Perceived pubertal timing and recent substance abuse among adolescents: A longitudinal perspective. *Addiction, 108*(10), 1845–1854.

Casbon, T. S., Curtin, J. J., Lang, A. R., & Patrick, C. J. (2003). Deleterious effects of alcohol intoxication: Diminished cognitive control and its behavioral consequences. *Journal of Abnormal Psychology, 112*(3), 476.

Casey, B. J., Getz, S., & Galvan, A. (2008). The adolescent brain. *Developmental Review, 28*(1), 62–77.

Caspi, A., Elder, G. H., & Bem, D. J. (1987). Moving against the world: Life-course patterns of explosive children. *Developmental Psychology, 23,* 308–313.

Caspi, A., McClay, J., Moffitt, T. E., Mill, J., Martin, J., Craig, I. W., Taylor, A., & Poulton, R. (2002). Role of genotype in the cycle of violence in maltreated children. *Science, 297*(5582), 851–854.

Caspi, A., Moffitt, T. E., Silva P. A., Stouthamer-Loeber, M., Krueger, R. F., & Schmutte, P. S. (1994). Are some people crime prone? Replications of the personality–crime relationship across countries, genders, races, and methods. *Criminology, 32*(2), 163–196.

Caspi, A., Roberts, B. W., & Shiner R. L. (2005). Personality development: Stability and change. *Annual Review of Psychology, 56,* 453–484.

Cauffman, E., Steinberg, L., & Piquero, A. R. (2005). Psychological, neuropsychological, and physiological correlates of serious antisocial behavior in adolescence: The role of self-control. *Criminology, 43*(1), 133–176.

Centers for Disease Control and Prevention. (2013). *Insufficient sleep is a public health epidemic.* Retrieved May 1, 2014, from http://www.cdc.gov/features/dssleep/

Chapple, C. L. (2005). Self-control, peer relations, and delinquency. *Justice Quarterly, 22*(1), 89–106.

Chapple, C. L., & Hope, T. L. (2003). An analysis of the self-control and criminal versatility of gang and dating violence offenders. *Violence and Victims, 18*(6), 671–690.

Charney, E. (2008). Genes and ideologies. *Perspectives on Politics, 6*(2), 299–319.

Christianson, S. (2003, February 8). "Bad seed or bad science?" *New York Times*. Retrieved from http://www.nytimes.com/2003/02/08/arts/bad-seed-or-bad-science.html?src=pm&page wanted=1

Clinkinbeard, S. S., Simi, P., Evans, M. K., & Anderson, A. L. (2011). Sleep and delinquency: Does the amount of sleep matter? *Journal of Youth and Adolescence, 40*(7), 916–931.

Cloninger, S. C. (1996). *Personality: Description, dynamics, and development.* Worth Publishers.

Cochran, J. K., Wood, P. B., Sellers, C. S., Wilkerson, W., & Chamlin, M. B. (1998). Academic dishonesty and low self-control: An empirical test of a general theory of crime. *Deviant Behavior, 19*(3), 227–255.

Collins, W. A., Maccoby, E. E., Steinberg, L., Hetherington, E. M., & Bornstein, M. H. (2000). Contemporary research on parenting: The case for nature and nurture. *American Psychologist, 55*(2), 218–232.

Collins, W. A., Madsen, S. D., & Susman-Stillman, A. (2002). *Parenting during middle childhood.* Mahwah, NJ: Lawrence Erlbaum.

Colman, R. A., Hardy, S. A., Albert, M., Raffaelli, M., & Crockett, L. (2006). Early predictors of self-regulation in middle childhood. *Infant and Child Development, 15*(4), 421–437.

Colten, H. R., & Altevogt, B. M. (Eds.). (2006). *Sleep disorders and sleep deprivation: An unmet public health problem.* Committee on Sleep Medicine and Research, Board on Health Sciences Policy. Washington, DC: Institute of Medicine, National Academies Press.

Conger, R. D., Wallace, L. E., Sun, Y., Simons, R. L., McLoyd, V. C., & Brody, G. H. (2002). Economic pressure in African American families: A replication and extension of the family stress model. *Developmental Psychology, 38*(2), 179.

Connolly, E. J., & Beaver, K. M. (2014). Examining the genetic and environmental influences on self-control and delinquency: Results from a genetically informative analysis of sibling pairs. *Journal of Interpersonal Violence, 29*(4), 707–735.

Conradt, E., Measelle, J., & Ablow, J. C. (2013). Poverty, problem behavior, and promise: Differential susceptibility among infants reared in poverty. *Psychological Science, 24*(3), 235–242.

Crescioni, A. W., Ehrlinger, J., Alquist, J. L., Conlon, K. E., Baumeister, R. F., Schatschneider, C., & Dutton, G. R. (2011). High trait self-control predicts positive health behaviors and success in weight loss. *Journal of Health Psychology, 16*(5), 750–759.

Crimesider Staff. (2014, August 20). Father of "affluenza" teen arrested for impersonating police. *CBS News/Associated Press.* Retrieved from http://www.cbsnews.com/news/father-of-affluenza-teen-arrested-for-impersonating-police

Cullen, F. T. (2005). The twelve people who saved rehabilitation: How the science of criminology made a difference. *Criminology, 43*(1), 1–42.

Davis, A. D., Sanger, D. D., & Morris-Friehe, M. (1991). Language skills of delinquent and non-delinquent adolescent males. *Journal of Communication Disorders, 24,* 251–266.

Deater-Deckard, K. (2005). Parenting stress and children's development: Introduction to the special issue. *Infant and Child Development, 14*(2), 111–115.

DeLisi, M. (2011). Self-control theory: The "Tyrannosaurus rex" of criminology is poised to devour criminal justice. *Journal of Criminal Justice, 39*(2), 103–105.

DeLisi, M. (2013). Pandora's box: The consequences of low self-control into adulthood. In C. L. Gibson & M. D. Krohn (Eds.), *Handbook of life-course criminology: Emerging trends and directors for future research* (pp. 261–273). New York, NY: Springer.

de Ridder, D. T., Lensvelt-Mulders, G., Finkenauer, C., Stok, F. M., & Baumeister, R. F. (2012). Taking stock of self-control: A meta-analysis of how trait self-control relates to a wide range of behaviors. *Personality and Social Psychology Review, 16*(1), 76–99.

Desmond, S. A., Bruce, A. S., & Stacer, M. J. (2012). Self-control, opportunity, and substance use. *Deviant Behavior, 33*(6), 425–447.

DeWall, C. N., Baumeister, R. F., Stillman, T. F., & Gailliot, M. T. (2007). Violence restrained: Effects of self-regulation and its depletion on aggression. *Journal of Experimental Social Psychology, 43*(1), 62–76.

DeWall, C. N., Deckman, T., Gailliot, M. T., & Bushman, B. J. (2011). Sweetened blood cools hot tempers: Physiological self-control and aggression. *Aggressive Behavior, 37*(1), 73–80.

Dobbs, D. (2011). Beautiful brains. *National Geographic, 220*(4), 36.

Doherty, E. E. (2006). Self-control, social bonds, and desistance: A test of life-course interdependence. *Criminology, 44*(4), 807–833.

Doherty, E. E., & Ensminger, M. E. (2013). Marriage and offending among a cohort of disadvantaged African Americans. *Journal of Research in Crime and Delinquency, 50*(1), 104–131.

Drummond, H., Bolland, J. M., & Harris, A. W. (2011). Becoming violent: Evaluating the mediating effect of hopelessness on the code of the street thesis. *Deviant Behavior, 32*(3), 191–223.

Duckworth, A. L., & Seligman, M. E. (2005). Self-discipline outdoes IQ in predicting academic performance of adolescents. *Psychological Science, 16*(12), 939–944.

Duckworth, A. L., Tsukayama, E., & Geier, A. B. (2010). Self-controlled children stay leaner in the transition to adolescence. *Appetite, 54*(2), 304–308.

Dugdale, R. L. 1910. *The Jukes: A study in crime, pauperism, disease, and heredity* (4th ed.). New York: NY: Knickerbocker Press.

Dunn, L. M., & Dunn, L. M. (1981). *Peabody picture vocabulary test: Forms L and M.* American Guidance Service.

Durkheim, E. (1893) *The division of labour in society.* New York, NY: Free Press.

Dvorak, R. D., & Simons, J. S. (2009). Moderation of resource depletion in the self-control strength model: Differing effects of two modes of self-control. *Personality and Social Psychology Bulletin, 35*(5), 572–583.

Elder, G. H., Jr. (1969). Occupational mobility, life patterns, and personality. *Journal of Health and Social Behavior, 10,* 308–323.

Elder, G. H., Jr. (1985). Perspectives on the life course. In G. H. Elder, Jr. (Ed.), *Life course dynamics.* Ithaca, NY: Cornell University Press.

Elias, N. (1939). *The civilizing process: Sociogenetic and psychogenetic investigations* (Rev. ed.). Cambridge, MA: Blackwell.

Ellis, L., Beaver, K. M., & Wright, J. (2009). *Handbook of crime correlates.* San Diego, CA: Elsevier.

Emirbayer, M., & Mische, A. (1998). What is agency? *American Journal of Sociology, 103*(4), 962–1023. Cincinnati, OH: Anderson Publishing Company.

Enos, R., & Southern, S. (1996). *Correctional case management.* Anderson.

Evans, G. W., Chen, E., Miller, G., & Seeman, T. (2012). How poverty gets under the skin: A life course perspective. In V. Maholmes & R. B. King (Eds.), *The Oxford handbook of poverty and child development.* New York, NY: Oxford University Press.

Evans, T. D., Cullen, F. T., Burton, V. S., Dunaway, R. G., & Benson, M. L. (1997). The social consequences of self-control: Testing the general theory of crime. *Criminology, 35*(3), 475–504.

Eysenck, S., & Zuckerman, M. (1978). The relationship between sensation-seeking and Eysenck's dimensions of personality. *British Journal of Psychology, 69*(4), 483–487.

Farrington, D. P., & Welsh, B. C. (2003). Family-based prevention of offending: A meta-analysis. *Australian and New Zealand Journal of Criminology, 36*(2), 127–151.

Farrington, D. P., & Welsh, B. C. (2007). *Saving children from a life of crime.* Boulder, CO: Westview.

Farrington, D. P., Welsh, B. C., & MacKenzie, D. L. (2002). *Evidence-based crime prevention* (p. 10). London, UK: Routledge.

Feldman, R., Rosenthal, Z., & Eidelman, A. I. (2014). Maternal–preterm skin-to-skin contact enhances child physiologic organization and cognitive control across the first 10 years of life. *Biological Psychiatry, 75*(1), 56–64.

Feldman, S. S., & Weinberger, D. A. (1994). Self-restraint as a mediator of family influences on boys' delinquent behavior: A longitudinal study. *Child Development, 65*(1), 195–211.

Felson, R. B., & Haynie, D. L. (2002). Pubertal development, social factors, and delinquency among adolescent boys. *Criminology, 40*(4), 967–988.

Fergus, S., & Zimmerman, M. A. (2005). Adolescent resilience: A framework for understanding healthy development in the face of risk. *Annual Review of Public Health, 26,* 399–419.

Finkel, E. J., & Campbell, W. K. (2001). Self-control and accommodation in close relationships: An interdependence analysis. *Journal of Personality and Social Psychology, 81*(2), 263.

Finkenauer, C., Engels, R. C., & Baumeister, R. F. (2005). Parenting behaviour and adolescent behavioural and emotional problems: The role of self-control. *International Journal of Behavioral Development, 29*(1), 58–69.

Fishbein, D. (2001). *Biobehavioral perspectives in criminology.* Belmont, CA: Wadsworth.

Flinn, M., Geary, D., & Ward, C. (2005). Ecological dominance, social competition, and coalitionary arms races: Why humans evolved extraordinary intelligence. *Evolution and Human Behavior, 26,* 10–46.

Ford, D. (2014, February 6). Judge orders Texas teen Ethan Couch to rehab for drunk driving, killing 4. *CNN.* Retrieved from http://www.cnn.com/2014/02/05/us/texas-affluenza-teen/

Forrest, W., & Hay, C. (2011). Life-course transitions, self-control and desistance from crime. *Criminology and Criminal Justice, 11*(5), 487–513.

Fox, K. A., Lane, J., & Akers, R. L. (2013). Understanding gang membership and crime victimization among jail inmates: Testing the effects of self-control. *Crime and Delinquency, 59*(5), 764–787.

Franzek, E. J., Sprangers, N., Janssens, A. C. J. W., Van Duijn, C. M., & Van De Wetering, B. J. (2008). Prenatal exposure to the 1944–45 Dutch "hunger winter" and addiction later in life. *Addiction, 103*(3), 433–438.

Funder, D. C. (2001). Personality. *Annual Review of Psychology, 52,* 197–221.

Gaertner, B. M., Spinrad, T. L., & Eisenberg, N. (2008). Focused attention in toddlers: Measurement, stability, and relations to negative emotion and parenting. *Infant and Child Development, 17*(4), 339.

Gailliot, M. T., Baumeister, R. F., DeWall, C. N., Maner, J. K., Plant, E. A., Tice, D. M., Brewer, L. E., & Schmeichel, B. J. (2007). Self-control relies on glucose as a limited energy source: Willpower is more than a metaphor. *Journal of Personality and Social Psychology, 92*(2), 325–336.

Gailliot, M. T., Schmeichel, B. J., & Baumeister, R. F. (2006). Self-regulatory processes defend against the threat of death: Effects of self-control depletion and trait self-control on thoughts and fears of dying. *Journal of Personality and Social Psychology, 91*(1), 49.

Gailliot, M. T., Schmeichel, B. J., & Maner, J. K. (2007). Differentiating the effects of self-control and self-esteem on reactions to mortality salience. *Journal of Experimental Social Psychology, 43*(6), 894–901.

Gallagher, T. M. (1999). Interrelationships among children's language, behavior, and emotional problems. *Topics in Language Disorders, 19,* 1–15.

Gardner, M., & Steinberg, L. (2005). Peer influence on risk taking, risk preference, and risky decision making in adolescence and adulthood: An experimental study. *Developmental Psychology, 41*(4), 625.

Geary, D. (2005). *The origin of mind: Evolution of brain, cognition, and general intelligence.* Washington, DC: American Psychological Association.

Gerich, J. (2014). The inhibiting function of self-control and social control on alcohol consumption. *Journal of Drug Issues, 44(2),* 120–131.

Gershoff, E. T. (2002). Corporal punishment by parents and associated child behaviors and experiences: A meta-analytic and theoretical review. *Psychological Bulletin, 128*(4), 539.

Gibbs, J. J., & Giever, D. (1995). Self-control and its manifestations among university students: An empirical test of Gottfredson and Hirschi's general theory. *Justice Quarterly, 12*(2), 231–255.

Gibbs, J. J., Giever, D., & Martin, J. S. (1998). Parental management and self-control: An empirical test of Gottfredson and Hirschi's general theory. *Journal of Research in Crime and Delinquency, 35*(1), 40–70.

Gibson, C. L. (2012). An investigation of neighborhood disadvantage, low self-control, and violent victimization among youth. *Youth Violence and Juvenile Justice, 10*(1), 41–63.

Gibson, C. L., Ward, J. T., Wright, J. P., Beaver, K. M., & Delisi, M. (2010). Where does gender fit in the measurement of self-control? *Criminal Justice and Behavior, 37*(8), 883–903.

Gillis, J. R. (1974). *Youth and history: Tradition and change in European age relations, 1770– present* (pp. 1–35). New York, NY: Academic Press.

Ginsberg, M. (2011, July 16). "Breaking Bad" star Bryan Cranston on Walter White: "He's well on his way to bad-ass." *Hollywood Reporter.* Retrieved from http://www.hollywoodreporter .com/live-feed/breaking-bad-star-bryan-cranston-212262

Giordano, P. C., Cernkovich, S. A., & Rudolph, J. L. (2002). Gender, crime, and desistance: Toward a theory of cognitive transformation. *American Journal of Sociology, 107*(4), 990–1064.

Glick, B., & Gibbs, J. C. (2011). *Aggression replacement training: A comprehensive intervention for aggressive youth.* Champaign, IL: Research Press.

Glueck, S., & Glueck, E. (1950). *Unraveling juvenile delinquency.* Cambridge, MA: Harvard University Press.

Gopnik, A. (2012, January 28). "What's wrong with the teenage mind?" *Wall Street Journal.* Retrieved April 9, 2014, from http://online.wsj.com/news/articles/SB100014240529702038 06504577181351486558984

Gordon, D. A., Graves, K., & Arbuthnot, J. (1995). The effect of Functional Family Therapy for delinquents on adult criminal behavior. *Criminal Justice and Behavior, 22*(1), 60–73.

Gottfredson, D. C., Gottfredson, G. D., & Weisman, S. A. (2001). The timing of delinquent behavior and its implications for after-school programs. *Criminology and Public Policy, 1*(1), 61–86.

Gottfredson, M., & Hirschi, T. (1990). *A general theory of crime.* Stanford, CA: Stanford University Press.

Gottfredson, M. R., & Hirschi, T. (2003). Self-control and opportunity. In C. L. Britt & M. R. Gottfredson (Eds.), *Control theories of crime and delinquency* (pp. 5–19). New Brunswick, NJ : Transaction Publishers.

Gough, H. G. (1975). *Manual for the California psychological inventory.* Palo Alto, CA: Consulting Psychologists Press.

Gouin, K., Murphy, K., & Shah, P. S. (2011). Effects of cocaine use during pregnancy on low birthweight and preterm birth: Systematic review and metaanalyses. *American Journal of Obstetrics and Gynecology, 204*(4), 340-e1.

Grasmick, H. G., Tittle, C. R., Bursik, R. J., & Arneklev, B. J. (1993). Testing the core empirical implications of Gottfredson and Hirschi's general theory of crime. *Journal of Research in Crime and Delinquency, 30*(1), 5–29.

Gray, M. R., & Steinberg, L. (1999). Unpacking authoritative parenting: Reassessing a multidi- mensional construct. *Journal of Marriage and the Family,* 574–587.

Graziano, P. A., Calkins, S. D., & Keane, S. P. (2011). Sustained attention development during the toddlerhood to preschool period: Associations with toddlers' emotion regulation strategies and maternal behaviour. *Infant and Child Development, 20*(6), 389–408.

Greenberg, M. T., Kusche, C. A., Cook, E. T., & Quamma, J. P. (1995). Promoting emotional competence in school-aged children: The effects of the PATHS curriculum. Development and Psychopathology, 7, 117-136.

Greenberg, M. T., & Kusché, C. A. (1998). Preventive interventions for school-age deaf children: The PATHS curriculum. *Journal of Deaf Studies and Deaf Education, 3*(1), 49–63.

Greenstein, T. N. (2006). *Methods of family research.* Thousand Oaks, CA: SAGE.

Greenwood, P. W. (2006). *Changing lives: Delinquency prevention as crime-control policy.* Chicago, IL: University of Chicago Press.

Greenwood, P. W., Karoly, L. A., Everingham, S. S., Houbé, J., Kilburn, M. R., Rydell, C. P., . . . Chiesa, J. (2001). Estimating the costs and benefits of early childhood interventions: Nurse home visits and the Perry Preschool. In B. Welsh, D. Farrington, & L. Sherman, *Costs and Benefits of Preventing Crime* (pp. 123–148), Boulder, CO: Westview.

Grossman, J. B., & Tierney, J. P. (1998). Does mentoring work? An impact study of the Big Brothers Big Sisters program. *Evaluation Review, 22*(3), 403–426.

Hack, M., Klein, N. K., & Taylor, H. G. (1995). Long-term developmental outcomes of low birth weight infants. *Future of Children,* pp. 176–196.

Hagger, M. S. (2013, November 20). *Willpower and carbs: A recipe for success?* Retrieved from http://spsptalks.wordpress.com/main/new-posts/page/3/

Hagger, M. S., & Chatzisarantis, N. L. (2012). Transferring motivation from educational to extramural contexts: A review of the trans-contextual model. *European Journal of Psychology of Education, 27*(2), 195–212.

Hagger, M. S., Wood, C., Stiff, C., & Chatzisarantis, N. L. D. (2010). Ego depletion and the strength model of self-control: A meta-analysis. *Psychological Bulletin, 136,* 495–525.

Hall, G. S. (1904). *Adolescence* (2 vols.). New York, NY: Appleton.

Hannaford, A. (2011). 127 hours: Aron Ralston's story of survival. *The Telegraph.* Retrieved from http://www.telegraph.co.uk/culture/film/8223925/127-Hours-Aron-Ralstons-story-of-survival.html

Harlow, J. M. (1869). Recovery: Passage of an iron bar through the head. *Publications of the Massachusetts Medical Society, 2,* 327–347.

Hart, B., & Risley, T. R. (1995). *Meaningful differences in the everyday experiences of young American children.* Baltimore, MD: Paul H. Brookes.

Hawkins, J. D., Catalano, R. F., & Arthur, M. W. (2002). Promoting science-based prevention in communities. *Addictive Behaviors, 27*(6), 951–976.

Hay, C. (2001). Parenting, self-control, and delinquency: A test of self-control theory. *Criminology, 39*(3), 707–736.

Hay, C., & Forrest, W. (2006). The development of self-control: Examining self-control theory's stability thesis. *Criminology, 44,* 739–774.

Hay, C., & Forrest, W. (2008). Self-control theory and the concept of opportunity: The case for a more systematic union. *Criminology, 46*(4), 1039–1072.

Hay, C., & Meldrum, R. (2010). Bullying victimization and adolescent self-harm: Testing hypotheses from general strain theory. *Journal of Youth and Adolescence, 39*(5), 446–459.

Hay, C., Meldrum, R. C., & Piquero, A. R. (2013). Negative cases in the nexus between self-control, social bonds, and delinquency. *Youth Violence and Juvenile Justice, 11,* 3–25.

Healey, K. M. (1999). *Case management in the criminal justice system* (Vol. 2, No. 2). Washington, DC: U.S. Department of Justice, Office of Justice Programs, National Institute of Justice.

Heckman, J. J. (2006). Skill formation and the economics of investing in disadvantaged children. *Science, 312*(5782), 1900–1902.

Heckman, J. J., & Masterov, D. V. (2007). The productivity argument for investing in young children. *Applied Economic Perspectives and Policy, 29*(3), 446–493.

Henggeler, S. W., Schoenwald, S. K., Borduin, C. M., Rowland, M. D., & Cunningham, P. B. (1998). *Multisystemic treatment of antisocial behavior in children and adolescents.* New York, NY: Guilford Press.

Higgins, G. E., Jennings, W. G., Tewksbury, R., & Gibson, C. L. (2009). Exploring the link between low self-control and violent victimization trajectories in adolescents. *Criminal Justice and Behavior, 36*(10), 1070–1084.

Hirschi, T. (1969) *Causes of delinquency.* Berkeley, CA: University of California Press.

Hirschi, T. (2004). Self-control and crime. In R. F. Baumeister & K. D. Vohs, *Handbook of self-regulation: Research, theory, and applications* (pp. 537–552). New York, NY: Guilford Press.

Hirschi, T., & Gottfredson, M. R. (1993). Commentary: Testing the general theory of crime. *Journal of Research in Crime and Delinquency, 30,* 47–54.

Hirschi, T., & Gottfredson, M. (2001). Self-control theory. In R. Paternoster & R. Bachman (Eds.), *Explaining criminals and crime* (pp. 81–96). Los Angeles, CA: Roxbury Press.

Hitlin, S., & Elder, G. H., Jr. (2007). Time, self, and the curiously abstract concept of agency. *Sociological Theory, 25*(2), 170–191.

Hofmann, W., Baumeister, R. F., Förster, G., & Vohs, K. D. (2012). Everyday temptations: An experience sampling study of desire, conflict, and self-control. *Journal of Personality and Social Psychology, 102,* 1318–1335.

Hofmann, W., Luhmann, M., Fisher, R. R., Vohs, K. D., & Baumeister, R. F. (2013). Yes, but are they happy? Effects of trait self-control on affective well-being and life satisfaction. *Journal of Personality, 82(4),* 265–277.

Holden, G. W., & Miller, P. C. (1999). Enduring and different: A meta-analysis of the similarity in parents' child rearing. *Psychological Bulletin, 125*(2), 223–254.

Holtfreter, K., Reisig, M. D., & Pratt, T. C. (2008). Low self-control, routine activities, and fraud victimization. *Criminology, 46*(1), 189–220.

Hope, T. (1995). Community crime prevention. *Crime and Justice, 19,* 21–89.

Hope, T. L., Grasmick, H. G., & Pointon, L. J. (2003). The family in Gottfredson and Hirschi's general theory of crime: Structure, parenting, and self-control. *Sociological Focus, 36*(4), 291–311.

Horney, J., Osgood, D. W., & Marshall, I. H. (1995). Criminal careers in the short-term: Intraindividual variability in crime and its relation to local life circumstances. *American Sociological Review, 60*(5), 655–673.

Jackson, D. B., & Beaver, K. M. (2013). The influence of neuropsychological deficits in early childhood on low self-control and misconduct through early adolescence. *Journal of Criminal Justice, 41*(4), 243–251.

James, W. (1890). *The principles of psychology* (Vol. 1). New York, NY: Holt.

Jennings, W. G., Higgins, G. E., Akers, R. L., Khey, D. N., & Dobrow, J. (2013). Examining the influence of delinquent peer association on the stability of self-control in late childhood and early adolescence: Toward an integrated theoretical model. *Deviant Behavior, 34*(5), 407–422.

Jennings, W. G., Higgins, G. E., Tewksbury, R., Gover, A. R., & Piquero, A. R. (2010). A longitudinal assessment of the victim–offender overlap. *Journal of Interpersonal Violence, 25*(12), 2147–2174.

Jennings, W. G., Piquero, A. R., & Reingle, J. M. (2012). On the overlap between victimization and offending: A review of the literature. *Aggression and Violent Behavior, 17*(1), 16–26.

Jensen-Campbell, L. A., Knack, J. M., Waldrip, A. M., & Campbell, S. D. (2007). Do Big Five personality traits associated with self-control influence the regulation of anger and aggression? *Journal of Research in Personality, 41*(2), 403–424.

Johnson, W. L., Giordano, P. C., Manning, W. D., & Longmore, M. A. (2011). Parent–child relations and offending during young adulthood. *Journal of Youth and Adolescence, 40*(7), 786–799

Jones, S., & Lynam, D. R. (2009). In the eye of the impulsive beholder: The interaction between impulsivity and perceived informal social control on offending. *Criminal Justice and Behavior, 36*(3), 307–321.

Jones, S. E., Miller, J. D., & Lynam, D. R. (2012). Personality and antisocial behavior, and aggression: A meta-analytic review. *Journal of Criminal Justice, 39,* 329–337.

Junger, M., & Tremblay, R. E. (1999). Self-control, accidents, and crime. *Criminal Justice and Behavior, 26*(4), 485–501.

Junger, M., & van Kampen, M. (2010). Cognitive ability and self-control in relation to dietary habits, physical activity and bodyweight in adolescents. *International Journal of Behavioral Nutrition and Physical Activity, 7,* 22–34.

Jussim, L., & Harber, K. D. (2005). Teacher expectations and self-fulfilling prophecies: Knowns and unknowns, resolved and unresolved controversies. *Personality and Social Psychology Review, 9*(2), 131–155.

Kam, C. M., Greenberg, M. T., & Kusché, C. A. (2004). Sustained effects of the PATHS curriculum on the social and psychological adjustment of children in special education. *Journal of Emotional and Behavioral Disorders, 12*(2), 66–78.

Kamphuis, J., Meerlo, P., Koolhaas, J. M., & Lancel, M. (2012). Poor sleep as a potential causal factor in aggression and violence. *Sleep Medicine, 13*(4), 327–334.

Kandel, D. B., & Wu. (1995). Disentangling mother–child effects in the development of antisocial behavior. In J. McCord (Ed.), *Coercion and punishment in long-term perspectives* (pp. 106–123). New York, NY: Cambridge University Press.

Kearney, M. S., & Levine, P. B. (2014). *Media influences on social outcomes: The Impact of MTV's* 16 and Pregnant *on teen childbearing.* NBER Working Paper No. 19795. National Bureau of Economic Research.

Kerr, M., Stattin, H., & Burk, W. J. (2010). A reinterpretation of parental monitoring in longitudinal perspective. *Journal of Research on Adolescence, 20*(1), 39–64.

Kett, J. F. (1977). *Rites of passage: Adolescence in America, 1790 to the present* (p. 327). New York, NY: Basic Books.

Kett, J. F. (2003). Reflections on the history of adolescence in America. *History of the Family, 8*(3), 355–373.

Kidd, C., Palmeri, H., & Aslin, R. N. (2013). Rational snacking: Young children's decision-making on the marshmallow task is moderated by beliefs about environmental reliability. *Cognition, 126*(1), 109–114.

Kiewitz, C., Restubog, S. L. D., Zagenczyk, T. J., Scott, K. D., Garcia, P. R. J. M., & Tang, R. L. (2012). Sins of the parents: Self-control as a buffer between supervisors' previous experience of family undermining and subordinates' perceptions of abusive supervision. *Leadership Quarterly, 23*(5), 869–882.

Killias, M., Gilliéron, G., Kissling, I., & Villettaz, P. (2010). Community service versus electronic monitoring: What works better? Results of a randomized trial. *British Journal of Criminology,* azq050.

King, R. B., & Gaerlan, M. J. M. (2014). High self-control predicts more positive emotions, better engagement, and higher achievement in school. *European Journal of Psychology of Education, 29,* 81–100.

King, R. D., Massoglia, M., & MacMillan, R. (2007). The context of marriage and crime: Gender, the propensity to marry, and offending in early adulthood. *Criminology, 45*(1), 33–65.

Kochanska, G. (1997). Multiple pathways to conscience for children with different temperaments: From toddlerhood to age 5. *Developmental Psychology, 33*(2), 228.

Kochanska, G. (2002). Mutually responsive orientation between mothers and their young children: A context for the early development of conscience. *Current Directions in Psychological Science, 11*(6), 191–195.

Kochanska, G., & Kim, S. (2014). A complex interplay among the parent–child relationship, effortful control, and internalized, rule-compatible conduct in young children: Evidence from two studies. *Developmental Psychology, 50*(1), 8–21.

Kochanska, G., & Murray, K. T. (2000). Mother–child mutually responsive orientation and conscience development: From toddler to early school age. *Child Development, 71*(2), 417–431.

Kochanska, G., Philibert, R. A., & Barry, R. A. (2009). Interplay of genes and early mother–child relationship in the development of self-regulation from toddler to preschool age. *Journal of Child Psychology and Psychiatry, 50*(11), 1331–1338.

Kocher, M., Rutzler, D., Sutter, M., & Trautmann, S. (2012). Cognitive skills, self-control, and life outcomes: The early detection of at-risk youth. *VOX.* Retrieved from http://www.voxeu.org/article/should-governments-teach-self-control

Kopasz, M., Loessl, B., Hornyak, M., Riemann, D., Nissen, C., Piosczyk, H., & Voderholzer, U. (2010). Sleep and memory in healthy children and adolescents—a critical review. *Sleep Medicine Reviews, 14,* 167–177.

Korkman, M., Kettunen, S., & Autti-Rämö, I. (2003). Neurocognitive impairment in early adolescence following prenatal alcohol exposure of varying duration. *Child Neuropsychology, 9*(2), 117–128.

Kovac, S. (2014, July 23). Spanking the gray matter out of our kids. *CNN Health.* Retrieved from http://www.cnn.com/2014/07/23/health/effects-spanking-brain/

Kruglanski, A. W., & Kopetz, C. (2013). Unpacking the self-control dilemma and its modes of resolution. In R. R. Hassin, K. N. Ochsner, & Y. Trope (Eds.), *Self-control in society, mind, and brain* (pp. 297–311). Oxford, UK: Oxford University Press.

Kuhn, E. S., & Laird, R. D. (2013). Parent and peer restrictions of opportunities attenuate the link between low self-control and antisocial behavior. *Social Development, 22*(4), 813–830.

LaGrange, T. C., & Silverman, R. A. (1999). Low self-control and opportunity: Testing the general theory of crime as an explanation for gender differences in delinquency. *Criminology, 37*(1), 41–72.

Laible, D., Panfile, T., & Makariev, D. (2008). The quality and frequency of mother–toddler conflict: Links with attachment and temperament. *Child Development, 79*(2), 426–443.

Laible, D. J., & Thompson, R. A. (2002). Mother–child conflict in the toddler years: Lessons in emotion, morality, and relationships. *Child Development, 73*(4), 1187–1203.

Landenberger, N. A., & Lipsey, M. W. (2005). The positive effects of cognitive–behavioral programs for offenders: A meta-analysis of factors associated with effective treatment. *Journal of Experimental Criminology, 1*(4), 451–476.

Larzelere, R. E., Morris, A. S. E., & Harrist, A. W. (2013). *Authoritative parenting: Synthesizing nurturance and discipline for optimal child development.* Washington, DC: American Psychological Association.

Laub, J. H. (2004). The life course of criminology in the United States: The American Society of Criminology 2003 presidential address. *Criminology, 42*(1), 1–26.

Laub, J. H. (2006). Edwin H. Sutherland and the Michael-Adler report: Searching for the soul of criminology seventy years later. *Criminology, 44*(2), 235–257.

Laub, J. H., & Sampson, R. J. (1993). Turning points in the life course: Why change matters to the study of crime. *Criminology, 31*(3), 301–325.

Laub, J. H., & Sampson, R. J. (2003). *Shared beginnings, divergent lives: Delinquent boys to age 70.* Cambridge, MA: Harvard University Press.

Laub, J. H., & Sampson, R. J. (2004). Strategies for bridging the quantitative and qualitative divide: Studying crime over the life course. *Research in Human Development, 1*(1/2), 81–99.

Lawrence, S., Mears, D. P., Dubin, G., & Travis, J. (2002). *The practice and promise of prison programming.* Washington, DC: Urban Institute.

Leahey, T. M., Xu, X., Unick, J. L., & Wing, R. R. (2013). A preliminary investigation of the role of self-control in behavioral weight loss treatment. *Obesity Research and Clinical Practice, 8,* 115–120.

Lee, G. Y., & Kisilevsky, B. S. (2014). Fetuses respond to father's voice but prefer mother's voice after birth. *Developmental Psychobiology, 56*(1), 1–11.

Lewis, K. M., Schure, M. B., Bavarian, N., DuBois, D. L., Day, J., Ji, P., . . . Flay, B. R. (2013). Problem behavior and urban, low-income youth: A randomized controlled trial of Positive Action in Chicago. *American Journal of Preventive Medicine, 44*(6), 622–630.

Li, S. D. (2004). The impacts of self-control and social bonds on juvenile delinquency in a national sample of midadolescents. *Deviant Behavior, 25*(4), 351–373.

Liem, M., & Richardson, N. J. (2014). The role of transformation narratives in desistance among released lifers. *Criminal Justice and Behavior.* doi: 10.1177/0093854813515445

Liu, J., Raine, A., Wuerker, A., Venables, P. H., & Mednick, S. (2009). The association of birth complications and externalizing behavior in early adolescents: Direct and mediating effects. *Journal of Research on Adolescence, 19*(1), 93–111.

Loeber, R., Drinkwater, M., Yin, Y., Anderson, S. J., Schmidt, L. C., & Crawford, A. (2000). Stability of family interaction from ages 6 to 18. *Journal of Abnormal Child Psychology, 28*(4), 353–369.

Lombardo, P. A. (2012). Return of the Jukes: Eugenic mythologies and internet evangelism. *Journal of Legal Medicine, 33*(2), 207–233.

Longshore, D. (1998). Self-control and criminal opportunity: A prospective test of the general theory of crime. *Social Problems,* 102–113.

Longshore, D., Chang, E., & Messina, N. (2005). Self-control and social bonds: A combined control perspective on juvenile offending. *Journal of Quantitative Criminology, 21*(4), 419–437.

Longshore, D., Rand, S. T., & Stein, J. A. (1996). Self-control in a criminal sample: An examination of construct validity. *Criminology, 34*(2), 209–228.

Longshore, D., & Turner, S. (1998). Self-control and criminal opportunity: Cross-sectional test of the general theory of crime. *Criminal Justice and Behavior, 25*(1), 81–98.

Lösel, F., & Beelmann, A. (2003). Effects of child skills training in preventing antisocial behavior: A systematic review of randomized evaluations. *Annals of the American Academy of Political and Social Science, 587*(1), 84–109.

Lowenkamp, C. T., Hubbard, D., Makarios, M. D., & Latessa, E. J. (2009). A quasi-experimental evaluation of thinking for a change: A "real-world" application. *Criminal Justice and Behavior, 36*(2), 137–146.

Luthar, S. S. (Ed.). (2003). *Resilience and vulnerability: Adaptation in the context of childhood adversities.* Cambridge University Press.

Lynam, D. R., Caspi, A., Moffit, T. E., Wikström, P. O., Loeber, R., & Novak, S. (2000). The interaction between impulsivity and neighborhood context on offending: The effects of impulsivity are stronger in poorer neighborhoods. *Journal of Abnormal Psychology, 109*(4), 563.

Lynam, D., Moffitt, T., & Stouthamer-Loeber, M. (1993). Explaining the relation between IQ and delinquency: Class, race, test motivation, school failure, or self-control? *Journal of Abnormal Psychology, 102*(2), 187.

Maccoby, E. E. (2000). Parenting and its effects on children: On reading and misreading behavior genetics. *Annual Review of Psychology, 51,* 1–27.

Maccoby, E. E., & Martin, J. A. (1983). Socialization in the context of the family: Parent–child interaction. In P. H. Mussen (Ed.), *Handbook of child psychology* (formerly *Carmichael's manual of child psychology*; Vol. 4, pp. 1–101). New York, NY: Wiley.

MacDonald, T. K., Zanna, M. P., & Fong, G. T. (1996). Why common sense goes out the window: Effects of alcohol on intentions to use condoms. *Personality and Social Psychology Bulletin, 22*(8), 763–775.

Maholmes, V., & King, R. B. (Eds.). (2012). *The Oxford handbook of poverty and child develop-ment.* New York, NY: Oxford University Press.

Maruna, S. (2001). *Defining desistance.* Washington, DC: American Psychological Association.

Masse, L. N., & Barnett, W. S. (2002). *A benefit cost analysis of the Abecedarian early childhood intervention.* New Brunswick, NJ: National Institute for Early Education Research.

Massey, D. S., & Denton, N. A. (1993). *American apartheid: Segregation and the making of the underclass.* Harvard University Press.

Masten, A. S. (2001). Ordinary magic: Resilience processes in development. *American Psychologist, 56*(3), 227.

McClelland, M. M., & Wanless, S. B. (2012). Growing up with assets and risks: The importance of self-regulation for academic achievement. *Research in Human Development, 9*(4), 278–297.

McCord, W., & McCord, J. (1959). *Origins of crime.* New York, NY: Columbia University Press.

McCrae, R. R., & Allik, J. (2002). *The five factor model of personality across cultures.* Boston, MA: Kluwer Academic.

McCullough, M. E., & Willoughby, B. L. (2009). Religion, self-regulation, and self-control: Associations, explanations, and implications. *Psychological Bulletin, 135*(1), 69.

McLaughlin, K. A., Sheridan, M. A., Winter, W., Fox, N. A., Zeanah, C. H., & Nelson, C. A. (2013). Widespread reductions in cortical thickness following severe early-life deprivation: A neurodevelopmental pathway to attention-deficit/hyperactivity disorder. *Biological Psychiatry, 76*(8), 629–638.

Meaney, M. J. (2001). Nature, nurture, and the disunity of knowledge. *Annals of the New York Academy of Sciences, 935*(1), 50–61.

Meier, M. H., Slutske, W. S., Arndt, S., & Cadoret, R. J. (2008). Impulsive and callous traits are more strongly associated with delinquent behavior in higher risk neighborhoods among boys and girls. *Journal of Abnormal Psychology, 117*(2), 377.

Meisels, S. J., Marsden, D. B., Wiske, M. S., & Henderson, L. W. (1997). *Early screening inventory, revised: Examiner's Manual.* Ann Arbor, MI: Rebus.

Meldrum, R. C. (2008). Beyond parenting: An examination of the etiology of self-control. *Journal of Criminal Justice, 36*(3), 244–251.

Meldrum, R. C., Barnes, J. C., & Hay, C. (2013). Sleep deprivation, low self-control, and delin-quency: A test of the strength model of self-control. *Journal of Youth and Adolescence,* pp. 1–13. doi: 10.1007/s10964-013-0024-4

Meldrum, R., & Hay, C. (2012). Do peers matter in the development of self-control? Evidence from a longitudinal study of youth. *Journal of Youth and Adolescence, 41*(6), 691–703.

Meldrum, R. C., & Restivo, E. (2014). The behavioral and health consequences of sleep depriva-tion among U.S. high school students: Relative deprivation matters. *Preventative Medicine 63,* 24–28.

Meldrum, R. C., Young, J. T., Hay, C., & Flexon, J. L. (2012). Does self-control influence mater-nal attachment? A reciprocal effects analysis from early childhood through middle adoles-cence. *Journal of Quantitative Criminology, 28*(4), 673–699.

Meldrum, R. C., Young, J. T., & Weerman, F. M. (2009). Reconsidering the effect of self-control and delinquent peers: Implications of measurement for theoretical significance. *Journal of Research in Crime and Delinquency, 46*(3), 353–376.

Meldrum, R. C., Young, J. T., & Weerman, F. M. (2012). Changes in self-control during adoles-cence: Investigating the influence of the adolescent peer network. *Journal of Criminal Justice, 40*(6), 452–462.

Mendelsohn, A. L., Huberman, H. S., Berkule, S. B., Brockmeyer, C. A., Morrow, L. M., & Dreyer, B. P. (2011). Primary care strategies for promoting parent–child interactions and school readiness in at-risk families: The Bellevue Project for Early Language, Literacy, and Education Success. *Archives of Pediatric and Adolescent Medicine, 165*(1), 33–41.

Menting, A. T., Orobio de Castro, B., & Matthys, W. (2013). Effectiveness of the Incredible Years parent training to modify disruptive and prosocial child behavior: A meta-analytic review. *Clinical Psychology Review, 33*(8), 901–913.

Merton, R. K. (1938). Social structure and anomie. *American Sociological Review, 3*(5), 672–682.

Milkman, H. B., & Wanberg, K. W. (2007). *Cognitive-behavioral treatment: A review and discussion for corrections professionals.* Washington, DC: U.S. Department of Justice, National Institute of Corrections.

Miller, H. V., Barnes, J. C., & Beaver, K. M. (2011). Self-control and health outcomes in a nationally representative sample. *American Journal of Health Behavior, 35*(1), 15–27.

Miller, J. D., & Lynam, D. (2001). Structural models of personality and their relation to antisocial behavior: A meta-analytic review. *Criminology, 39,* 765–798.

Minnes, S., Singer, L. T., Min, M. O., Lang, A. M., Ben-Harush, A., Short, E., & Wu, M. (2014). Comparison of 12-year-old children with prenatal exposure to cocaine and non-exposed controls on caregiver ratings of executive function. *Journal of Youth and Adolescence, 43*(1), 53–69.

Mischel, W. (1977). On the future of personality measurement. *American Psychologist, 32*(4), 246.

Mischel, W., & Ebbesen, E. B. (1970). Attention in delay of gratification. *Journal of Personality and Social Psychology, 16*(2), 329–337.

Mischel, W., Shoda, Y., & Peake, P. K. (1988). The nature of adolescent competencies predicted by preschool delay of gratification. *Journal of Personality and Social Psychology, 54*(4), 687.

Moffitt, T. E. (1993). Adolescence-limited and life-course-persistent antisocial behavior: A developmental taxonomy. *Psychological Review, 100*(4), 674–701.

Moffitt, T. E., Arseneault, L., Belsky, D., Dickson, N., Hancox, R. J., Harrington, H., . . . Caspi, A. (2011). A gradient of childhood self-control predicts health, wealth, and public safety. *Proceedings of the National Academy of Sciences, 108*(7), 2693–2698.

Moffitt, T. E., Poulton, R., & Caspi, A. (2013). Lifelong impact of early self-control. *American Scientist, 101*(5).

Monahan, K. C., Hawkins, J. D., & Abbott, R. D. (2013). The application of meta-analysis within a matched-pair randomized control trial: An illustration testing the effects of Communities That Care on delinquent behavior. *Prevention Science, 14*(1), 1–12.

Morgane, P. J., Austin-LaFrance, R., Bronzino, J., Tonkiss, J., Diaz-Cintra, S., Cintra, L., . . . Galler, J. R. (1993). Prenatal malnutrition and development of the brain. *Neuroscience and Biobehavioral Reviews, 17*(1), 91–128.

Muraven, M., Collins, R. L., Shiffman, S., & Paty, J. A. (2005). Daily fluctuations in self-control demands and alcohol intake. *Psychology of Addictive Behaviors, 19*(2), 140.

Muraven, M., Tice, D. M., & Baumeister, R. F. (1998). Self-control as limited resource: Regulatory depletion patterns. *Journal of Personality and Social Psychology, 74,* 774–789.

Na, C., & Paternoster, R. (2012). Can self-control change substantially over time? Rethinking the relationship between self- and social control. *Criminology, 50*(2), 427–462.

Nagin, D. S. (1999). Analyzing developmental trajectories: A semiparametric, group-based approach. *Psychological Methods, 4*(2), 139.

Nagin, D. S., & Paternoster, R. (1991). On the relationship of past to future participation in delinquency. *Criminology, 29*(2), 163–189.

Nagin, D. S., & Paternoster, R. (1994). Personal capital and social control: The deterrence implications of a theory of individual differences in criminal offending. *Criminology, 32*(4), 581–606.

Nagin, D., & Paternoster, R. (2000). Population heterogeneity and state dependence: State of the evidence and directions for future research. *Journal of Quantitative Criminology, 16*(2), 117–144.

Narag, R. E., Pizarro, J., & Gibbs, C. (2009). Lead exposure and its implications for criminological theory. *Criminal Justice and Behavior, 36*(9), 954–973.

National Public Radio. (2014). "Is *16 and Pregnant* an effective form of birth control?" *National Public Radio.* Retrieved April 15, 2014, from http://www.npr.org/ 2014/01/13/262175399/is-16-and-pregnant-an-effective-form-of-birth-control

National Sleep Foundation. (2013). *Teens and sleep.* Retrieved May 14, 2013, from www.sleep foundation.org/article/sleep-topics/teens-and-sleep

Neugebauer, R., Hoek, H. W., & Susser, E. (1999). Prenatal exposure to wartime famine and development of antisocial personality disorder in early adulthood. *JAMA, 282*(5), 455–462.

Nicpon, M. F., Allmon, A., Sieck, B., & Stinson, R. D. (2011). Empirical investigation of twice-exceptionality: Where have we been and where are we going? *Gifted Child Quarterly, 55*(1), 3–17.

Nofziger, S. (2008). The "cause" of low self-control: The influence of maternal self-control. *Journal of Research in Crime and Delinquency, 45*(2), 191–224.

O'Brien, E. M., & Mindell, J. A. (2005). Sleep and risk-taking behavior in adolescents. *Behavioral Sleep Medicine, 3,* 113–133.

O'Gorman, J. G., & Baxter, E. (2002). Self-control as a personality measure. *Personality and Individual Differences, 32*(3), 533–539.

Olds, D., Henderson, C. R., Jr., Cole, R., Eckenrode, J., Kitzman, H., Luckey, D., . . . Powers, J. (1998). Long-term effects of nurse home visitation on children's criminal and antisocial behavior: 15-year follow-up of a randomized controlled trial. *JAMA, 280*(14), 1238–1244.

Olds, D. L., Henderson, C. R., Jr., Tatelbaum, R., & Chamberlin, R. (1986). Improving the delivery of prenatal care and outcomes of pregnancy: A randomized trial of nurse home visitation. *Pediatrics, 77*(1), 16–28.

Olds, D. L., Kitzman, H., Hanks, C., Cole, R, Anson, E., Sidora-Arcoleo, K., . . . Bondy, J. (2007). Effects of nurse home visiting on maternal and child functioning: Age-9 follow-up of a randomized trial. *Pediatrics, 120*(4), e832–e845.

Olson, S. L. (1989). Assessment of impulsivity in preschoolers: Cross-measure convergences, longitudinal stability, and relevance to social competence. *Journal of Clinical Child Psychology, 18*(2), 176–183.

Osgood, D. W., & Lee, H. (1993). Leisure activities, age, and adult roles across the lifespan. *Society and Leisure, 16*(1), 181–207.

Osgood, D. W., Wilson, J. K., O'Malley, P. M., Bachman, J. G., & Johnston, L. D. (1996). Routine activities and individual deviant behavior. *American Sociological Review,* 635–655.

Ouscy, G. C., & Wilcox, P. (2007). The interaction of antisocial propensity and life-course varying predictors of delinquent behavior: Differences by method of estimation and implications for theory. *Criminology, 45*(2), 313–354.

Padgett, K. G., Bales, W. D., & Blomberg, T. G. (2006). Under surveillance: An empirical test of the effectiveness and consequences of electronic monitoring. *Criminology and Public Policy, 5*(1), 61–91.

Palmer, T. (1975). Martinson revisited. *Journal of Research in Crime and Delinquency, 12*(2), 133–152.

"Parents of affluent teen drunk driver put under intense scrutiny" [Video file]. (2013, December 18). *ABC News*. Retrieved from http://abcnews.go.com/GMA/video/ethan-couch-affluenza-parents-affluent-teen-drunk-driver-put-intense-scrutiny-21258453

Paternoster, R., & Bushway, S. (2009). Desistance and the "feared self": Toward an identity theory of criminal desistance. *Journal of Criminal Law and Criminology, 99*(4), 1103–1156.

Paternoster, R., McGloin, J., Nguyen, H., & Thomas, K. (2013). The causal impact of exposure to deviant peers: An experimental investigation. *Journal of Research in Crime and Delinquency, 50*(4), 476–503.

Peach, H. D., & Gaultney, J. F. (2013). Sleep, impulse control, and sensation-seeking predict delinquent behavior in adolescents, emerging adults, and adults. *Journal of Adolescent Health, 53*(2), 293–299.

Perrone, D., Sullivan, C. J., Pratt, T. C., & Margaryan, S. (2004). Parental efficacy, self-control, and delinquency: A test of a general theory of crime on a nationally representative sample of youth. *International Journal of Offender Therapy and Comparative Criminology, 48*(3), 298–312.

Perry, A. (2013). *Willpower: Regain your self-control and rediscover your willpower instinct*. Moondance. Retrieved from http://www.amazon.com/Willpower-Self-Control-Rediscover-Instinct-Empowerment/dp/0615871119.

Peters, J. (2013). "Dumb criminals don't get much dumber than this bumbling burglar." *Slate*. Retrieved April 9, 2014, from http://www.slate.com/blogs/crime/2013/11/21/dumb_criminal_of_the_week_brandon_campbell_dumb_criminals_don_t_get_much.html

Peterson, J. L., & Zill, N. (1986). Marital disruption, parent–child relationships, and behavior problems in children. *Journal of Marriage and Family, 48*(2), 295–307.

Pew Charitable Trusts. (2012). *Pursuing the American Dream: Economic mobility across generations*. Washington, DC: Pew Charitable Trusts.

Pinker, S. (2011). *The better angels of our nature: Why violence has declined*. New York, NY: Penguin Books.

Piquero, A. R. (2014). "Take my license n'all that jive, I can't see . . . 35": Little hope for the future encourages offending over time. *Justice Quarterly*, pp. 1–27.

Piquero, A. R., Jennings, W. G., & Farrington, D. P. (2010). On the malleability of self-control: Theoretical and policy implications regarding a general theory of crime. *Justice Quarterly, 27*(6), 803–834.

Piquero, A. R., MacDonald, J., Dobrin, A., Daigle, L. E., & Cullen, F. T. (2005). Self-control, violent offending, and homicide victimization: Assessing the general theory of crime. *Journal of Quantitative Criminology, 21*(1), 55–71.

Piquero, A. R., Paternoster, R., Pogarsky, G., & Loughran, T. (2011). Elaborating the individual difference component in deterrence theory. *Annual Review of Law and Social Science, 7*, 335–360.

Piquero, A. R., & Pogarsky, G. (2002). Beyond Stafford and Warr's reconceptualization of deterrence: Personal and vicarious experiences, impulsivity, and offending behavior. *Journal of Research in Crime and Delinquency, 39*(2), 153–186.

Piquero, A. R., & Rosay, A. B. (1998). The reliability and validity of Grasmick et al.'s self-control scale: A comment on Longshore et al. *Criminology, 36*(1), 157–174.

Piquero, A., & Tibbetts, S. (1996). Specifying the direct and indirect effects of low self-control and situational factors in offenders' decision making: Toward a more complete model of rational offending. *Justice quarterly, 13*(3), 481–510.

Pirutinsky, S. (2014). Does religiousness increase self-control and reduce criminal behavior? A longitudinal analysis of adolescent offenders. *Criminal Justice and Behavior, 41*, 1290–1307.

Pogarsky, G. (2002). Identifying "deterrable" offenders: Implications for research on deterrence. *Justice Quarterly, 19*(3), 431–452.

Pogarsky, G. (2007). Deterrence and individual differences among convicted offenders. *Journal of Quantitative Criminology, 23*(1), 59–74.

Polakowski, M. (1994). Linking self-and social control with deviance: Illuminating the structure underlying a general theory of crime and its relation to deviant activity. *Journal of Quantitative Criminology, 10*(1), 41–78.

Power, T. G., & Chapieski, M. L. (1986). Childrearing and impulse control in toddlers: A naturalistic investigation. *Developmental Psychology, 22*(2), 271.

Prado, E. L., & Dewey, K. G. (2014). Nutrition and brain development in early life. *Nutrition Reviews, 72*(4), 267–284.

Pratt, T. C. (2009). *Addicted to incarceration: Corrections policy and the politics of misinformation in the United States.* Thousand Oaks, CA: SAGE.

Pratt, T. C., & Cullen, F. T. (2000). The empirical status of Gottfredson and Hirschi's general theory of crime: A meta-analysis. *Criminology, 38*(3), 931–964.

Pratt, T. C., Turanovic, J. J., Fox, K. A., & Wright, K. A. (2014). Self-control and victimization: A meta-analysis. *Criminology, 52*(1), 87–116.

Pratt, T. C., Turner, M. G., & Piquero, A. R. (2004). Parental socialization and community context: A longitudinal analysis of the structural sources of low self-control. *Journal of Research in Crime and Delinquency, 41,* 219–243.

Pronk, T. M., Karremans, J. C., & Wigboldus, D. H. (2011). How can you resist? Executive control helps romantically involved individuals to stay faithful. *Journal of Personality and Social Psychology, 100*(5), 827.

Raffaelli, M., Crockett, L. J., & Shen, Y. (2005). Developmental stability and change in self-regulation from childhood to adolescence. *Journal of Genetic Psychology: Research and Theory on Human Development, 166*(1), 54–76.

Raine, A., & Liu, J. (1998). Biological predispositions to violence and their implications for biosocial treatment and prevention. *Psychology, Crime and Law, 4*(2), 107–125.

Raine, A., Phil, D., Stoddard, J., Bihrle, S., & Buchsbaum, M. (1998). Prefrontal glucose deficits in murderers lacking psychosocial deprivation. *Cognitive and Behavioral Neurology, 11*(1), 1–7.

Ratchford, M., & Beaver, K. M. (2009). Neuropsychological deficits, low self-control, and delinquent involvement toward a biosocial explanation of delinquency. *Criminal Justice and Behavior, 36*(2), 147–162.

Ray, J. V., Jones, S., Loughran, T. A., & Jennings, W. G. (2013). Testing the stability of self-control: Identifying unique developmental patterns and associated risk factors. *Criminal Justice and Behavior, 40*(6), 588–607.

Rebellon, C. J., & Manasse, M. (2004). Do "bad boys" really get the girls? Delinquency as a cause and consequence of dating behavior among adolescents. *Justice Quarterly, 21*(2), 355–389.

Rebellon, C. J., Straus, M. A., & Medeiros, R. (2008). Self-control in global perspective: An empirical assessment of Gottfredson and Hirschi's general theory within and across 32 national settings. *European Journal of Criminology, 5*(3), 331–361.

Reisig, M. D., Pratt, T. C., & Holtfreter, K. (2009). Perceived risk of Internet theft victimization: Examining the effects of self-control vulnerability and financial impulsivity. *Criminal Justice and Behavior, 36,* 369–384.

Reisig, M. D., Wolfe, S. E., & Pratt, T. C. (2012). Low self-control and the religiosity–crime relationship. *Criminal Justice and Behavior, 39*(9), 1172–1191.

Riggs, N. R., Greenberg, M. T., Kusché, C. A., & Pentz, M. A. (2006). The mediational role of neurocognition in the behavioral outcomes of a social-emotional prevention program in elementary school students: Effects of the PATHS curriculum. *Prevention Science, 7*(1), 91–102.

Righetti, F., & Finkenauer, C. (2011). If you are able to control yourself, I will trust you: The role of perceived self-control in interpersonal trust. *Journal of Personality and Social Psychology, 100*(5), 874.

Rijlaarsdam, J., Stevens, G. W., van der Ende, J., Hofman, A., Jaddoe, V. W., Mackenbach, J. P., ... Tiemeier, H. (2013). Economic disadvantage and young children's emotional and behavioral problems: Mechanisms of risk. *Journal of Abnormal Child Psychology, 41*(1), 125–137.

Roberts, B. W., Caspi, A., & Moffitt, T. E. (2003). Work experiences and personality development in young adulthood. *Journal of Personality and Social Psychology, 84*(3), 582.

Roberts, B. W., & DelVecchio, W. F. (2000). The rank-order consistency of personality traits from childhood to old age: A quantitative review of longitudinal studies. *Psychological Bulletin, 126*(1), 3–25.

Roberts, B. W., & Mroczek, D. (2008). Personality trait change in adulthood. *Current Directions in Psychological Science, 17*(1), 31–35.

Roberts, B. W., Walton, K. E., & Viechtbauer, W. (2006). Patterns of mean-level change in personality traits across the life course: A meta-analysis of longitudinal studies. *Psychological Bulletin, 132*(1), 1–25.

Roberts, B. W., Wood, D., & Caspi, A. (2008). The development of personality traits in adulthood. *Handbook of Personality: Theory and Research, 3*, 375–398.

Rocque, M., Welsh, B. C., & Raine, A. (2012). Biosocial criminology and modern crime prevention. *Journal of Criminal Justice, 40*(4), 306–312.

Rogozov, V., & Bermel, N. (2009). Christmas 2009 auto-appendectomy in the Antarctic: Case report. *British Medical Journal* (International ed.), 339.

Rosenthal, R., & Jacobson, L. (1968). *Pygmalion in the classroom: Teacher expectation and pupils' intellectual development.* New York, NY: Holt, Rinehart and Winston.

Rounding, K., Lee, A., Jacobson, J. A., & Ji, L. J. (2012). Religion replenishes self-control. *Psychological Science, 23*(6), 635–642.

Rueda, M. R., Posner, M. I., & Rothbart, M. K. (2005). The development of executive attention: Contributions to the emergence of self-regulation. *Developmental Neuropsychology, 28*(2), 573–594.

Rutter, M. (2012). Gene–environment interdependence. *European Journal of Developmental Psychology, 9*(4), 391–412.

Sampson, R. J. (2013). The place of context: A theory and strategy for criminology's hard problems. *Criminology, 51*(1), 1–31.

Sampson, R. J., & Laub, J. H. (1993) *Crime in the making: Pathways and turning points through life.* Cambridge, MA: Harvard University Press.

Sampson, R. J., & Laub, J. H. (1995). *Crime in the making: Pathways and turning points through life. Cambridge, MA:* Harvard University Press.

Sampson, R. J., & Laub, J. H. (1997). A life-course theory of cumulative disadvantage and the stability of delinquency. *Developmental Theories of Crime and Delinquency, 7*, 133–161.

Sampson, R. J., & Laub, J. H. (2005). A general age-graded theory of crime: Lessons learned and the future of life-course criminology. *Integrated Developmental and Life Course Theories of Offending, 14*, 165–182.

Sampson, R. J., Laub, J. H., & Wimer, C. (2006). Does marriage reduce crime? A counterfactual approach to within-individual causal effects. *Criminology, 44*(3), 465–508.

Sanders, M. R., Dittman, C. K., Farruggia, S. P., & Keown, L. J. (2014). A comparison of online versus workbook delivery of a self-help positive parenting program. *Journal of Primary Prevention, 35*(3), 125–133.

Sanders, M. R., & Mazzucchelli, T. G. (2013). The promotion of self-regulation through parenting interventions. *Clinical Child and Family Psychology Review, 16*(1), 1–17.

Scharf, M., & Mayseless, O. (2007). Putting eggs in more than one basket: A new look at developmental processes of attachment in adolescence. *New Directions for Child and Adolescent Development, 117,* 1–22.

Schlam, T. R., Wilson, N. L., Shoda, Y., Mischel, W., & Ayduk, O. (2013). Preschoolers' delay of gratification predicts their body mass 30 years later. *Journal of Pediatrics, 162*(1), 90–93.

Schoepfer, A., & Piquero, A. R. (2006). Self-control, moral beliefs, and criminal activity. *Deviant Behavior, 27*(1), 51–71.

Schreck, C. J. (1999). Criminal victimization and low self-control: An extension and test of a general theory of crime. *Justice Quarterly, 16*(3), 633–654.

Schreck, C. J., Stewart, E. A., & Fisher, B. S. (2006). Self-control, victimization, and their influence on risky lifestyles: A longitudinal analysis using panel data. *Journal of Quantitative Criminology, 22*(4), 319–340.

Schreck, C. J., Wright, R. A., & Miller, J. M. (2002). A study of individual and situational antecedents of violent victimization. *Justice Quarterly, 19*(1), 159–180.

Schroder, K. E., & Schwarzer, R. (2005). Habitual self-control and the management of health behavior among heart patients. *Social Science and Medicine, 60*(4), 859–875.

Schroeder, R. D., & Frana, J. F. (2009). Spirituality and religion, emotional coping, and criminal desistance: A qualitative study of men undergoing change. *Sociological Spectrum, 29*(6), 718–741.

Serketich, W. J., & Dumas, J. E. (1996). The effectiveness of behavioral parent training to modify antisocial behavior in children: A meta-analysis. *Behavior Therapy, 27*(2), 171–186.

Sexton, T., & Turner, C. W. (2010). The effectiveness of Functional Family Therapy for youth with behavioral problems in a community practice setting. *Journal of Family Psychology, 24*(3), 339.

Shaw, C. R., & McKay, H. D. (1969). *Juvenile delinquency and urban areas* (Rev. ed.). Chicago, IL: University of Chicago Press.

Sheridan, M. A., Fox, N. A., Zeanah, C. H., McLaughlin, K. A., & Nelson, C. A. (2012). Variation in neural development as a result of exposure to institutionalization early in childhood. *Proceedings of the National Academy of Sciences, 109*(32), 12927–12932.

Sherman, L. W., Farrington, D. P., Welsh, B. C., & MacKenzie, D. L. (2002). *Evidence-based crime prevention.* New York, NY: Routledge.

Shonkoff, J. P., Garner, A. S., Siegel, B. S., Dobbins, M. I., Earls, M. F., McGuinn, L., . . . Wood, D. L. (2012). The lifelong effects of early childhood adversity and toxic stress. *Pediatrics, 129*(1), e232–e246.

Siennick, S. (2011). Tough love? Crime and parental assistance in young adulthood. *Criminology, 49*(1), 163–196.

Silva, P. A., & Stanton, W. R. (1996). *From child to adult: The Dunedin multidisciplinary health and development study.* Oxford, UK: Oxford University Press.

Silver, E., & Ulmer, J. T. (2012). Future selves and self-control motivation. *Deviant Behavior, 33*(9), 699–714.

Simons, R. L., & Burt, C. H. (2011). Learning to be bad: Adverse social conditions, social schemas, and crime. *Criminology, 49*(2), 553–598.

Smetana, J. G., Campione-Barr, N., & Metzger, A. (2006). Adolescent development in interpersonal and societal contexts. *Annual Review of Psychology, 57,* 255–284.

Smiles, S. (1866). *Self-help: With illustrations of character, conduct, and perseverance* (2nd ed.). London, UK: John Murray.

Smith, B. L. (2012). The case against spanking. *Monitor on Psychology, 43*(4).

Solnick, S. J., & Hemenway, D. (2012). The "Twinkie Defense": The relationship between carbonated non-diet soft drinks and violence perpetration among Boston high school students. *Injury Prevention, 18*(4), 259–263.

Somerville, L. H. (2013). The teenage brain sensitivity to social evaluation. *Current Directions in Psychological Science, 22*(2), 121–127.

Stattin, H., & Klackenberg-Larsson, I. (1993). Early language and intelligence development and their relationship to future criminal behavior. *Journal of Abnormal Psychology, 102,* 369–378.

Steinberg, L. (2010a). A behavioral scientist looks at the science of adolescent brain development. *Brain and Cognition, 72*(1), 160–164.

Steinberg, L. (2010b). A dual systems model of adolescent risk-taking. *Developmental Psychobiology, 52*(3), 216–224.

Steinberg, L., & Silk, J. S. (2002). *Parenting adolescents.* Mahwah, NJ: Lawrence Erlbaum.

Stevens, A. (2012). "I am the person now I was always meant to be": Identity reconstruction and narrative reframing in therapeutic community prisons. *Criminology and Criminal Justice, 12*(5), 527–547.

Stewart, E. A., Elifson, K. W., & Sterk, C. E. (2004). Integrating the general theory of crime into an explanation of violent victimization among female offenders. *Justice Quarterly, 21*(1), 159–181.

Stewart, E. A., & Simons, R. L. (2006). Structure and culture in African American adolescent violence: A partial test of the "Code of the Street" thesis. *Justice Quarterly, 23*(1), 1–33.

Stix, G. (2013). "Sleep's role in obesity, schizophrenia, diabetes . . . everything." *Scientific American Blogs.*

Stout, D., Toth, N., Shick, K., & Chaminade, T. (2008). Neural correlates of early Stone Age toolmaking: Technology, language, and cognition in human evolution. *Philosophical Transactions of the Royal Society, 363,* 1939–1949.

Sullivan, E. V., Harris, R. A., & Pfefferbaum, A. (2010). Alcohol's effects on brain and behavior. *Alcohol Research and Health: The Journal of the National Institute on Alcohol Abuse and Alcoholism, 33*(1), 127.

Tangney, J. P., Baumeister, R. F., & Boone, A. L. (2004). High self-control predicts good adjustment, less pathology, better grades, and interpersonal success. *Journal of Personality, 72*(2), 271–324.

Teasdale, B., & Silver, E. (2009). Neighborhoods and self-control: Toward an expanded view of socialization. *Social Problems, 56*(1), 205–222.

Tibbetts, S. G., & Myers, D. L. (1999). Low self-control, rational choice, and student test cheating. *American Journal of Criminal Justice, 23*(2), 179–200.

TIME Staff. (2009). Top 10 skanky reality shows. *TIME Magazine.* Retrieved from http://entertainment.time.com/2009/06/02/top-10-skanky-reality-shows/slide/temptation-island/

Tittle, C. R. (2011). Self-control and the management of violence. In W. Heitmeyer, H. Haupt, S. Malthaner, & A. Kirschner (Eds.), *Control of violence: Historical and international perspectives on violence* (pp. 91–120). New York, NY: Springer.

Tittle, C. R., & P. McCall. (2006). *Collective self-control and homicide in U.S. cities.* Presented at the annual meetings of the American Society of Criminology in Los Angeles, CA.

Tittle, C. R., Ward, D. A., & Grasmick, H. G. (2003). Self-control and crime/deviance: Cognitive vs. behavioral measures. *Journal of Quantitative Criminology, 19*(4), 333–365.

Tittle, C. R., Ward, D. A., & Grasmick, H. G. (2004). Capacity for self-control and individuals' interest in exercising self-control. *Journal of Quantitative Criminology, 20,* 143–172.

Tobin, R. M., Graziano, W. G., & Vanman, E. J. (2000). Personality, emotional experience, and efforts to control emotions. *Journal of Personality and Social Psychology, 79*(4), 656–669.

Toga, A. W., & Thompson, P. M. (2005). Genetics of brain structure and intelligence. *Annual Review of Neuroscience, 28,* 1–23.

Tonry, M., Ohlin, L., & Farrington, D. P. (1991). *Human development and criminal behavior.* New York, NY: Springer-Verlag.

Triandis, H. C., & Suh, E. M. (2002). Cultural influences on personality. *Annual Review of Psychology, 53,* 133–160.

Trope, I., Lopez-Villegas, D., Cecil, K. M., & Lenkinski, R. E. (2001). Exposure to lead appears to selectively alter metabolism of cortical gray matter. *Pediatrics, 107*(6), 1437–1442.

Tsukayama, E., Toomey, S. L., Faith, M. S., & Duckworth, A. L. (2010). Self-control as a protective factor against overweight status in the transition from childhood to adolescence. *Archives of Pediatrics and Adolescent Medicine, 164*(7), 631.

Tucker, R., & Dugas, J. (2009). *The runner's body: How the latest exercise science can help you run stronger, longer, and faster.* New York, NY: Rodale.

Turner, M. G., Livecchi, C. M., Beaver, K. M., & Booth, J. (2011). Moving beyond the socialization hypothesis: The effects of maternal smoking during pregnancy on the development of self-control. *Journal of Criminal Justice, 39*(2), 120–127.

Turner, M. G., & Piquero, A. R. (2002). The stability of self-control. *Journal of Criminal Justice, 30*(6), 457.

Twomey, S. (Jan. 2010). "Phineas Gage: Neuroscience's most famous patient." *Smithsonian Magazine.* Retrieved April 30, 2014, from http://www.smithsonianmag.com/history/phineas-gage-neurosciences-most-famous-patient-11390067/?page=2

Tyler, J. M., & Burns, K. C. (2008). After depletion: The replenishment of the self's regulatory resources. *Self and Identity, 7,* 305–321.

Uggen, C. (2000). Work as a turning point in the life course of criminals: A duration model of age, employment, and recidivism. *American Sociological Review,* 529–546.

Unnever, J. D., & Cornell, D. G. (2003). Bullying, self-control, and ADHD. *Journal of Interpersonal Violence, 18*(2), 129–147.

Unnever, J. D., Cullen, F. T., & Pratt, T. C. (2003). Parental management, ADHD, and delinquent involvement: Reassessing Gottfredson and Hirschi's general theory. *Justice Quarterly, 20*(3), 471–500.

vanDellen, M. R., & Hoyle, R. H. (2010). Regulatory accessibility and social influences on state self-control. *Personality and Social Psychology Bulletin, 36*(2), 251–263.

Van Gelder, J., & de Vries, R. E. (2012). Traits and states: Integrating personality and affect into a model of criminal decision making. *Criminology, 50*(3), 637–672.

Van Horn, J. D., Irimia, A., Torgerson, C. M., Chambers, M. C., Kikinis, R., & Toga, A. W. (2012). Mapping connectivity damage in the case of Phineas Gage. *PloS One, 7*(5), e37454.

Vaske, J., Galyean, K., & Cullen, F. T. (2011). Toward a biosocial theory of offender rehabilitation: Why does cognitive-behavioral therapy work? *Journal of Criminal Justice, 39*(1), 90–102.

Vazsonyi, A. T., & Belliston, L. M. (2007). The family→ low self-control→ deviance: A cross-cultural and cross-national test of self-control theory. *Criminal Justice and Behavior, 34*(4), 505–530.

Vazsonyi, A. T., Cleveland, H. H., & Wiebe, R. P. (2006). Does the effect of impulsivity on delinquency vary by level of neighborhood disadvantage? *Criminal Justice and Behavior, 33*(4), 511–541.

Vazsonyi, A. T., Machackova, H., Sevcikova, A., Smahel, D., & Cerna, A. (2012). Cyberbullying in context: Direct and indirect effects by low self-control across 25 European countries. *European Journal of Developmental Psychology, 9*(2), 210–227.

Vazsonyi, A. T., Pickering, L. E., Junger, M., & Hessing, D. (2001). An empirical test of a general theory of crime: A four-nation comparative study of self-control and the prediction of deviance. *Journal of Research in Crime and Delinquency, 38*(2), 91–131.

Vazsonyi, A. T., Wittekind, J. E. C., Belliston, L. M., & Van Loh, T. D. (2004). Extending the general theory of crime to "the East": Low self-control in Japanese late adolescents. *Journal of Quantitative Criminology, 20*(3), 189–216.

Vergano, D. (2012, June 30). "Myth of "the Jukes" offers cautionary genetics tale." *USA Today.* Retrieved from http://usatoday30.usatoday.com/tech/science/columnist/vergano/story/2012–07–02/eugenics-jukes-family/55944082/1

Virkkunen, M., & Huttunen, M. O. (1982). Evidence for abnormal glucose tolerance test among violent offenders. *Neuropsychobiology, 8,* 30–34.

Vohs, K. D., & Faber, R. J. (2007). Spent resources: Self-regulatory resource availability affects impulse buying. *Journal of Consumer Research, 33*(4), 537–547.

Vohs, K. D., Finkenauer, C., & Baumeister, R. F. (2011). The sum of friends' and lovers' self-control scores predicts relationship quality. *Social Psychological and Personality Science, 2*(2), 138–145.

Wakschlag, L. S., Pickett, K. E., Cook, E., Jr., Benowitz, N. L., & Leventhal, B. L. (2002). Maternal smoking during pregnancy and severe antisocial behavior in offspring: A review. *American Journal of Public Health, 92*(6), 966–974.

Waldo, G. P., & Dinitz, S. (1967). Personality attributes of the criminal: An analysis of research studies, 1950–65. *Journal of Research in Crime and Delinquency, 4*(2), 185–202.

Walker, T. (2013). Ethan Couch: Texas quadruple murderer—or a victim of 'affluenza'? *The Independent.* Retrieved from http://www.independent.co.uk/news/world/americas/ethan-couch-texas-quadruple-murderer—or-a-victim-of-affluenza-9004308.html

Walsh, A. (2009). *Biology and criminology: The biosocial synthesis.* New York, NY: Routledge.

Warfield, M. E. (2005). Family and work predictors of parenting role stress among two-earner families of children with disabilities. *Infant and Child Development, 14*(2), 155–176.

Warr, M. (1993). Age, peers, and delinquency. *Criminology, 31*(1), 17; 17–40; 40.

Warr, M. (1998). Life-course transitions and desistance from crime. *Criminology, 36*(2), 183–216.

Warr, M. (2002). *Companions in crime: The social aspects of criminal conduct.* Cambridge, UK: Cambridge University Press.

Weafer, J., & Fillmore, M. T. (2012). Acute tolerance to alcohol impairment of behavioral and cognitive mechanisms related to driving: Drinking and driving on the descending limb. *Psychopharmacology, 220*(4), 697–706.

WebMD. (n.d.). *Diabetes health center.* Retrieved from http://www.webmd.com/diabetes/diabetes-hyperglycemia

Weissberg, R. P., & Greenberg, M. T. (1998). School and community competence-enhancement and prevention programs. In W. Damon (Series Ed.) & I. E. Sigel & K. A. Renninger (Vol. Eds.), *Handbook of child psychology: Vol. 4. Child psychology in practice* (5th ed., pp. 877–954). New York, NY: Wiley.

Wellesley College. (2014, January 13). New study finds MTV's *16 and Pregnant, Teen Mom* contributed to record decline in U.S. teen childbearing rate. *ScienceDaily.* Retrieved from http://www.sciencedaily.com/releases/2014/01/140113095145.htm

Welsh, B. C., & Farrington, D. P. (2007). *Preventing crime.* New York, NY: Springer Science/ Business Media.

Welsh, B. C., Lipsey, M. W., Rivara, F. P., Hawkins, D. J., Aos, S., Peel, M. E., & Petechuk, D. (2013). *Bulletin 6: Changing lives: Prevention and intervention to reduce serious offending.* National Institute of Justice.

Werstein, K. M. (2013). An examination of the role of self-control in the health and wealth connection. *Graduate Theses and Dissertations,* Paper 13116.

Widiger, T. A., & Costa, P. T., Jr. (2002). *Personality disorders and the five-factor model of personality.* Washington, DC: American Psychological Association.

Wikström, P. O. (2004). Crime as alternative: Towards a cross-level situational action theory of crime causation. *Beyond Empiricism: Institutions and Intentions in the Study of Crime,* 1–38.

Wikström, P. O. H., & Svensson, R. (2010). When does self-control matter? The interaction between morality and self-control in crime causation. *European Journal of Criminology,* 7(5), 395–410.

Wills, T. A., Isasi, C. R., Mendoza, D., & Ainette, M. G. (2007). Self-control constructs related to measures of dietary intake and physical activity in adolescents. *Journal of Adolescent Health, 41*(6), 551–558.

Wilson, D. B., Gallagher, C. A., & MacKenzie, D. L. (2000). A meta-analysis of corrections-based education, vocation, and work programs for adult offenders. *Journal of Research in Crime and Delinquency, 37*(4), 347–368.

Wilson, J. Q., & Herrnstein, R. (1985). *Crime and human nature.* New York, NY: Simon & Schuster.

Winfree, L. T., Jr., Taylor, T. J., He, N., & Esbensen, F. (2006). Self-control and variability over time: Multivariate results using a 5-year, multisite panel of youths. *Crime and Delinquency,* 52(2), 253–286.

Wise, J. (2010) "The most amazing feat of self-control ever." *Psychology Today.* Retrieved from http://www.stumbleupon.com/su/2MeUhB/www.psychologytoday.com/blog/extreme-fear/201005/the-most-amazing-feat-self-control-ever

Wright, B. R., Caspi, A., Moffitt, T. E., & Paternoster, R. (2004). Does the perceived risk of punishment deter criminally prone individuals? Rational choice, self-control, and crime. *Journal of Research in Crime and Delinquency, 41*(2), 180–213.

Wright, B. R. E., Caspi, A., Moffitt, T. E., & Silva, P. A. (1999). Low self-control, social bonds, and crime: Social causation, social selection, or both? *Criminology, 37*(3), 479–514.

Wright, B. R. E., Caspi, A., Moffitt, T. E., & Silva, P. A. (2001). The effects of social ties on crime vary by criminal propensity: A life-courses model of interdependence. *Criminology, 39*(2), 321–348.

Wright, J. P., & Beaver, K. M. (2009). A systematic approach to understanding human variability in serious, persistent offending. In J. Savage (Eds.), *The development of persistent criminality* (pp. 163–178). New York, NY: Oxford University Press.

Wright, J. P., Tibbetts, S. G., & Daigle, L. E. (2008). *Criminals in the making: Criminality across the life course.* Thousand Oaks, CA: SAGE.

Wyatt, W. (2014). *Self discipline now! Proven strategies to develop unstoppable self discipline and self control in 10 days or less.* Indie Print Publishing. Retrieved from:http://www.amazon.com/Self-Discipline-Strategies-Unstoppable-Willpower-ebook/dp/B00F5FVW7A

Young, J. T. (2010). How do they "end up together"? A social network analysis of self-control, homophily, and adolescent relationships. *Journal of Quantitative Criminology, 27*(3), 251–273.

Zimmerman, G. M. (2010). Impulsivity, offending, and the neighborhood: Investigating the person–context nexus. *Journal of Quantitative Criminology, 26*(3), 301–332.

Zimmerman, G. M., Botchkovar, E. V., Antonaccio, O., & Hughes, L. A. (2012). Low self-control in "bad" neighborhoods: Assessing the role of context on the relationship between self-control and crime. *Justice Quarterly* (ahead-of-print), 1–29.

INDEX

Note: Italic page numbers indicate figures, tables, and boxed material.

ABOUT THE AUTHORS

Carter Hay is a Professor and the Director of Graduate Studies in the College of Criminology and Criminal Justice at Florida State University in Tallahassee, Florida. He received his PhD in Sociology from the University of Texas at Austin in 1999. His articles, chapters, and books have focused on the causes and consequences of crime and deviance over the life course, with a special focus on self-control and its early-in-life precursors.

Ryan C. Meldrum is an Assistant Professor in the Department of Criminal Justice at Florida International University in Miami, Florida. He received his PhD from Florida State University in 2010. His research addresses individual-level correlates of delinquent behavior, with a particular emphasis on child development and the role of self-control.